One Hundred Years of
Surrealist Poetry

T0244399

One Hundred Years of Surrealist Poetry

Theory and Practice

Willard Bohn

BLOOMSBURY ACADEMIC

NEW YORK · LONDON · OXFORD · NEW DELHI · SYDNEY

BLOOMSBURY ACADEMIC
Bloomsbury Publishing Inc
1385 Broadway, New York, NY 10018, USA
50 Bedford Square, London, WC1B 3DP, UK
29 Earlsfort Terrace, Dublin 2, Ireland

BLOOMSBURY, BLOOMSBURY ACADEMIC and the Diana logo
are trademarks of Bloomsbury Publishing Plc

First published in the United States of America 2023

Cover design by Eleanor Rose
Cover image © Getty Images

Library of Congress Cataloging-in-Publication Data
Names: Bohn, Willard, 1939- author.
Title: One hundred years of Surrealist poetry: theory and practice / Willard Bohn.
Description: New York: Bloomsbury Academic, 2022. | Includes
bibliographical references and index. | Summary: "Tells the story of the
origins and growth of Surrealist literature - primarily through poetry
written in French, Spanish, Catalan, and Portuguese - throughout the
western hemisphere, examining its popularity, influence, and variety"–
Provided by publisher.
Identifiers: LCCN 2022018621 (print) | LCCN 2022018622 (ebook) | ISBN
9781501393723 (hardback) | ISBN 9781501393730 (paperback) | ISBN
9781501393747 (eBook) | ISBN 9781501393761 (ePDF) | ISBN
9781501393754 (electonic)
Subjects: LCSH: Surrealism (Literature) | Romance-language poetry–History
and criticism. | LCGFT: Literary criticism.
Classification: LCC PN56.S87 B66 2022 (print) | LCC PN56.S87 (ebook) |
DDC 840–dc23/eng/20220608
LC record available at https://lccn.loc.gov/2022018621
LC ebook record available at https://lccn.loc.gov/2022018622

ISBN: HB: 978-1-5013-9372-3
         PB: 978-1-5013-9373-0
       ePDF: 978-1-5013-9376-1
      eBook: 978-1-5013-9374-7

Typeset by Integra Software Sevices Pvt. Ltd.
Printed and bound in the United States of America

To find out more about our authors and books visit www.bloomsbury.com
and sign up for our newsletters.

To Anita and Heather
One More Time.

Contents

Introduction

In view of Surrealism's vitality and continual popularity, it is amazing to realize that a hundred years have passed since the movement was founded. Today virtually everyone is familiar with Salvador Dalí's melting watches and René Magritte's pipe that insists it is not a pipe. Examples of the two images appear everywhere—on refrigerator magnets, for example, in advertisements, and as the subject of innumerable parodies. However, it wasn't always that way. In the beginning, the Surrealists were met with widespread incomprehension, mercilessly ridiculed, and treated as madmen. Indeed, that is how some people still regard them today. Surprisingly, the chief art critic for the *London Times* recently complained that the Surrealist movement was "a magnet for the untalented" and that many works are simply "poor art," forgetting that Surrealism explicitly rejects aesthetic judgments.[1] At the present moment, nevertheless, plans are being made around the world to celebrate the one-hundredth anniversary of the *Manifeste du surréalisme*, published on October 15, 1924. Entitled *The Milk of Dreams*, the current Venice Biennale is likewise concerned with Surrealism

Let me say at the outset that the poems discussed here do not cover this entire time period. The title of the present book refers both to Surrealist poetry's success and to the critical interest it has generated during the past one hundred years. People have encountered this poetry and tried to appreciate it for the past century. As critics have struggled to make sense of Surrealist compositions—always a challenging task—they have developed strategies that provide keys to what is admittedly a highly recalcitrant genre. This book seeks not only to shed light on the poems that I have chosen to investigate but also to illustrate some of the more fruitful critical approaches that have been devised over the years.

With the exception of Dada, which has successfully reinvented itself as neo-Dada, no other early avant-garde movement has lasted even half as long as Surrealism. Consigned to oblivion after a few years, Fauvism, Cubism, Simultanism, Expressionism, Ultraism, Nunism, Futurism, Acmeism, Cubo-Futurism, Rayonism, Vorticism, Imagism, Creationism, Hallucinism, Constructivism, Suprematism, Plasticism, Purism, Dimensionism, Stridentism, Vibrationism, Integralism, impulsionism, Dynamism, Paroxysm, Dramatism, Synchronism, Synchromism, and other movements have only been preserved through the efforts of a small band of enthusiasts. By contrast, the term "surreal" and its bastard child "surrealistic" entered the lexicon long ago and have become household words. The fact that three of the poets examined here have received the Nobel Prize in Literature has also increased the movement's prestige.

The five years leading up to the manifesto were filled with ceaseless activity on the part of Breton and his colleagues, all of which prepared him to compose his magnum opus. Following the end of the First World War, Breton immersed himself in the Dada movement like many other members of the Parisian avant-garde. In March 1919, together with Philippe Soupault and Louis Aragon, he published the first issue of the journal *Littérature*. In addition to numerous articles, *Mont de piété* (*Pawnshop*) appeared in 1919, *Les Champs magnétiques* (*Magnetic Fields*, co-authored with Soupault) in 1920, and *Les Pas perdus* (*Public Lobby*) early in 1924. When the *Manifeste* finally appeared in October, therefore, the groundwork was well out of the way. So excited was Breton at the prospect of unveiling the unconscious, that he even interviewed Sigmund Freud in Vienna (on October 10, 1921) while he and his wife were on their honeymoon. Not only was the manifesto extremely timely, but the fact that it included a collection of automatic texts entitled *Poisson soluble* (*Soluble Fish*) made it invaluable as well. The first chapter of the following study examines some of these works as well as similar examples taken from *Les Champs magnétiques*.

The second chapter considers the historical and theoretical forces that shaped the Surrealist image and analyzes poems by three of the most important Surrealist poets. By contrast, Chapter 3 is devoted entirely to Paul Eluard, who is often considered to be the most lyrical of the French Surrealists.

With the publication of the first manifesto, poets living anywhere in the world could learn what Surrealism was all about and could experiment with psychic automatism themselves. Even before the manifesto appeared in print, word of what was going on in Paris had begun to seep out. For years an international network of avant-garde journals had ensured that the latest experiments and the latest theories would be disseminated throughout Europe and the Americas. The journals tended not to exist for very long, but as soon as one disappeared, another sprang up to take its place. After the Surrealists founded their own journals, especially *Littérature* (1919–24), *La Révolution Surréaliste* (1924–9), and *Le Surréalisme au Service de la Révolution* (1930–3), their influence increased accordingly. In many ways, paradoxically, the *Manifeste du surréalisme* represents the movement's high point. Situated at the beginning of the Surrealist adventure, rather than at the middle or near the end when it reached its full stride, it positively vibrates with excitement. At this stage, Breton and his fellow Surrealists were filled with hope, optimism, boundless energy, and unlimited expectations. By the time the next two manifestoes appeared (in 1930 and 1942), some of their initial precepts—for example, that Surrealist poets should merely act as recording devices—had been modified and several new precepts added.

Containing both detailed instructions and copious examples, the first manifesto served essentially as an operating manual. This made it especially attractive to poets who lived elsewhere and who wished either to join the movement or to learn more about it. Before long, accordingly, Surrealists and Surrealist groups began to appear in other countries. A number of poets even traveled to Paris so they could experience Surrealism at first hand. Those who remained at home listened to their tales when they returned, absorbed the manifesto's lessons, and imitated the sample constructions. Chapter 4 focuses on three poets in particular, two of whom were citizens of other countries, who created examples of Surrealist metapoetry. Robert Desnos was from France, Vicente Aleixandre from Spain, and Pablo Neruda from Chile. Each author composed a poem about poetry and/or poets that expressed his own personal insights. The next two chapters after that are each devoted to a poet from Andalucía—to José María Hinojosa, who is not well known, and to Federico García Lorca, who is famous. Tragically, both were executed by adversaries belonging to opposite political parties during the Spanish Civil War. The seventh chapter is concerned with J[osep] V[icenç] Foix, the best Surrealist poet in Catalonia during his lifetime and a popular candidate for the Nobel Prize. Chapter 8 contains a discussion of Portuguese Surrealism, which deserves to be better known, and Chapter 9 is preoccupied with Octavio Paz who, like Aleixandre and Neruda, was awarded a Nobel Prize in literature. The final chapter expands the discussion of Latin American Surrealism to include three poets living in Argentina, Peru, and Chile respectively who, despite their geographical isolation, were among Breton's most faithful disciples. As much as anything, therefore, the following chapters illustrate the remarkable diversity and the widespread geographic distribution that the movement assumed. Where Surrealism was concerned, even broad oceans and tall mountains were unable to prevent its spread to other continents and other countries.

It remains to say a word about the principles that have guided the selections included in the present book, which is intended to be an analytical survey rather than a proper history.[2]

The following discussion is meant above all for readers who are poetry enthusiasts, who are fascinated by the mechanics of poetry and the way in which Surrealist poetry functions at its most basic level. In addition to examining how the latter signifies, the book discusses some of the common strategies employed by Surrealist poets to produce a maximum of meaning with a minimum of effort. The main problem facing anyone who proposes to demonstrate the skill, the diversity, and widespread appeal of Surrealist poetry is that there are so many interesting poets to choose from. This problem is especially acute among French-speaking Surrealists, but it characterizes Spanish speakers as well, who are equally numerous and equally talented.

In the beginning, I cast my critical net as widely as possible, hoping to obtain a broad cross-section of all the poets, past and present, who ever practiced Surrealism. However, those I collected were so numerous that I was quickly forced to narrow my search. Both for historical reasons and because of my limited linguistic competence, I decided to concentrate on poets writing in the Romance languages. Despite Surrealism's worldwide distribution, Spanish and French speakers have been largely responsible for its spread. Although the movement's roots are thoroughly French, the first individuals to embrace the movement outside of France resided on the Iberian Peninsula. Beginning initially in Catalonia, the enthusiasm for Surrealism soon spread to the rest of Spain (including the Canary Islands) and from there to Hispanic America and the Caribbean. Regrettably, there was no coherent Surrealist movement in either Italy or Germany. Under the leadership of F. T. Marinetti, Futurism continued to preoccupy Italian poets and painters until the end of the Second World War. A similar situation prevailed in Germany, where Expressionism eclipsed everything else. For these reasons, I limited my pool to major Surrealist poets residing in the aforementioned regions. Besides their poetry, the selection process examined their critical reputation and their contribution to the development of Surrealism in their respective countries. The outcome was thus determined by a combination of intrinsic merit, critical evaluation, and historical importance.

Inevitably, a number of fine poets had to be excluded for these reasons, unfortunately including a number of women. The truth is that Surrealism was a man's game from the very beginning. As Gwen Raaberg points out, no women belonged to the original Surrealist group, nor did they sign the original manifestoes.[3] "The Surrealists lived in their own masculine world," Rudolf E. Kuenzli adds, "the better to construct their male phantasms of the feminine."[4] When women eventually joined the movement, they found themselves forced to operate within a masculine paradigm that was already established. Although the deck was stacked against them, they managed nevertheless to create some excellent Surrealist poetry.[5] For better or worse, therefore, the present survey is far from complete. It simply attempts to document the spread of Surrealism throughout the Western hemisphere, while examining some of the shapes that it assumed. In every instance, since I planned to submit the poetry to detailed analysis, I chose prominent individuals who were considered to be among the most important Surrealist poets in their respective countries. In most cases, they were either the first to introduce Surrealism to their colleagues or to found a local Surrealist group or both. Although different poets tended to emphasize different principles, they were united by a common devotion to André Breton and the *Manifeste du surréalisme*. Without exception, all of them strove to free human beings from their unconscious chains so that they could develop their true potential.

Notes

1	Waldemar Januszczak, "Surrealism beyond Borders—Tate Modern Can't Tell Good Art from Bad," *London Times*, February 27, 2022, pp. 14–5.
2	See, for example, Gérard Durozoi, *History of the Surrealist Movement*, tr. Alison Anderson (Chicago: University of Chicago Press, 2002).
3	Gwen Raaberg, "The Problematics of Women and Surrealism," *Surrealism and Women*, ed. Mary Ann Caws et al (Cambridge: MIT Press, 1991), pp. 1–2.
4	Rudolf E. Kuenzli, "Surrealism and Misogyny," ibid., p. 18.
5	Besides Caws et al., *Surrealism and Women*, see Katharine Conley, *Automatic Woman: The Representation of Woman in Surrealism* (Lincoln: University of Nebraska Press, 2008), Katharine Conley, *Surrealist Ghostliness* (Lincoln: University of Nebraska Press, 2013), Mary Ann Caws, ed., *The Milk Bowl of Feathers* (New York: New Directions, 2018), and *Dada/Surrealism*, No. 18 (1990).

1

André Breton and Automatic Writing

Ironically, the first Surrealist text was published five years before Surrealism was invented. More precisely, it appeared during the period leading up to the *Manifeste du surréalisme* (1924), while André Breton and his colleagues were battling several rival groups for the right to call themselves Surrealists.[1] In homage to Guillaume Apollinaire, who had recently died and who had previously coined the term "surrealist," several people claiming to be his poetic heirs had begun using the name too.[2] Unlike the latter, for whom "surrealist" was simply another term for "avant-garde," Breton and his friends had begun to create an actual movement. Motivated by the theories of Sigmund Freud in particular, their investigations led to a series of discoveries that promised to revolutionize not only poetry but also life itself. Encouraged by the use of automatic diagnostic tools in psychiatry, which as a young intern he had witnessed and to some extent employed, Breton proposed to explore both the unconscious and chance verbal encounters. When the *Manifeste* was eventually published five years later, it defined Surrealism as "automatisme psychique pur, par lequel on propose d'exprimer ... le fonctionnement réel de la pensée" ("pure psychic automatism, by which we propose to express... the true functioning of thought"). In addition, the manifesto added, the Surrealists believed in "la réalité supérieure de certaines formes d'associations négligées jusqu'à lui, à la toute puissance du rêve, au jeu désintéressé de la pensée" ("the superior reality of certain forms of association neglected until now, the omnipotence of dream, and the disinterested play of thought").[3]

In the midst of the turbulent period extending from 1918 to 1924, Breton teamed up with Philippe Soupault to create a collection of automatic texts entitled *Les Champs magnétiques* (*Magnetic Fields*). Like the names of many of the individual compositions, the volume's title seems to have been added just before it was published in May 1920.[4] Like the magnetic field surrounding the twin poles of a magnet, the collection was centered around the two authors, whose symbiotic relationship made it hard to tell their (unsigned) contributions apart. As Louis Aragon declared, it was "l'oeuvre d'un seul auteur à deux têtes" ("the work of a single author with two heads").[5] In addition, the title evoked the mysterious way in which the words were assembled on the page—according to invisible but powerful lines of attraction. According to Breton, the texts were originally composed during May and the first two weeks of June 1919.[6] Eager to display the fruit of their automatic experiments, he and Soupault published various parts of the book in *Littérature* from September 1919 to February 1920. Working daily from eight to ten hours at a stretch, they collaborated on most of the texts, with each of them contributing different sections of a given composition. Several works were also conceived as Surrealist dialogues as if the two men were actually talking to each other. However, some of the works were also composed by a single author. Where automatic texts differ from ordinary texts, Michael Riffaterre explains, is in their "total departure from logic, temporality, and referentiality." They are different because they violate "the rules of verisimilitude and the representation of the real."[7] Although normal syntax is respected, they make only limited sense.

What originally motivated Breton to write *Les Champs magnétiques*, he confides in the manifesto and elsewhere, was a series of striking phrases that suddenly occurred to him as he was falling asleep.[8] Since these clearly originated in his unconscious, he set out to duplicate the original conditions as far as possible. Before sitting down to work on *Les Champs magnétiques* each day, he and Soupault immersed themselves in an ecstatic, dream-like state that they maintained as long as they could. Picking up a pen, they wrote as quickly as possible without stopping to think or to let reality intrude.[9] In order to maintain continuity, they even left their sentences unpunctuated. If a phrase suddenly began to make sense, they stopped and substituted another word—beginning with the letter "l"—for the previous word. Although the two men managed to produce a number of striking phrases, the texts that resulted were far from poetic. For this reason Breton thought it important to distinguish between Surrealist poems, which were artistic achievements, and Surrealist texts, which were purely experimental.

Mutual Affections

Composed by Breton, the two compositions examined initially were taken from a section entitled "Ne bougeons plus" ("Let's not budge"), which also contained several texts by Soupault. Reviewing *Les Champs magnétiques* many years later, Aragon was struck by the section's fragmentary nature: "Le photographe ne fait guère poser longtemps, se contente par moments de l'instantané d'une phrase" ("the photographer barely has time to record a pose; from time to time he settles for the snapshot of a phrase").[10] Entitled "Lune de miel" ("Honeymoon"), the first text is surprisingly easy to decipher. Even without the title, it is obvious that it describes a young couple on their honeymoon:

A quoi tiennent les inclinations réciproques? Il y a des jalousies plus touchantes les unes que les autres. La rivalité d'une femme et d'un livre, je me promène volontiers dans cette obscurité. Le doigt sur la tempe n'est pas le canon d'un revolver. Je crois que nous nous écoutions penser mais le machinal "A rien" qui est le plus fier de nos refus n'eut pas à être prononcé de tout ce voyage de noces. Moins haut que les astres il n'y a rien à regarder fixement. Dans quelque train que ce soit, il est dangereux de se pencher par la portière. Les stations étaient clairement reparties sur un golfe. La mer qui pour l'oeil humain n'est jamais si belle que le ciel ne nous quittait pas. Au fond de nos yeux se perdaient de jolis calculs orientés ver l'avenir comme ceux des murs de prisons.

(How to account for mutual affections? Some jealousies are more touching than others. The rivalry of a woman and a book, I enjoy going for a walk in the dark. A finger touching a temple is not a revolver barrel. I believe we are listening to each other think, but the mechanical "Of nothing," which is the proudest of our refusals, did not need to be pronounced during the whole honeymoon. There is nothing to stare at under the stars. In any train, it is dangerous to stick your head out the carriage door. The stations were clearly spaced along a gulf. The sea, which to the human eye never seems as beautiful as the sky, did not abandon us. Pleasing calculations about the future were lost in the depths of our eyes, like those on prison walls.)

Compared to most of the other texts in *Les Champs magnétiques*, which leave the reader puzzled and a bit confused, "Lune de miel" is fairly transparent. It contains none of the logical, temporal, and/or referential problems mentioned previously that are typical of Surrealism. Although the text was published in *Littérature* in January 1920, it looks as if it were composed quite a bit earlier. Consisting of a series of memories, the scenario is perfectly straightforward. The reader progresses logically and chronologically from each subject to the next without encountering any serious difficulties. The individual scenes were all generated metonymically by the umbrella title, which covers a large area. Each one illustrates a different aspect of the central theme: "honeymoon." Beginning in the present tense, the speaker, who may or may not be Breton, switches to the past tense mid-way through the composition.

Finding himself alone with his new bride after the wedding ceremony, the speaker indulges in multiple reflections. Isn't it strange, he wonders, how two people can fall in love as he and his bride have done? There are so many variables, so many unpredictable twists and turns before two strangers meet and eventually decide to get married. The subject of love next leads him to consider jealousy, which, in this context, suggests that someone they know envies their good fortune. Because they occupy opposite sides of the same coin, the theme of jealousy is followed by that of rivalry. Perhaps one of the couple has triumphed over a jealous adversary for the hand of his or her partner. The only rivalry that interests the husband, however, is the competition for his attention between an attractive woman and an interesting book. Sometimes he prefers to take long walks at dusk. Since he seems to lead a quiet life, perhaps it is his wife who is the object of the jealousy encountered earlier. Perhaps another woman wishes the husband had married her instead. While all these thoughts are passing through the speaker's mind, his wife makes a quizzical gesture and asks what he is thinking about. Instead of brushing her off with a simple: "Nothing"— in other words refusing to communicate—he attentively shares his thoughts with her. Only at this point do we learn that the couple have been traveling by train the whole time. Their trip has taken them along a beautiful gulf coast somewhere, where the sky is even more lovely than the sea. Gazing deep into each other's eyes, they make plans for the future. Like a prisoner calculating how soon he will be released, they are excited by the prospect of spending the rest of their lives together.

Although "Lune de miel" is firmly embedded in *Les Champs magnétiques*, which Breton called "le premier ouvrage purement surréaliste" ("the first purely Surrealist work"), it is only tangentially related to Surrealism. While it lacks the visual dislocation typical of "Forêt-Noire" or "Monsieur V," it is essentially a Cubist composition. Like most of Breton's early poetry, "Lune de miel" relies heavily on parataxis. It consists of a series of nonsequiturs punctuated by impersonal constructions and vague generalizations. Although the text possesses a linear structure, the relationship between successive sentences is hopelessly obscure. Isolated pronouncements are juxtaposed with other isolated pronouncements to create a giant jigsaw puzzle. The only Surreal touch is provided by the intriguing statement: "Le doigt sur la tempe n'est pas le canon d'un revolver," but Breton makes no effort to capitalize on it. More importantly, he makes no attempt to create an atmosphere of mystery or to evoke the marvelous.[11]

Abandoned Shells

The second text chosen for examination has no title but comes from "Ne bougeons plus" ("Let's not budge") like the first. For convenience's sake, I will call it "Les Nocturnes." Unlike the previous work, it bears all the hallmarks of a Surrealist composition. Although it is much more demanding than the first text, it is also more intriguing and more beautiful. At first glance, to be sure, nothing appears to make any sense. As others have pointed out before me, this is a common reaction to most, if not all, Surrealist texts. One of the things that characterize automatic writing, Sarane Alexandrian notes, is the intensive production of images.[12] Unfortunately, Riffaterre adds, these tend to be "obscure and disconcerting—even absurd."[13] Since Surrealist creations are deliberately irrational, this is not terribly surprising. Their rejection of logic and reason is precisely what makes their contributions to art and literature so valuable. In contrast to "Lune de miel," the second text cannot really be "deciphered," i.e., reduced to a more manageable version. No underlying subtext or allegorical interpretation is readily available. Nor is there meant to be. The author's refusal to capitulate to the reader's impatient demands forces him or her to examine the text more closely. This is really where the ultimate reward lies. On the one hand, much of the pleasure of reading a Surrealist composition derives from its surprising imagery and marvelous encounters. On the other hand, much of the enjoyment also comes from disentangling its various thematic strands, figuring out which elements are related to which, and reconstructing the composition's genesis. As we will see, the unconscious has a grammar all of its own. The first half of "Les Nocturnes" introduces the reader to a strange world inhabited by zombie musicians, moving shrubs, and metamorphic seashells:

> Les nocturnes des musiciens morts bercent les villes à jamais endormies. Sur le perron d'un hôtel de la trentième avenue s'ébattent un bébé et un tout jeune chien. Non, vous ne pouvez vous faire une idée des moeurs aquatiques en regardant à travers les larmes, ce n'est pas vrai. L'espace doux comme la main d'une femme appartient à la vitesse. De jour en jour, on approche des maquis et des marchés. La profondeur des Halles est moindre que celle de l'océan Pacifique. Les livres épais souvent feuilletés deviennent des coquillages abandonnés et pleins de terre.

(The dead musicians' nocturnes lull the towns that have fallen asleep forever. On the front steps of a hotel on 30th Avenue, a baby and a very young dog are playing. No, you cannot learn about aquatic manners by looking through tears; that's not true. Space as soft as a woman's hand belongs to speed. From day to day, some shrubs and some markets move closer together. The depth of Les Halles is less than that of the Pacific Ocean. The thick, much thumbed-through books become abandoned shells full of dirt.)

While some Surrealist compositions evolve from a single sentence or group of sentences, as Riffaterre has impressively demonstrated, this does not describe all of them by any means.[14] So long as a text originates entirely and without interruption during a single unconscious session, his theory is undoubtedly correct. As soon as one of these conditions is violated, however, it is no longer automatically valid. If the session is interrupted before continuing, the text will suffer from a lack of continuity. If it does not originate wholly in the unconscious, it will be unavoidably contaminated. The different sections will be inconsistent at best and totally unrelated at worst. The present composition is a case in point. "Les Nocturnes" is composed of twelve declarative sentences, none of which appear to have anything to do with the others. For this reason, it is hard to believe that the work evolved from a single sentence or that it was generated during an unconscious session. Although we have no idea how the text was actually created, the third sentence appears to be both a joke and a conscious interjection. Not only is it more abrupt than the other sentences, but it is also a response to an earlier (implicit) question: "Can you learn about aquatic manners by looking through tears?" This is the first indication we have had that another person is present. It is also the first time that the speaker has revealed his presence. Like most of the composition, the previous two sentences were studiously impersonal. Unfortunately, while the implicit question and subsequent answer are amusing, they clash with the rest of the text. Although "Les Nocturnes" seems initially to be a collection of random sentences, a closer look reveals that they are bound together by a complex web of interrelated references. As Roman Jakobson has demonstrated, metaphor and metonymy govern all known symbolic systems.[15] The progression of any form of discourse takes place according to two separate but complementary criteria. One subject may lead to another via similarity (the metaphoric way) or through contiguity (the metonymic way). At first glance, "Les Nocturnes" seems to begin in a rather ominous manner. Not only do we encounter dead musicians playing ghostly music, but the towns themselves also appear to be dead. Upon reflection, however, the situation turns out to be less serious than it initially appears. In reality, most Classical composers are dead simply because they lived a long time ago not because anything recently happened to them. Although they are gone, their beautiful music remains for others to enjoy. While the specter of death also hangs over the towns in the text, the situation is not especially menacing. Consciously or unconsciously, Breton compares the towns to babies who have been lulled to sleep by musicians' lullabies.

The second sentence continues some of the themes introduced in the first. It focuses on a single town and its metonymic features, which include broad avenues and sumptuous hotels. Just as each avenue possesses a particular street number, each hotel also possesses a set of front steps. On the steps of one of the hotels, a baby and a puppy are playing. Thus the description continues to progress, via metonymy, from the general to the particular. The focus tightens accordingly from one subject to the next. Pursuing this generative approach, one can summarize the rest of the first two lines by the following diagram: nocturnes→ musiciens + (bercent→ bébé→ jeune chien) + (endormies ←morts). Nocturnes were traditionally associated with musicians, and both of them with rocking cradles— which in turn were associated with sleeping infants, represented here by the "bébé." In addition, "endormies" ("asleep") is reinforced by its resemblance to death, which precedes it in the initial sentence. Like the different parts of the town, most of the remaining images exploit metonymy. By contrast, the transition from "morts" to "endormies," like that from "bébé" to "chien," was generated via metaphor. Thus the members of each couple resemble each other in some way. The first pair are characterized by immobility, the second pair embody the concept of youth.

While it would be tedious to list every single example of metaphor and metonymy, they shape the rest of the text as well. The next three sentences break with the previous two networks, which combine to form a larger, imbricated structure. The fourth sentence, which attempts to combine space and speed, makes no sense and is completely isolated. The fifth sentence, which contains a puzzling reference to moving markets (and shrubs), continues the catalogue of city features begun earlier. It and the humorous third sentence join forces to create the sixth sentence. The allusion to markets engenders the image of Les Halles, while the theme of water (tears and aquatic manners) leads to the Pacific Ocean plus the banal observation that it is deeper than the market. Next the Pacific Ocean generates the abandoned "coquillages" (shells) in the seventh sentence, which turn out to be miraculous transformations of battered books. Since the two are paired with each other, one suspects that the books contain numerous *coquilles* (misprints). That the shells are full of dirt instead of sand is interesting as well. Discussing a similar image in *Poisson soluble* (*Soluble Fish*), which originally accompanied the *Manifeste du surréalisme*, Riffaterre calls attention to the following sentence: "Là des pêcheurs débarquaient des paniers pleins de coquillages terrestres" ("There, some fishermen were unloading baskets full of terrestrial shells"). All that Breton's unconscious needed to do, he explains, was to replace the stock epithet in *coquillages marins* (sea shells) by its antonym: *terrestres* to create "a negative mimesis of the real."[16] As Jakobson declares, antithesis is an important metaphoric principle.[17] Similarity and dissimilarity are simply opposite sides of the same conceptual coin.

Sur les rampes d'agate et les trottoirs roulants on remarque de petites étoiles à la craie qui n'ont jamais signifié que la nostalgie des tapissiers et des marins. L'antiquité est une fontaine nacrée par places, mais la gorge des sphinx a verdi. La grêle horizontale des prisons, ce merveilleux trousseau de clés, nous empêche de voir le soleil. Une danseuse sur la corde raide, c'est notre patience changeante. A l'abri des injures posthumes, nous regrettons l'amour de toutes les femmes, nous relisons des indices barométriques à toutes les devantures de jardin.

(On the agate flight of stairs and the moving sidewalks one notices tiny chalk stars that have never signified anything but the nostalgia of tapestry-makers and sailors. Antiquity is a lustrous fountain, but the sphinxes' throats have turned green. The prisons' horizontal hail, that marvelous ring of keys, prevents us from seeing the sun. A tight rope walker, that's our changeable patience. Sheltered from posthumous harm, we miss all the women's love, we study barometric readings at all the garden shop-windows.)

The second half of "Les Nocturnes" extends the catalogue of city features even further. The hotels and avenues encountered in the first half are supplemented by flights of stairs, sidewalks, a fountain, prisons, and shop-windows. That the sidewalks are moving is a nice touch, as is the fact that they are covered with chalk stars, but why the latter should be associated with nostalgia is unclear. Like the shells examined previously, the nostalgic sailors are probably related to the Pacific Ocean. Perhaps they have been assigned to shore duty and would rather be back on their ship. Although the equation between antiquity and the lustrous fountain is ostensibly a metaphor, its principal function is to inform the reader that the fountain is very old. That it is surrounded by statues of sphinxes seems to be a recurring motif in Breton's work. The same juxtaposition occurs in a poem entitled "Femme et oiseau" (Woman and Bird"), where the fountain represents the source of inspiration and the sphinx the source of wisdom.[18] Whether that is the case here is difficult to say since the reference is so fleeting. The reader has just enough time to note the green patina on the sphinxes' throats, which is a sign that they are made of bronze.

Except for the references to prisons and shop-windows, the metonymic trail grows cold at this point. In exchange, Breton introduces several striking metaphors. "La grêle horizontale des prisons" would appear to describe prison bars except that, for some reason, these are horizontal rather than vertical. A second metaphor establishes an equation between the horizontal hail and a ring of keys, which is even harder to imagine. However, the tightrope walker in the penultimate sentence is an excellent metaphor for someone who is trying not to lose patience. These two sentences confirm our earlier suspicion that Breton is accompanied by somebody else. "La grêle horizontale ... *nous* empêche de voir le soleil," he confides; the tightrope walker "C'est *notre* patience changeante" (emphasis added). The first person plural also occurs twice in the final sentence. As the text continues, it becomes increasingly evident that the speaker and his companion(s) are in prison themselves. They cannot see the sun because they are incarcerated. If they are growing impatient, it is because they are anxious to be released. This means that the relationship between the horizontal bars and the ring of keys (which presumably belong to a jailer) is metonymic rather than metaphorical. Both are common features of prison life. Although Breton and his friend(s) are protected from harm, this is only because they are locked up. For the same reason, they are forbidden to have any contact with women, amorous or otherwise. The term "posthumous" echoes the theme of apparent death introduced at the beginning of the text. Locked away and deprived of any contact with the opposite sex, the prisoners might as well be dead.

A Haunting Refrain

Nineteen twenty-four was a bellwether year for Breton and his fellow Surrealists. He published a collection of essays entitled *Les Pas perdus* (*The Waiting Room*) in February, engaged in a violent war of words for possession of the term "surréalisme" during the summer, and put the finishing touches on the *Manifeste du surréalisme* in October, just before it appeared in print. The same month witnessed the opening of the Bureau de Recherches Surréalistes in the rue Grenelle and the founding of *La Revolution Surrealiste* in December, directed by Pierre Naville and Benjamin Peret. At last a coherent program existed for what Breton and his colleagues had been doing for quite some time.

It was clear that Surrealism would prosper during the long years ahead. Attached to the *Manifeste* was another document, drafted during the previous spring, in which Breton continued his experiments with psychic automatism. Entitled *Poisson Soluble* (*Soluble Fish*), it included thirty-two unrelated automatic texts selected from a total of over one hundred. Since each possesses the semantic autonomy characteristic of a piece of poetry, Riffaterre contends that they are prose poems.[19] The collection's delightful title was added at the last moment, while Breton was correcting the proofs. "N'est-ce pas moi le poisson soluble," he asked at one point in the *Manifeste*; "je suis né sous le signe des Poissons, et l'homme est soluble dans sa pensée!" ("Isn't the soluble fish really me? I was born under the sign of Pisces, and man is soluble in his thought!").[20] Marguerite Bonnet speculates that the title represents "une figure emblématique de l'écriture automatique elle-même" ("an emblematic figure for automatic writing itself").[21]

According to Laurent Jenny, *Poisson soluble* belongs to Surrealism's most radical period, where it made the most decisive contribution to Surrealist writing experiments.[22] In Ferdinand Alquié's opinion, *Poisson soluble* constitutes "la plus significative des oeuvres surréalistes" ("the most significant of the Surrealist works").[23] Like the other automatic texts, however, it has received relatively little critical attention. Nor is there much consensus as to what the work is really about. According to Anna Balakian, its basic subject is "self-identification," i.e., memories of love, liberty, and adventure in Paris. In her opinion, it foresees all the fundamental images of Breton's future poetry.[24] For Sarane Alexandrian, on the contrary, it resembles an imaginary autobiography. "Jamais l'inspiration de Breton," he writes, "ne sera plus légère, plus ensoleillée, plus insouciante que dans ce texte merveilleux" ("Never will Breton's inspiration be lighter, sunnier, more carefree than in this marvelous text").[25] In return, Bonnet vehemently attacks his autobiographical interpretation as well as his ecstatic praise. In her opinion, *Poisson soluble* suffers from "une insécurité et une instabilité géneralisées [qui] minent le récit" ("a generalized insecurity and instability [that] undermine the story").[26] Nevertheless, since both Balakian and

Alexandrian compare the compositions to dreams, a certain amount of spatiotemporal disruption is to be expected. As noted previously, the unconscious operates according to its own unique grammar. The degree of automatism also varies from one work to the next and even within a single composition.

As Alexandrian declares, *Poisson soluble* possesses "une plénitude qui laisse bien loin derrière lui *Les Champs magnétiques*" ("a completeness that leaves *Les Champs magnétiques* far behind"). Not only are the paragraphs longer and more developed, but the finished texts resemble miniature short stories. Some of them are situated in Paris, some in the countryside, and some in both locations. Like several other compositions in the collection, Number 24 takes place initially in the capital and is divided into four parts. The first paragraph introduces an obsessive refrain that runs throughout the composition:

> "Un baiser est si vite oublié" j'écoutais passer ce refrain dans les grandes promenades de ma tête, dans la province de ma tête et je ne savais plus rien de ma vie, qui se déroulait sur sa piste blonde. Vouloir entendre plus loin que soi, plus loin que cette roué dont un rayon, à l'avant de moi, effleure à peine les ornières, quelle folie! J'avais passé la nuit en compagnie d'une femme frêle et avertie, tapi dans les hautes herbes d'une place publique, du côté du Pont-Neuf. Une heure durant nous avions ri des serments qu' échangeaient par surprise les tardifs promeneurs, qui venaient tour à tour s'asseoir sur le banc le plus proche. Nous étendions la main vers les capucines coulant d'un balcon de City-Hôtel, avec l'intention d'abolir dans l'air tout ce qui sonne en trébuchant comme les monnaies anciennes qui exceptionellement avaient cours cette nuit-là.

> ("A kiss is so quickly forgotten." I listened to this refrain traversing my head's broad avenues, in my head's province, and I forgot everything about my life, which was unfolding on the blonde path. Trying to understand more than oneself, more than this wheel before me from which a spoke touches the ruts, what madness! I spent the night hidden in a public square's tall grass near the Pont-Neuf with a frail, experienced woman. We laughed for one whole hour at the surprising

declarations late strollers made to each other and who came to sit on the closest bench one after the other. We reached toward the nasturtiums flowing from the City Hotel's balcony, intending to eliminate every awkward aerial thing that rings like old coins—which, unbelievably, were legal tender that night.)

If a kiss is so quickly forgotten, as the refrain repeatedly insists, that clearly does not describe the kiss in this song, which pursues Breton with unbelievable tenacity. It appears over and over like clockwork. It is important nevertheless to note that it is also fundamentally perverse. Kisses are *not* quickly forgotten because they express love, tenderness, and/or passion. For this reason, people still remember a kiss many years later. Suffice it to say that the basic situation evoked in the text is familiar to just about everyone. While apparently thinking about some aspect of his life, Breton either hears or remembers a line from a song that reminds him of an exciting experience with a woman. The memory is so powerful that it causes him to forget about everything else, including the subject he was just considering. In Bonnet's opinion, the first sentence is "une allusion à l'operation même de l'écriture automatique" ("an allusion to the process of automatic writing").[27] The incident itself is evoked by means of an extended geographical metaphor. Breton's thoughts are compared, first, to broad avenues and then to a whole province, while his life is described as "blonde piste." Since the path is blonde, it is probably a simple dirt (or sandy) track. Overcome by the immensity of everything beyond his immediate sphere, which includes a bicycle wheel lying on the ground before him, he despairs of ever trying to comprehend it all.

At this point, contrary to what the refrain proclaims, Breton remembers a previous adventure with a mysterious woman—probably the woman he has been thinking about. For some reason, the two of them were hiding in a public square near the Pont-Neuf. We never find out whom they are hiding from or why. As Riffaterre points out, "tapi dans les hautes herbes" is a cliché generated by the first word in the sequence."[28] Thus next four words fall into place effortlessly and automatically. Bonnet identifies the square in question as the place Dauphine, located on the western tip of the Isle de la Cité.[29] Since Breton used to live there, as he notes in *Nadja*, he knew the area well.[30] Although the park is well kept today, in 1924 it was apparently terribly neglected. Breton confided four years later that it was "un des pires terrains vagues qui soient à Paris" ("one of the worst no man's lands in Paris"). Thus the tall grass in the text may well have been generated by a cliché, as Riffaterre implies, or it may have actually been a historical fact. As passing lovers whisper endearments to each other, Breton and the woman reach out toward a mass of nasturtiums tumbling from the balcony of the City-Hotel, where he formerly resided. For some strange reason, they think the flowers are unsightly and wish to destroy them.

> Mon amie parlait par aphorismes tels que "Qui souvent me baise mieux s'oublie" mais il n'était question que d'une partie de paradis et, tandis que nous rejetions autour de nous des drapeaux qui allaient se poser aux fenêtres, nous abdiquions peu à peu toute insouciance, de sorte qu'au matin il ne resta de nous que cette chanson qui lappait un peu d'eau de la nuit au centre de la place: "Un baiser est si vite oublié." Les laitiers conduisaient avec fracas leurs voitures aurifères au lieu des fuites éternelles. Nous nous étions séparés en criant de toute la force de notre coeur. J'étais seul et, le long de la Seine, je découvrais des bancs d'oiseaux, des bancs de poissons, je m'enfonçais avec précaution dans les buissons d'orties d'un village blanc. Ce village était encombré de ces bobines de télégraphe qu'on voit suspendues à égale distance, de part et d'autre des poteaux des grandes routes. Il avait l'aspect d'une de ces pages de romance que l'on achète pour quelques sous dans les rassemblements suburbains. "Un baiser est si vite oublié." Sur la couverture du village, tournée vers la terre, et qui était tout ce qui restait de la campagne, on distinguait mal une sorte de lorette sautant à la corde à l'orée d'un bois de laurier gris.

> (My woman friend spoke in aphorisms, such as "Whoever kisses me often will be forgotten the quickest," but it was only a game of Paradise and, while we wrapped some flags around us that were supposed to be hanging from the windows, we gradually renounced all unconcern,

so that in the morning all that remained of us was that song, which
lapped up a little night water in the center of the square: "A kiss is so
quickly forgotten." The milkmen drove their noisy gold-bearing trucks
instead of eternal leaks. Upon parting we shouted with all the force
in our hearts. I was alone and, along the Seine, I discovered shoals of
birds and shoals of fish. I carefully thrust myself into the nettle bushes
in a white village. This village was crammed with those telegraph
spools one sees, equally spaced and hanging from the poles on either
side of major highways. It looked like one of those romance booklets
for sale at suburban gatherings. "A kiss is so quickly forgotten." On the
village's roof, turned toward the earth, which was all that remained of
the countryside, one could barely discern a young woman jumping
rope near a copse of gray laurel.)

Although we know virtually nothing about Breton's companion, we
learn in the second paragraph that she expresses herself via aphorisms.
The first example is basically a variation on the haunting refrain. "Un
baiser est si vite oublié" is transformed into "Qui souvent me baise
mieux s'oublie." Disguised as a sweeping generalization, the original
refrain is fundamentally ambiguous. It is impossible to tell whether
it represents a complaint, for example, or an ironic observation. One
also wonders exactly who is speaking. Fortunately, the answers to
these questions are provided by Breton's woman friend, who adds two
intensifiers (*souvent* and *mieux*) and an indirect object pronoun to the
original refrain. Two things are immediately apparent: (1) the degree
of forgetfulness is directly proportional to the intensity of the kiss and
(2) she is talking about her own experience. She could very well be the
author of the original refrain as well. Unfortunately, the portrait of her
that emerges is far from flattering. Not only do kisses mean nothing
to her, but she is also incapable of responding to passion. At best, she
is fickle; at the worst she is pathological. Although Breton claims that
the expanded refrain is an aphorism, moreover, the situation is exactly
the reverse. Since an aphorism is a short, pithy statement containing
a general truth, it describes the original refrain but not the expanded
version. Everything is not always as it appears to be when automatic
writing is involved.

Following a game of Paradise, whatever that may be, Breton and the woman wrap themselves in holiday flags and drift off to sleep on the grass. By the time the next morning dawns, they have been completely absorbed by the refrain which, transformed into an animal, laps up water from a puddle. Since it is morning, milkmen are noisily delivering milk to their customers. Electing to go their separate ways, the two adventurers, who have somehow regained their original form, utter a cry "with all the force of their hearts." Here again an automatic mechanism is at work, this time involving repetition and substitution instead of addition. The basic model is provided by the cliché: "with all the force of their lungs." Eager to economize, the unconscious adopts this readymade phrase and substitutes *coeur* for *poumons*. As such, it gives new meaning to the principle of conservation of energy. Since both words belong to the same category, namely "internal organs," the substitution encounters minimal resistance.

Striking out on his own, Breton discovers shoals of fish swimming in the Seine and shoals of birds flying in the air. Like the English adjective, *banc* ("shoal") in French is reserved for fish not for birds. Here and elsewhere, repetition provides another unconscious shortcut. Perversely thrusting himself into some nettles, which one would normally avoid, Breton discovers a village filled with large telegraph spools. For some reason, the scene reminds him of cheap romance booklets sold in the suburbs rather than the cities, and in public gatherings rather than stores, where one would expect to find them. Triggered perhaps by Breton's decision to enter a thicket of nettles, the sentence contains two unexpected antonyms. As noted previously, the unconscious occasionally likes to replace metaphors with their opposites. Following the refrain, which appears one more time, the reader learns two more surprising things, both of which are definitely abnormal. Not only is the village covered by a roof, but the latter is oriented toward the ground rather than toward the sky. Equally implausibly, a young woman is jumping rope on top of the (upside down) roof. Remarking the similarity between "lorette" and "laurier," Bonnet perceptively deduces that the woman is Marie Laurencin, who was Apollinaire's lover for many years.[31] In the latter's *Poète assassiné*, she appears as a character named Tristouse Ballerinette, who, like Marie herself, is fond of jumping rope.

> Je pénétrai dans ce bois, où les noisettes étaient rouges. Noisettes rouillés, étiez-vous les persiennes du baiser qui me poursuivait pour que je l'oubliasse? J'en avais peur, je m'écartais brusquement de chaque buisson. Mes yeux étaient les fleurs de noisetier, l'oeil droit la fleur mâle, le gauche la fleur femelle. Mais j'avais cessé de me plaire depuis longtemps. Des sentiers sifflaient de toutes parts devant moi. Près d'une source la belle de la nuit me rejoignit haletante. Un baiser est si vite oublié. Ses cheveux n'étaient plus qu'une levée de champignons roses, parmi les aiguilles de pin et de très fines verreries de feuilles sèches.

> (I entered this copse whose hazel-nuts were red. Rusty hazel-nuts, were you the Venetian blinds of the kiss pursuing me so I would forget it? I was afraid, I suddenly moved away from each bush. My eyes were hazel-nut flowers, the right the male flower, the left the female flower. But I had ceased to please myself a long time ago. Paths whistled from every direction before me. Near a spring, the nocturnal beauty rejoined me out of breath. A kiss is so quickly forgotten. Her hair was no more than a swell of pink mushrooms, among the pine needles and some very fine glassware made of dry leaves.)

As Breton enters a grove of hazel bushes, he is surprised to discover that their nuts are red. Wondering if they can block the kiss that has been pursuing him, like Venetian blinds blocking the light, he suddenly feels afraid. Although he quickly moves away, hoping to escape the hallucinatory experience awaiting him, he is not successful. While the converging paths utter mysterious whistling sounds, his eyes are both transformed into hazel-nut flowers. Wandering over to a nearby spring, Breton is joined by his female companion in the previous paragraph. Once again she is accompanied by the haunting refrain, which by now has become her *leitmotiv*: "Un baiser est si vite oublieé." The fact that Breton associates her with mushrooms, pine needles, and dry leaves suggests that she may be an Earth Mother figure.

> Nous gagnâmes ainsi la ville d'Ecureil-sur-mer. Là des pêcheurs débarquaient des paniers pleins de coquillages terrestres, parmi

lesquels beaucoup d'oreilles, que des étoiles circulant à travers la ville s'appliquaient douloureusement sur le coeur pour entendre le bruit de la terre. C'est ainsi qu'elles avaient pu reconstituer pour leur plaisir le bruit des tramways et des grandes orgues, tout comme nous recherchons dans notre solitude les sonneries des paliers soumarins, le ronflement des ascenseurs aquatiques. Nous passâmes inaperçus des courbes de céans, sinusoïdes, paraboles, geysers, pluies. Nous n'appartenions plus qu'au désespoir de notre chanson, à la sempiternelle évidence de ces mots touchant le baiser. Nous nous anéantîmes, d'ailleurs, tout près de là, dans un étalage où n'apparaissait des hommes et des femmes que ce qui de leur nudité nous est le plus géneralement visible: soit le visage et les mains, à peu de chose près. Une jeune fille était pourtant nu-pieds. Nous endossâmes à notre tour les vêtements de l'air pur.

(Thus we reached the town of Squirrel-on-the-Sea. There, fishermen were unloading baskets full of terrestrial shells, among which were numerous ears that some starfish, circulating around town, painfully pressed to their hearts in order to hear the sound of the earth. In this manner, they were able to recreate the sound of streetcars and powerful church organs for their pleasure, just as we, in our solitude, listen for doorbells ringing on submarine stairwells and the rumbling of aquatic elevators. We passed by unnoticed by the curves within, sinusoidal curves, parabolas, geysers, rains. Henceforth we belonged exclusively to our song's despair, to the eternal evidence of those words concerning the kiss. We disappeared into a nearby display where all we could see of the men's and women's nudity was what is generally visible: their faces and their hands. One girl was barefoot. When our turn came, we put on clothes of pure air.)

Whether the meeting at the fountain occurs by chance or by prearrangement, Breton and the woman act like an actual couple from that moment on. All of their subsequent experiences are recounted in the first person plural. Reaching a town with a ridiculous name, they witness several fishermen unloading "coquillages terrestres" as well as batches of human ears. Although the terrestrial shells were discussed earlier in the context of "Les Nocturnes," the fact that they are accompanied by ears comes as a surprise. In point of fact, however, each one traditionally serves as a metaphor for the other. Thus the Spanish Surrealist Vicente Aleixandre deliberately juxtaposes them in a phrase from "Mi voz" ("My Voice"): "palabras sin sentido/que ruedan como oídos, caracoles" ("senseless words/rolling around like ears, seashells").[32] In both literature and art, Wendy Steiner explains, "the ear … is frequently depicted as a shell—that is, both the hearer of the sea sounds and their receptacle."[33] And since the metaphor is reversible, shells are often depicted as ears. Thus Paul Eluard's portrait of Paul Klee contains the following line: "Sur la plage la mer a laissé ses oreilles" ("On the beach, the sea has left its ears").[34] Technically, since their tenors are never stated, both are implicit metaphors. Because ears and shells serve as receptacles for sound, they are united by functional similarity. Breton embellishes the metaphorical exchange in *Poisson soluble* by introducing several starfish, which engage in a bizarre ritual. Pressing their ears to their hearts, they listen to the sound of the earth. This is an example of what Riffaterre identifies as a "conversion," where a sentence is completely transformed by a simultaneous transformation of all of its components.[35] Beginning with the stereotypical phrase: "pressing the shells to their ears, they listen to the sound of the sea," the unconscious perverts each of the nouns in turn. The final sentence plays on two registers (ears and shells) at the same time, one implicit and the other explicit.

Ironically, the sounds that the starfish manage to detect are associated not with the earth but with the modern city. The sound of streetcars vies with other noises for their attention. Despite this apparent setback, the starfish find these sounds pleasing—just like Breton and his female companion, who enjoy the sound of doorbells and elevators. The fact that these sounds emanate from under the water is surprising but apparently not a serious problem. Concentrating on the relentless refrain, the poet and the woman immerse themselves in the song's despair: "Un baiser est si vite oublié." At long last, we learn how this ambiguous line is meant to be interpreted—as a mournful protest against the transience of love. The last few sentences combine to form a marvelous conclusion, literally and figuratively. Dismayed by the realization that love is fleeting, the two adventurers discover a group of mannequins in a nearby store window. Like all mannequins, which occupy a position of honor in the Surrealist pantheon, they embody *le merveilleux* ("the marvelous").[36] Perhaps this explains how Breton and his companion manage to join them behind the glass, where they wait to be transformed into mannequins themselves. Against all odds, they have found a way to escape the fate reserved for them. Never again will they be troubled by kisses that are quickly forgotten.

Reviewing the Surrealists' contributions to art and literature, which were more extensive than is often recognized, Anna Balakian calls attention to their "systematic cult of the latent possibilities of language."[37] Although Surrealist art has attracted much more attention than Surrealist writing over the years, this is primarily because it is more accessible. By contrast, Surrealist texts are much more demanding. Readers basically need to recreate the work in question by filtering the author's words through their own network of memories and personal associations. To be sure, reader response critics have demonstrated that this describes works of literature in general. The difference is that Surrealist texts are a great deal harder to interpret. This is especially true of the experiments with automatic writing, which lack a conscious structure. Interestingly, Breton concluded in 1933 that verbal inspiration was "infinitely richer" from a visual perspective than anything an artist could create.[38] "Voilà ... la véritable révolution déclenchée par Breton dans le langage poétique," Alexandrian concludes: "on se laisse emporter par son cours comme un fétu par un torrent" ("That is ... the real revolution in poetic language launched by Breton: writers let themselves be carried away by the flow of their writing like a piece of straw in a flood").[39] The degree of freedom experienced by automatic authors is not only unparalleled but exhilarating as well. By 1933, the Surrealists had begun to modify their initial experiments with automatic writing and were experimenting with new means of tapping the unconscious. Nevertheless, *Les Champs magnétiques* and *Poisson soluble* would always occupy a special place in their hearts. As Breton noted the same year, "la volonté d'ouvrir toutes grandes les écluses [de l'inconscient] restera sans nul doute l'idée génératrice du surréalisme" ("the desire to fling open the flood gates [of the unconscious] will forever remain the seminal principle of Surrealism").[40]

Despite the undeniable attractions of automatic writing, Breton realized from the beginning that a certain amount of risk was involved. Indeed, that appears to have been part of his initial motivation. What originally inspired him, he admitted in his notes for *Les Champs magnétiques*, "c'est le désir d'écrire un livre dangereux" ("it is the desire to write a dangerous book").[41] This explains why his experiments were limited to such a relatively short period. By 1925, when Breton abandoned this fascinating genre, they had become too dangerous. Writing in 1933, he addressed the problem directly: "L'écriture automatique, pratiqueé avec quelque ferveur, mène tout droit à l'hallucination visuelle, j'en ai fait personnellement l'expérience" ("Practiced with some fervor, automatic writing leads directly to visual hallucination; I have personally experienced it").[42] Although this admission was intriguing, to say the least, it was all anyone knew about Breton's experience with unconscious dictation until a copy of *Les Champs magnétiques* surfaced with a note in his handwriting opposite the phrase "Pneus pattes de velours" ("tires velvet paws") (from "Eclipses"): "Cette phrase ... m'a joué les plus mauvais tours. C'est à elle que j'ai dû de me croire un après-midi ... traqué place de l'Etoile par des chats qui étaient peut-être ... seulement des autos" ("This phrase ... played terrible tricks on me. Thanks to it, I believed I was being hunted by some cats at the place de l'Etoile one afternoon, which were perhaps only ... some cars").[43] Although the Surrealists were very interested in mental patients, Breton had no wish to become one himself. While he admired their untrammeled imagination, the price he would have had to pay was simply too great.

Notes

1   See, for example, Michel Décaudin, "Autour du premier manifeste,"
     Quaderni del Novecento Francese, No. 2 (1974), pp. 27–47 and Paul Ilie,
     "The Term 'Surrealism' and Its Philological Imperative," *Romanic Review*,
     Vol. 69, Nos. 1–2 (January–March, 1978), pp. 90–102.

2   L. C. Breunig, "Le Sur-réalisme," *Revue des Lettres Modernes*, Nos. 123–126 (1965), pp. 25–7.

3   André Breton, *Manifeste du surréalisme, Oeuvres complètes*, Vol. 1, ed. Marguerite Bonnet et al. (Paris: Gallimard, 1988), p. 328.

4   Cited by Philippe Audoin in *Breton* (Paris: Gallimard, 1970), p. 17.

5   Cited by Jacqueline Chénieux-Gendron in *Surrealism*, tr. Vivian Folkenflik (New York: Columbia University Press, 1990), p. 33.

6   See André Breton and Philippe Soupault, *Les Champs magnétiques: Le Manuscrit original fac-similé et transcription*, ed. Serge Faucherau and Lydia Lachenal (Paris: Lachenal and Ritter, 1988).

7   Michael Riffaterre, *Text Production*, tr. Terese Lyons (New York: Columbia University Press, 1983), p. 221.

8   Breton, *Manifeste*, pp. 325–6. See also André Breton, *Les Pas perdus, Oeuvres complètes*, pp. 274–5.

9   Breton, *Manifeste*, pp. 331–2.

10 Louis Aragon, "L'Homme coupé en deux," *Les Lettres Françaises*, May 9–15, 1968, p. 7.

11 For the difference between these two concepts, see André Breton, "Le Merveilleux contre le mystère," in *La Clé des champs, Oeuvres complètes*, Vol. 3, ed. Marguerite Bonnet et al. (Paris: Gallimard, 1999), pp. 653–8.

12 Sarane Alexandrian, *André Breton par lui-même* (Paris: Seuil, n.d.), p. 40.

13 Riffaterre, *Text Production*, p. 202.

14 Michael Riffaterre, *Semiotics of Poetry* (Bloomington: Indiana University Press, 1978), pp. 19–22.

15 Roman Jakobson, "Two Aspects of Language and Two Types of Aphasic Disturbances," in *Fundamentals of Language*, ed. Roman Jakobson and Morris Halle, 2nd ed. (The Hague: Mouton, 1971), pp. 90–6.

16 Riffaterre, *Semiotics of Poetry*, pp. 218–19.

17 See Jakobson, "Two Aspects of Language," p. 91.

18 André Breton, "Femme et oiseau," *Signe ascendant suivi de …Constellations* (Paris: Gallimard, 1968), p. 143. See Willard Bohn, *The Rise of Surrealism: Cubism, Dada, and the Pursuit of the Marvelous* (Albany: State University of New York Press, 2002), pp. 195–209.

19 Riffaterre, *Text Production*, p. 222.

20 Breton, *Manifeste*, p. 340.

21   Marguerite Bonnet, "Notice" in Breton, *Oeuvres complètes*, Vol. 1, p. 1373.

22   Laurent Jenny, "La Surréalité et ses signes narratifs," *Poétique*, No. 16 (1973), p. 499.

23   Ferdinand Alquié, *Philosophie du surréalisme* (Paris: Flammarion, 1955), p. 13.

24   Anna Balakian, *André Breton* (New York: Oxford University Press, 1971), pp. 65 and 67.

25   Alexandrian, *André Breton par lui même*, pp. 40 and 42.

26   Bonnet, "Notice," pp. 1374–6.

27   Ibid., p. 1388.

28   Riffaterre, *Text Production*, p. 207.

29   Bonnet, "Notice," p. 1388. See Breton, "Pont-Neuf," in *La Clé des champs, Oeuvres complètes*, Vol. 3, 888–95.

30   André Breton, *Nadja* in *Oeuvres complètes*, Vol. 1, pp. 693–5.

31   Bonnet, "Notice," pp. 1388–9.

32   Vicente Aleixandre, *Poesía completa*, ed. Alejandro Sanz (Barcelona: Lumen, 2017), p. 171.

33   Wendy Steiner, *The Colors of Rhetoric: Problems in the Relation between Modern Literature and Painting* (Chicago: University of Chicago Press, 1982), p. 72.

34   Paul Eluard, *Oeuvres complètes*, Vol. 1, ed. Marcelle Dumas and Lucien Scheler (Paris: Gallimard, 1968), p.182.

35   Riffaterre, *Text Production*, p. 53.

36   Breton, *Manifeste*, p. 321.

37   Anna Balakian, *Surrealism: The Road to the Absolute* (Chicago: University of Chicago Press, 1986), p. 142.

38   André Breton, "Le Message automatique," *Point du jour in Oeuvres complètes*, Vol. 2, p. 389.

39   Alexandrian, *André Breton par lui-même*, p. 39.

40   Breton, "Le Message automatique," p. 380.

41   Quoted in Marguerite Bonnet, *André Breton: Naissance de l'aventure surréaliste* (Paris: Corti, 1975), p. 187.

42   Breton, "Le Message automatique," p. 390.

43   Breton and Soupault, *Les Champs magnétiques*, p. 93, line 6.

2

Revisiting the Surrealist Image

When André Breton undertook to write the *Manifeste du surréalisme* in 1924, after experimenting with automatic writing for five years, he chose to follow an illustrious example. Inspired by the Renaissance poet Joachim Du Bellay, who authored the *Défense et Illustration de la Langue Francaise* in 1549, he divided the manifesto into two (extremely disproportionate) halves.[1] Discussing the sources of poetic imagination in the first, smaller section, Breton proclaimed that realism, logic, and rationalism were to be avoided at all cost. Like descriptive passages, which he scornfully compared to postcards, they were boring and totally unsuited to poetry. A sentence like "La marquise sortit à cinq heures" ("The marquess went out at five o'clock") was simply and purely intended to convey information. It had no more poetic qualities than a realistic novel. Far better, Breton insisted, to cultivate qualities such as originality, imagination, and the "marvelous." Indeed, the third concept was to become one of Surrealism's guiding principles. Producing metaphysical shivers in the reader, Breton explained, *le merveilleux* reflected "l'irrémédiable inquiétude humaine" ("incurable human anxiety").[2] All three concepts were epitomized by two explorers whose discoveries were to have profound implications for the modern world. Like Christopher Columbus, who revolutionized the study of geography, Sigmund Freud transformed the study of psychology. To Breton the discovery of the unconscious was especially intriguing, and it caused him to wonder if dream and reality could somehow be combined to create an absolute reality, a *surréalité*. "C'est à sa conquête," he proclaimed, "que je vais" ("That's exactly what I am trying to accomplish").[3]

Pierre Reverdy

The remainder of the first manifesto, that reserved for the "illustration" of Surrealism, described Breton's project in great detail. Dismissing his earlier poetic attempts as "pseudo poetry," he hastened to introduce a second tenet of Surrealism that he clearly found exciting. So far, ironically, he had yet to introduce the movement itself. Convinced that Surrealist poetry should possess a marvelous dimension, Breton discussed one of the surest ways to accomplish this goal: through the use of marvelous imagery. Before he could proceed, however, he needed to examine this issue more closely. Fortunately, as numerous critics have noted previously, Pierre Reverdy had published an article in *Nord-Sud* six years earlier that caught his eye. Entitled "L'Image," it contained the following lines:

> L'image est une création pure de l'esprit.
> Elle ne peut naître d'une comparaison mais du rapprochement de deux
>   réalités plus ou moins éloignées.
> Plus les rapports des deux réalités rapprochées seront lointains et justes,
>   plus l'image sera forte—plus elle aura de puissance émotive et de
>   réalité poétique.[4]

(The image is a pure creation of the mind. It results not from a comparison but from the juxtaposition of two more or less distant realities. The more the relations between the two juxtaposed realities are distant and valid, the stronger the image will be—the more emotive power and poetic reality it will possess.)

Interestingly, these lines seem to describe how *metaphor* functions as opposed to a single isolated image. They evoke an image that is composed of two other images, which are juxtaposed to create a hybrid trope. Reverdy admits as much himself on the following page, where he calls the image an "analogie." Although he does not employ the language of metaphor, which revolves around similarity and substitution, his rejection of comparison confirms this identification.

Since similes have been excluded, metaphor is the only figurative device remaining that fits the basic description. Unfortunately, the term "image" tends to dissolve into confusion before long, as does the notion of "metaphor." For this reason Robert Champigny prefers to call Reverdy's creation an "S device" rather than a metaphor.[5] In order to distinguish between the two images that constitute the primary image, however, I. A. Richards's distinction between "tenor" and "vehicle" proves to be more useful. Appropriated by Breton six years later (with one key modification), the bipolar trope would lead to the creation of the Surrealist image. Widely regarded as "the most articulate aesthetician among the poets," to quote L. C. Breunig, Reverdy could also be extremely convincing.[6] Although he remained a cubist poet for as long as he lived, his discussion of metaphor had major repercussions for the nascent Surrealist movement. While Breton found his article fascinating, he decided, after lengthy reflection, that it was not entirely credible. Unfortunately, Reverdy's theory seemed to be lacking something. What that was and how he chose to deal with it is the subject of the present study.

As Breton instantly realized, Reverdy's article was a brilliant piece of structural analysis. His discussion of the dynamics of bipolar imagery produced at least two important insights. The first lesson was that juxtaposition was a more effective tool than comparison for creating vivid imagery. Because metaphors were more direct than similes, they were naturally more evocative and thus more powerful. As Marcel Lecomte observes, "La poésie reverdyenne implique ... la fin du jeu de la particule 'comme' à l'intérieur du poème. L'image doit surgir d'un rapprochement à la fois lointain et irremplaçable" ("Reverdy's poetry implies ... the end of poetry's 'like' game. The image must arise from a distant and unique connection").[7] Because the second lesson was counter-intuitive, it took a little more time to digest. The more distant (i.e., dissimilar) the tenor and the vehicle were from each other, Reverdy insisted, the more powerful the final image would be, so long as a valid bond continued to exist between them. Having authored five volumes of poetry, he spoke from personal experience. Two verses chosen at random will demonstrate what he meant:

Les coeurs brûlent à feu couvert
("Their hearts burn with a smoldering fire")
Un nuage passe à cheval
("A cloud passes by on horseback").[8]

The first example comes from "Paris-Noël" ("Paris Christmas"), published in *Quelques Poèmes* (*Several Poems*) in 1916. Although it is hard to be sure, the smoldering hearts seem to belong to members of the religious procession evoked in the preceding line. Because the equation between passion and fire was essentially a cliché by then, the distance between them was greatly reduced from what it was originally. As a consequence, the resulting metaphor is relatively weak. The second example is taken from "La Saison Dernière" ("Last Season"), included in *Les Ardoises du toit* (*Roof Slates*) in 1918. Unlike the previous line, the equation between the fast-moving cloud and a man on horseback is original and completely unexpected. Since the distance between tenor and vehicle is much greater than in the first example, the image is much more powerful. The next line confirms that it is a windy day and continues the theme of flight: "En courant le vent le dépasse" ("The wind runs right past it").

It would be interesting to know how Reverdy arrived at the dazzling epiphany described in "L'Image," which was destined to have long-lasting repercussions for him, for the Surrealists, and for modern French poetry. One also wonders if the article was entirely his own creation. These questions lead to an intriguing observation. Although Breton admits that he borrowed the bipolar image from Reverdy, no one seems to have any idea where Reverdy found it (if in fact he did). While in theory he could have authored the article himself, he could also have discovered it (or a portion of it) somewhere else. To be sure, the claim that a metaphor's force is proportional to the distance between its poles strikes one as completely original. Nevertheless, the image's structural model ("the juxtaposition of two realities") dates at least from Classical antiquity. Perceived as an important contribution to the modernist enterprise, metaphor attracted a huge amount of avant-garde attention at the beginning of the twentieth century. Writing in 1897, for instance, Mallarmé compared metaphors to parallel bonfires "prompts tous, avant extinction, à une réciprocité de feux distante" ("hurrying, before they are extinguished, to participate in a distant reciprocity of fires").[9] Returning to the same theme seven years later, he elaborated on the original line. This time, metaphors were portrayed as blazing reciprocal reflections in the Book of Life:

> L'Oeuvre pure implique la disparition élocutoire du poète, qui cède l'initiative aux mots, par le heurt de leur inégalité mobilisés; ils s'allument de reflets réciproques ... .

> (The pure Work implies the elocutionary disappearance of the poet, who cedes the initiative to the words, mobilized by the shock of their inequality; they catch fire from their parallel reflections ...).[10]

Although Mallarmé probably played a role in Reverdy's education, together with other nineteenth-century poets, one suspects that his influence was fairly minimal. By contrast Apollinaire, whom Reverdy knew personally and admired, almost certainly influenced him. Not only was he an accomplished poet, but he was also an excellent role model for a young poet who was just beginning his career. As early as 1909, for example, Jules Romains praised Apollinaire's poetry for "l'explosion d'analogies imprévues et qui juxtaposent si soudainement des parcelles de l'univers si distantes" ("the explosion of unforeseen analogies, which suddenly juxtapose such distant parcels of the universe").[11] Interestingly, Reverdy would employ the same devices— surprise and distance—in his own poetry before long. F. T. Marinetti, who was the leader of the Italian Futurists, was also a likely source for some of the ideas expressed in "L'Image." As Robert W. Greene, Herbert S. Gershman, and Gerald Mead have all pointed out, Marinetti published a *Manifeste technique de la littérature futuriste* in 1912 that may have served as Reverdy's blueprint six years later.[12] The Italian manifesto (written in French) includes two sentences in particular that closely resemble portions of "L'Image." Evoking the vastness of the universe at one point, Marinetti defined analogy as "l'amour immense qui rattache les choses distantes, apparamment différentes et hostiles" ("the immense love that connects distant things that appear to be different from, and hostile to, each other").[13] This definition recalls a similar remark by Reverdy, who, as has been noted previously, evoked the "rapprochement de deux réalités plus ou moins éloignées" ("the juxtaposition of two realities that are more or less distant from each other"). In both cases, the fact that the images are far apart emphasizes the power of analogy to transcend time and space. Inspired perhaps by Marinetti as well, Georges Duhamel made a similar point the following year. "Plus une image s'adresse à des objets naturellement distants dans le temps et l'espace," he declared, "plus elle est surprenante et suggestive" ("The more an image is addressed to objects naturally distant in time and space, the more surprising and suggestive it is").[14]

Returning to his discussion of the image a few lines later, Marinetti amplified his previous statement. "Plus les images contiennent de rapports vastes," he declared, "plus elles gardent longtemps leur force ahurissante" ("The more images possess vast connections, the more they retain their astonishing strength"). Once again, Marinetti's words are astonishingly close to Reverdy's. "Plus les rapports des deux réalités rapprochées seront lointains et justes," the latter wrote, "plus l'image sera forte" ("The more the relations between the two juxtaposed realities are distant and valid, the stronger the image will be"). As before, the resemblance between the two passages is striking. In some respects, the manifesto and the article are practically identical. The main difference between them is that there is no mention of a valid polar bond in Marinetti's text. Although the "distant things" are supposedly connected to each other by "love," what this actually means is far from clear. In any case, since the text alludes to multiple images rather than to pairs of images, it does not conform to Reverdy's definition. Marinetti may have been thinking of a similar line in *The Divine Comedy*, perhaps "l'amor che move i sole et l'altre stelle" ("love which moves the sun and the other stars").[15] Like God's love, which suffuses the universe, he implies, the power of analogy is all encompassing.

André Breton

By now Reverdy's contribution to the theory of the image has become clear. Taking the traditional structural model, he insisted that the two poles be juxtaposed, rather than compared, and that they be linked together by a bond of variable intensity. Judging from internal clues, that bond would seem to be constituted by similarity. Although Breton found "L'Image" exciting, he confides in the *Manifeste*, something about it continued to bother him.[16] The problem with Reverdy's theory, he eventually realized, was that everything had to be arranged beforehand. The tenor and the vehicle needed to be carefully selected in advance. Since the theory itself was created *a posteriori*, Breton complained, it confused cause with effect and vice versa. Not only that, but it assumed more prescience on the part of the poet than he was prepared to grant. While metaphors are normally created in exactly this manner, Breton denied that the process could produce the kind of dazzling images he was seeking. It exceeded the power of the human brain, he maintained, to create premeditated sentences such as:

> Dans le ruisseau il y a une chanson qui coule
> ("In the brook there is a song that flows"),
> Le jour s'est déplié comme une nappe blanche
> ("The day unfolded like a white tablecloth"), or
> Le monde rentre dans un sac
> ("The world retreats into a bag").

Images like these, Breton insisted, could only be created by the activity he called "Surrealist." At the same time, nevertheless, he admitted that the three verses were taken from poems by Reverdy.[17] The first line came from "Surprise d'en haut" ("Surprise from on High"), published in *La Lucarne ovale* (*The Oval Skylight*) in 1917. Like many of Reverdy's poems, it is filled with apocalyptic images but concludes with a nonsequitur, cited in the manifesto by Breton. The second verse was taken from "Glaçon dans l'air" ("*Icicle in the Air*"), included in *Cravates de chanvre* (*Hemp Neckties*) in 1922. It describes the early morning as night gradually disappears and the sun emerges from a thick red mist.

The third verse was borrowed from "L'Ombre du mur" ("The Wall's Shadow"), published in *Les Ardoises du toit* (*Roof Slates*) in 1918. It evokes the end of the day as night falls, the moon rises, and it begins to rain. Ironically, Breton appeared to be arguing against himself at this point in his discussion. If the three verses in question were really unpremeditated, as indeed he insisted they were, then his basic thesis had to be mistaken. Reverdy's theory of the image could apparently produce dazzling images after all. Seeking to demonstrate that the latter's poetry suffered from being consciously planned beforehand, Breton chose verses—admittedly for another purpose—that in point of fact were brilliant.

Since Breton never addressed this apparent contradiction, it is impossible to know what he was thinking at the time. In any event, he and Reverdy agreed that juxtaposition produced the strongest images. Compared to metaphors, Breton declared, similes tended to be ineffective—which did not prevent him from occasionally using one. However, this was effectively where the two men parted ways. Whereas Reverdy focused on a structural model of the image, Breton was attracted to a metaphorical model. Without naming the metaphorical object directly, he confided that its two poles could be juxtaposed to produce a special light. "La valeur de l'image," he added, "dépend de la beauté de l'étincelle obtenue; elle est par conséquent, fonction de la différence de potentiel entre les deux conducteurs" ("The value of the image depends on the beauty of the spark obtained; it thus results from the difference in potential between the two electrodes").[18] Curiously, generations of critics have read this passage without pausing to examine it more closely. Marguerite Bonnet merely notes that Breton uses "[le] vocabulaire de la décharge électrique" ("the vocabulary of electrical discharge").[19] Anna Balakian refers to "the light produced by the contact of two electrical conductors."[20] Léopold Peeters attributes the spark to "le court-circuit entre deux termes ou pôles d'un circuit électrique" ("a short circuit between two terms or poles of an electrical circuit").[21] All three critics simply paraphrase Breton's description, which borders on the abstract, without providing any more details.

Although their explanations are technically correct, they say nothing about the object to which he is referring.

In 1924, Breton's words would probably not have seemed as mysterious as they do to us today. A contemporary reader would presumably have recognized that the object in question was an arc light (also called a voltaic light). Invented in the early 1800s by Sir Humphry Davy in England and Vassily Petrov in Russia, arc lights were fairly rare until 1870, when a reliable dynamo was invented to power them. Consisting of an electric arc passing between two carbon electrodes inserted into a glass bulb, they were widely used for street lighting and for illuminating large buildings. This identification is confirmed a few lines later in the manifesto, where Breton expands his original metaphor to create a *métaphore filée* (extended metaphor). "La longueur de l'étincelle," he adds, "gagne à ce que celle-ci se produise à travers des gaz rarifiés" ("The length of the spark increases if it passes through rarefied gases"). Originally, arc lights were simply filled with air or with self-generated carbon vapor. After mercury vapor lamps were introduced in 1901, other gases such as xenon, argon, neon, and krypton began to be employed as well. Beginning in the 1910s and throughout the next two decades, however, most arc lights were gradually replaced by incandescent bulbs.

Like other early technological inventions such as airplanes, telephones, and wireless telegraphy, the arc light was quickly transformed into a modern icon. Artists and writers were attracted in particular because of its multiple symbolic possibilities. In 1904, the Symbolist poet Saint-Pol-Roux described some of his recent experiments in a passage that eerily anticipates Surrealism. Searching for secret affinities (his term) between a random group of words, he was delighted to find that two words occasionally combined to make sense—often in unexpected ways. As he described it, "la réconciliation d'un Mot négatif et d'un Mot affirmatif engendrait l'étincelle miraculeuse" ("the reconciliation of a negative Word and an affirmative Word would engender a miraculous spark").[22] To him, the process clearly resembled an electrical current passing between the poles of an arc light. Representing the moment of linguistic fusion, the spark evoked the physical activity on one level and the poet's surprise on another.

In 1909, two recent converts to Italian Futurism, founded by Marinetti the same year, painted pictures in which arc lights played a prominent role. In *Piazza del Duomo* (*Cathedral Square*), Carlo Carrà depicted downtown Milan filled with crowds of people at night. Beneath a tangle of overhead wires and suspended arc lights, numerous streetcars converged on the central square. By contrast, Giacomo Balla portrayed a single street lamp blazing like a torch in the middle of the night. Although the Museum of Modern Art, which owns the painting, calls it *Streetlight*, its Italian title is *Lampada ad Arco* (*Arc Light*). Literary references to arc lights abounded during this period, including a poem full of typographical effects by the chief Dada spokesman Tristan Tzara. Evoking a nocturnal street scene in 1916, he compared the single arc light to a neural impulse traveling across a synapse and then, a few lines later, its bright spark to an orgasm.[23] The following year, the Italian Dadaist Gino Cantarelli published a poem called "Lumières de mercure" in which he compared the rosy dawn to mercury vapor lights illuminating "les claires façades sur silencieux jardins" ("the bright facades above silent gardens"). In 1918, the Catalan Futurist Joan Salvat-Papasseit founded a journal entitled *Arc-Voltaic*, which published a single issue and then disappeared. The next year, Guillermo de Torre, who headed the Spanish Ultraist group, celebrated modern streetlights in a poem entitled "Arco Voltaico." Featuring an epigraph by Tzara, who mentioned arc lights again, it began by comparing the latter to night-blooming flowers: "Florescencia de corolas luminosas/en la noche hemiédrica" ("Florescence of luminous corollas/in the hemihedral night"). At the urging of André Breton, finally, the novelist, diplomat, and short story writer Paul Morand issued a book of poetry in 1920 entitled *Lampes à arc*.[24] The deluxe edition was covered in fine morocco leather with multiple gilded joints and silver titles symbolizing an arc lamp.

As the preceding paragraphs demonstrate, arc lights appeared not only as the subjects of various paintings but also as metaphors in a number of poems. Since they were common literary currency at the time, Breton's decision to appropriate one for the *Manifeste*, even though it was partially concealed, does not seem especially original. What *was* original, however, was how he eventually solved the problem he had discerned with "L'Image." The trouble with Reverdy's theory of the image, to recapitulate, was that it relied entirely on conscious mechanisms. It was unthinkable that a poet would deliberately juxtapose, say, a locomotive and a carrot or a padlock and a fish filet. The gap between each term and its companion was simply too great to overcome. To escape the numerous limitations imposed by the rational mind, Breton invented Surrealism, which, among other things, allowed him to plumb the depths of the human psyche. The solution to Reverdy's dilemma, he concluded, was to adopt procedures like automatic writing that exploited unconscious activity.

Almost from the very beginning, Gershman remarks, Breton and his colleagues regarded the Surrealist image as a key to *le merveilleux* "Its proper use," he explains, "could wrest revelation from indifferent matter."[25] Another strategy that produced excellent results was to exploit the possibilities of *le hasard objectif* ("objective chance"). When it was successful, the random juxtaposition of two unrelated objects replicated the dynamics of the Surrealist image. Unlike the latter, however, which originated in the unconscious brain, sense was imposed from without instead of being deduced from within. In both cases, however, it was up to the reader to discern an unexpected connection between the two objects in question. In contrast to Reverdy's images, which were almost entirely metaphorical, approximately half of the Surrealist images were metonymic.[26] Whereas those in the first group exploited similarity, those in the second group employed either similarity or contiguity. Although Surrealist images and Surrealist chance encounters originated in a totally different manner, they were otherwise indistinguishable from one another. Oblivious to their origins, readers reacted with the same surprise, the same revelatory shudder, when they encountered them.

"[L'image] la plus forte," Breton explained four-fifths of the way through the *Manifeste*, "est celle qui présente le degré d'arbitraire le plus élevé" ("The strongest [image] is that which presents the highest degree of arbitrariness").[27] Indeed, he specifies elsewhere in the manifesto that it must have "un très haut degré d'*absurdité immédiate*" ("a very high degree of *immediate absurdity*"—his emphasis).[28] As Johnnie Gratton observes, the concept of *l'arbitraire* represents "a specific alternative to the notion of *justesse*" ("validity") proposed by Reverdy.[29] According to Breton, the strongest Surrealist images are ones that are arbitrary— which is to say surprising—rather than valid. It is interesting to note that Breton's images resemble Reverdy's up to a certain point. As Marguerite Bonnet remarks, "L'arbitraire est fonction de la distance entre les termes rapprochés; il s'accroit avec elle" ("Gratuitousness is proportional to the distance between the juxtaposed terms; it increases with this distance").[30] Two images cited by Breton in the manifesto illustrate what Reverdy meant. An expression such as "le rubis du champagne" ("the champagne's ruby") borders on a cliché and is thus relatively weak. What links the drink to the jewel is simply the fact that they share the same color. By contrast, "la rosée à tête de chatte" ("the cat-headed dew") is surprising and thus much more powerful. It takes a while to realize that the cat and the dew share a common denominator—the glistening drops of precipitation resemble the animal's glistening eyes.

It is important nevertheless to realize that this is only half the story. Simply juxtaposing two random images will not automatically produce a Surrealist image. Breton was only speaking about arbitrary bonds that were *successful*. For the image to produce a marvelous spark, its two terms need to possess an implicit relationship at some level. The image must either originate in the poet's unconscious or activate the reader's unconscious (or both). Unexpectedly, the principle of *justesse* turns out to exist after all—at the unconscious level rather than the conscious level. At the core of every Surrealist image, arbitrariness is offset by the demand for validity and vice versa. Each principle serves as an effective check on the other. Neither one can exist independently if the final image is to be successful. Proof that the two principles are well balanced is provided by the surprise that they generate.

Discussing the interplay of word and image in Breton's poetry, Mary Ann Caws describes the *Manifeste* as "a testimony of wonder and acceptance in the face of the marvelous."[31] Acceptance not of the status quo, which the Surrealists were determined to completely transform, but of the revelatory power inherent in *le merveilleux*.[32] Indeed, accessing the marvelous was the ultimate goal of every Surrealist activity, from automatic writing to nonsense dialogues and elaborate word games. Not surprisingly, therefore, it is one of the principal themes running through the manifesto. Celebrating Surrealism's fierce dedication to the marvelous, Breton announced: "le merveilleux est toujours beau, n'importe quel merveilleux est beau, il n'y a même que le merveilleux qui soit beau" ("the marvelous is always beautiful, any kind of marvelous is beautiful, nothing but the marvelous is beautiful"). Because it participates in the particular sensibility that defines a given culture at a given time, Breton added, the marvelous varies from one era to another. For the Romantics it was epitomized by ancient ruins harking back to another time and another place. For contemporary society it is exemplified by modern mannequins, like those painted by Giorgio de Chirico, which possess an eerie, otherworldly identity of their own.

Since Surrealism was primarily a voyage of discovery, it would be more accurate to speak of wonder and *revelation* rather than acceptance. Above all, the Surrealists sought to open up new areas for exploration, experiment, and exploitation. "An authentic Surrealist image," J. H. Matthews explains, "brings before us something never seen before.... It is by departing from the norms of perception and representation that the Surrealist image makes its audience see."[33] In other words, by freeing people from their ossified reading habits it opens up exciting new vistas. Not only are words free to make love, as Breton announced in *Les Pas perdus* (*The Waiting Room*) (1924), but they are free to make love with different partners.[34]

The unexpected juxtaposition of words and images encourages serious readers—those who do not immediately give up—to search for a possible explanation. Breton views these surprising juxtapositions as trampolines that stimulate the reader's mind. Fortunately, he confides, "l'esprit est d'une merveilleuse promptitude à saisir le plus faible rapport qui peut exister entre deux objets" ("the mind is marvelously prompt in grasping the slightest relationship that can exist between two objects").[35] This ability can also be expanded to include the relationship between entire sentences. Thus a sentence like "le cadavre exquis boira le vin nouveau" ("the exquisite cadaver will drink the new wine"), which inaugurated a brand new round of Surrealist experiments in 1925, can be interpreted as a reference to Holy Communion.[36] As far as Breton is concerned, Jacqueline Chénieux-Gendron declares, metaphor is essentially "a creator of meaning ... through the medium of language."[37] The same thing can be said of the Surrealist image, which is a creator of Surrealist meaning. If language has been given to mankind to make Surrealist use of, as Breton insists in the *Manifeste*, it operates according to an entirely different set of rules than ordinary language.[38] The world it evokes is only tangentially related to the world we are familiar with.

Three Surrealist Poets

The original Surrealist group was composed of only four members: Breton, Philippe Soupault, Louis Aragon, and Paul Eluard. By the time the *Manifeste du surréalisme* appeared, their number had increased to twelve, and the movement was attracting considerable attention. On January 27, 1925, no fewer than twenty-six Surrealists published a *Déclaration* in which they proclaimed: "Le surréalisme est un moyen de libération de l'esprit et de tout ce qui lui ressemble" ("Surrealism is a means of liberating the mind and everything that resembles it"). By 1935, the movement was well established and included perhaps seventy-five individuals. From France it spread around the globe and interested many more artists, writers, choreographers, composers, film makers, and so forth. As Balakian notes, the creative role of language was strongly stressed initially by the Surrealists' concept of poetry.[39] Although Surrealist artists would be largely responsible for establishing the movement's future reputation, Breton doubted at first whether Surrealist literary principles could successfully be applied to art. Even so, the first exhibition of Surrealist paintings took place in November 1925 at the Galerie Pierre, with works by André Masson, Man Ray, Giorgio de Chirico, Joan Miró, and others. Since art was a form of human expression, Breton reasoned that paintings were just as open to Surrealist inquiry as literary works. "Qui dit expression," he explained in 1934, "dit langage." ("Whoever says 'expression' … says 'language.'")[40]

Paul Eluard

Although they represent two different modes of expression, Surrealist art and Surrealist literature exploit the very same principles. To the extent that both poetry and painting may be said to speak to us, their words and images are closely intertwined, either explicitly or implicitly. Poets possess one tool in particular, Breton declared the following year, that enables them to "forer toujours plus profondément, qui est l'*image* et, entre tous les types d'image, la *métaphore* (penetrate deeper and deeper, namely the *image* and, among all the types of images, *metaphor*").[41] By itself, an individual word can convey only so much information. Its mission is essentially denotative. Only when it is combined with other words does it manage to transcend its basic limitations. Only then can it be used to create virtual constructions that conjure up a whole new universe. This is what Eluard means in "Défense de savoir" when he says "Les images pensent pour moi" ("Images think for me").[42] Stopping to illustrate a previous point in "Position politique du surréalisme" (1935), Breton reproduced three poems that he admired for their depth of feeling, richness of intuition, and lively structure.[43] In the eleven years since his discussion of the Surrealist image in the *Manifeste du surréalisme*, Paul Eluard, Benjamin Péret, and Salvador Dalí had learned how to extract the maximum from their imagery. Entitled "Les Maîtres" ("The Masters"), the first poem was published the following year in *La Barre d'appui* (*The Hand-Rail*).

Au fort des rires secoués
Dans un cuvier de plomb
Quel bien-être d'avoir
Des ailes de chien
Qui tient un oiseau vivant dans sa gueule
Allez-vous faire l'obscurité
Pour conserver cette mine sombre
Ou bien allez-vous nous céder
Il y a de la graisse au plafond
De la salive sur les vitres
La lumière est horrible
O nuit perle perdue
Aveugle point de chute où le chagrin s'acharne.

(At the fortress of shaken laughs
In a tub made of lead
How comforting to have
The wings of a dog
Holding a live bird in its mouth
Go make yourself obscurity
In order to maintain that somber expression
Or else submit to us
There is grease on the ceiling
Saliva on the window panes
The light is horrible
O night lost pearl
Blind fall where grief persists).

The first thing one notices is that this is a very uncooperative poem. It possesses none of the usual rhetorical signposts that help readers find their way through a Surrealist work. Nor does it exploit such common linguistic strategies as repetition, elaboration, or contiguity. The presence of several ungrammaticalities complicates things even more.

While Riffaterre explains that they force readers to "hypothesize a figurative meaning," this is true of virtually every feature in the poem.[44] Then there is also the problem of the title, which appears to be totally gratuitous. Should it be translated as "The Masters," one wonders, or as "The Teachers"? In the absence of any meaningful context, it is difficult to say. If structured discontinuity characterizes Surrealist poetry in general, as Richard Stamelman maintains, the poem has plenty of discontinuity but very little structure.[45]

According to the first line, "Les Maîtres" takes place in a fortified stronghold somewhere. We have no idea initially who the disembodied speaker is, where he is located, or whom he is addressing. Not only is the first stanza strenuously impersonal, but the source of the shaking and laughter is never identified. Eluard utilizes passive constructions throughout the first stanza to evoke what is happening inside the fortress. In some respects, the poem resembles a game of Clue. Since there is no punctuation, one wonders who is doing what to whom and where. Although the heavy lead tub in the second line could conceivably be filled with "rires secoués," it is much more rewarding to put a period at the end of the first line and an actual person in the tub. According to all indications, the latter is the mysterious addressee, who continues to take a bath as the poem progresses.

In contrast to the first two lines, which are purely descriptive, the next three lines constitute an exclamation. The speaker's initial remarks give way to a splendid example of *le merveilleux*. All of a sudden, the reader encounters a dog that possesses wings and is presumably able to fly. Not just any winged dog, moreover, but one that holds a live bird securely in its jaws. The scene bears all the hallmarks of automatic writing. The unconscious has simply transferred the bird's wings to the animal that has caught it. Ultimately, of course, the wings are purely imaginary—like the marvelous dog itself. They are a doubly virtual construction that mirrors reality twice. The bird is contained by the dog which is contained by another character in the poem. While these relationships are implicit, they are also unmistakable. Although Eluard introduces the players in reverse order, they obey the internal logic of the poem. Nevertheless, a question still remains: Who is actually wearing the wings? That individual is almost certainly the man who is taking a bath in the second line. The two other characters are merely sources of the wings. The poem's focus narrows progressively from the fortress to the tub to the person inside it. One imagines a winged man scrubbing away in all his naked glory, secure in the belief that nobody can see him. For some reason, the speaker finds this scene comforting.

At this point, three questions naturally arise. Who is the man in the tub, who is the speaker, and what is the relationship between them? While avian humanoids figure prominently in mythology, folklore, and science fiction, a rapid survey fails to turn up any who resemble the winged man. One suspects that he is simply meant to be an impressive figure. By contrast, the speaker's identity is quickly revealed in the second stanza. Assuming a threatening pose, he offers the first man two choices, neither one of which is very appealing. Either he can run away and hide like a coward, or he can surrender to the enemy troops who are besieging his fortress. Unexpectedly, the poem turns out to have a structure after all, one that is very simple. As in most epic poems, its deep structure is divided into two halves, reflecting the confrontation between good and evil. One half is devoted to the attackers, the other half to the defenders. Although the speaker is clearly located outside the fortress, somehow he remains aware of everything taking place inside it. This curious ability is puzzling until one remembers that it is an epic convention. Not only is the speaker the enemy commander, but, like many epic narrators, he is also omniscient. Nothing escapes his attention no matter where it takes place.

The last five lines, which break abruptly with the preceding narrative, are equally puzzling. Following his double-barreled ultimatum to the man in the fortress, the speaker pauses to look around and suddenly notices that the place is filthy. How on earth, he thinks to himself, did all that grease get on the ceiling? What degenerate has been licking the windows? Thankfully, the glaring light shed by the lamp can be eliminated by adjusting the shade. At least that is how the scenario looks at first. I prefer to think the complaints are uttered not by a character in the poem but by Eluard himself. Tired of writing the work we have been reading, he waits for his unconscious to recharge itself. Eventually he adds two more lines:

> O nuit perle perdue
> Aveugle point de chute où le chagrin s'acharne.
> (O night lost pearl)
> Blind fall where grief persists

Since the poem concludes with an apostrophe to night, the sun seems to have set already. Night itself serves as the tenor of two metaphors that one assumes will be filled with praise. Unexpectedly, however, the examples that Eluard has chosen possess negative markers. The *perle* in the first line is "lost," and the *chute* in the second line is stricken with "grief." The poet compares the night to a lost pearl because both are associated with absence and loss. Like the precious bauble, which is nowhere to be found, night is characterized by absence—the absence of light. Since the pearl is round and shiny, its loss may also parallel the sun's recent disappearance. The final line, which vaguely recalls Mallarmé's poetry, continues these twin themes. Night is obviously associated with blindness because both involve the loss of light. However, its additional association with falling and grief turns out to involve metonymy rather than metaphor. Although the allusions are heavily veiled, with a little effort they can be deciphered. Eluard hints at the following scenario. Returning home late one night, someone unfortunately makes a misstep in the darkness, falls into a hole (or off a cliff), and is killed or seriously injured. Thus "aveugle" is meant to be understood figuratively. The individual is simply unable to see where he is going. Unexpectedly, what initially promised to become the account of an epic battle concludes with a single, unrelated tragedy. Thinking by images turns out to be as unpredictable as unconscious dictation.

Benjamin Péret

Of all the major Surrealists, Benjamin Péret has received the least critical attention. Not only are there relatively few studies devoted to his poetry, for example, but his poems are also rarely anthologized. The reasons for his lack of popularity are not hard to divine. His poetic works are very demanding, they seem to lack structure, and they strike some readers as self-indulgent. And yet there is widespread agreement among French specialists, as well as among Péret's colleagues, that he is one of the stars in the Surrealist pantheon. For Gershman he represents "one of [Surrealism's] finest practitioners."[46] In Matthews' opinion, he is "Surrealism's greatest poet."[47] One of the things that make Péret a delight to read is the amazing facility with which he produces image after image. As incredible as it seems, Robert Benayoun reports that each of his poems was written in a single draft with no corrections.[48]

Another thing most readers enjoy is the persistent playfulness that pervades his works. Although Péret has tremendous respect for poetry, he loves to play with his readers' expectations by introducing unexpected twists and turns. He is never happier than when he is making outrageous claims or introducing surprising juxtapositions. For these reasons, critics tend to associate his poetry with France's national beverage. Evoking Péret's remarkable facility, for example, Benayoun declares: "Il pratiquait la poésie comme on vide un verre de bordeaux" ("He wrote poetry like you empty a glass of Bordeaux"). And Breton devotes a section to Péret in his *Anthologie de l'humour noir*. "Jamais les mots ... n'avaient manifesté une telle liesse," he writes. "La joie panique est revenue. C 'est toute la magie dans un verre de vin blanc" ("Never have words ... exhibited such gaiety ... Frenzied joy has returned. It is magic itself in a glass of white wine").[49] Entitled "Parle-moi" ("Speak to Me"), the second poem selected by Breton was published the following year in *Je sublime*.

Le noir de fumée le noir animal le noir noir
se sont donné rendez-vous entre deux monuments aux morts

qui peuvent passer pour mes oreilles
où l'écho de ta voix de fantôme de mica marin
répète indéfiniment ton nom
qui ressemble tant au contraire d'une éclipse de soleil
que je me crois quand tu me regardes
un pied d'alouette dans une glacière dont tu ouvrirais la porte
dans l'espoir d'en voir s'échapper une hirondelle de pétrole enflammé
mais du pied d'alouette jaillira une source de pétrole flambant
si tu le veux
comme une hirondelle
veut l'heure d'été pour jouer la musique des orages
et la fabrique à la manière d'une mouche
qui rêve d'une toile d'araignée de sucre
dans un verre d'oeil
parfois bleu comme une étoile filante réfléchie par un oeuf
parfois vert comme une source suintant d'une horloge.

(Smoky black animal black and black black agreed to meet between two monuments to fallen soldiers which can pass for my ears where the echo of your phantom voice of marine mica repeats your name indefinitely which resembles so much contrary to a solar eclipse that I believe myself when you look at me to be a lark's foot in a glacier whose door you would open hoping to see a burning swallow of oil escape but a spring of flaming oil will spurt from the lark's foot if you want as a swallow waits for the summer's hour to play the storms' music and fabricates it like a fly who dreams of a spider's sugar web in a glass of eye which is blue sometimes like a shooting star reflected by an egg green sometimes like a spring seeping from a clock.)

Although the absence of punctuation tends to obscure this fact, the poem is composed of a single, very long sentence. Just when readers think they have come to the end of a line, Péret repeatedly adds a grammatical connector that introduces a new phrase. Instead of flowing like a river, the poem zig-zags down the page like a skier on a slalom course. The connectors are mainly prepositions (*à, de, dans,* and *pour*), conjunctions (*et, quand, mais,* and *comme*), and relative pronouns (*qui, que,* and *dont*). As Matthews observes, "Péret's poems seem to proceed by a series of non sequiturs that are deliberately misleading."[50] Like them, many of the examples in "Parle-Moi" promise more than they really deliver. The phrase that precedes the connector is usually perfectly reasonable, leading the reader to expect that the words following the connector will correspond to his or her expectations. When these actually arrive, however, they turn out to be totally unsuitable. While they fit the linguistic slot reserved for them, they either (1) make no sense or (2) are patently absurd or (3) introduce another subject altogether. The first problem is illustrated by the presence of a spider web "dans un verre d'oeil" in line 15. For some reason, Péret's unconscious has reversed the two terms in *oeil de verre* ("glass eye"). The second problem occurs in line 9, where one encounters "une hirondelle de pétrole enflammé." Not only is the swallow flaming, but it is the apparent victim of a lark that feeds the fire. The third problem is illustrated by the reference to "une glacière dont tu ouvrirais la porte" in line 8. The rest of the sentence focuses on what happens once the door is opened.

Besides numerous nonsequiturs, "Parle-Moi" employs several other devices to disrupt the flow of thought. One of these is the use of random interjections, such as "Si tu le veux," which are inserted in the middle of a sentence. Péret also introduces unrelated parenthetical phrases from time to time, such as "quand tu me regardes," which have essentially the same effect. At one point, he even interrupts the expression "tant que" to inject a parenthetical phrase: "*tant* au contraire d'une éclipse de soleil *que*." Additional connectors introduce phrases that attract attention because they are self-consciously bizarre. This describes the comparisons in the last two lines, for example, which have nothing to do with the color they are supposed to describe: "bleu comme une étoile filante réfléchie par un oeuf" and "vert comme une source suintant d'une horloge." One begins to understand why Matthews believes the basic characteristics of Péret's verse are arbitrariness, inconsequence, and impertinence.[51] He just writes down the first phrase that pops into his head with no regard for grammatical niceties or semantic continuity. However, this is not as high-handed as it first appears. Péret's refusal to embrace cultural norms is both deliberate and programmatic. As the sworn enemy of reason, which he believes has exerted tyrannical control over Western civilization since the Enlightenment, he looks to poetry to restore our imaginative freedom. As much as anything, therefore, his freewheeling poetry represents a form of rebellion.

Despite the disruptive tactics described previously, portions of "Parle-Moi" make a certain amount of sense. The first line, which lists three kinds of black, is an obvious exception. When a word pleases him, Benayoun explains, Péret will repeat it indefinitely.[52] *Noir* is apparently one of those words, for in his hands it becomes a kind of incantation, one that is miraculously endowed with agency. The fact that the two monuments where the blacks agree to meet resemble the poet's ears is amusing but not impossible. In theory, at least, they could have a similar shape. The next four or five lines introduce a romantic note. Péret is so enamored of a certain woman that he still hears her voice echoing in his ears after she has gone. Her glance exerts such a hypnotic spell on him that he believes he is a flaming lark's foot caught in a glacier but eager to liberate a flaming swallow. The latter waits for summer to arrive before it sings its stormy song, which Péret compares to a fly's longing for a sweet spider web. Like the anonymous woman, perhaps, both are attractive but also dangerous. Ultimately, the poem's interest lies not so much in its twisted itinerary as in the continual cascade of marvelous images. As Péret himself proclaimed a few years later, *le merveilleux* is "le coeur et le système nerveux de toute la poesie" ("the heart and nervous system of all poetry").[53]

Salvador Dalí

As Roger Rothman notes, Dalí was embraced by the Surrealists almost immediately upon his arrival in Paris in 1929.[54] Not only was he an accomplished artist with a brilliant career ahead of him, but he was eager to benefit from what Surrealism had to offer. Besides a brand new aesthetics, it seemed to hold the solutions to several problems that had been bothering him. "Le surréalisme [proposait] un langage sans réserve," Janine Mesaglio-Nevers explains, "et une nouvelle vision capable de révéler les pulsions à la fois" ("Surrealism [offered] a language without reservations and, at the same time, a new vision capable of revealing unconscious impulses").[55] Between 1929 and 1940, when he was expelled from the group, Dalí painted many of his best works. In addition, he developed his famous paranoiac-critical method, which provided an exciting new area for the Surrealists to explore.[56] "Next to André Breton," W. L. Courshon declares, "he was probably the most vital and explosive force to enter the Surrealist movement." [57] Although Dalí is known today for his extraordinary paintings, much of his time was spent writing poetry and articles. Indeed, according to Dawn Ades he wrote almost as much as he painted.[58] Not surprisingly, Dalí's poetry reflects many of the same preoccupations as his art. Since he was an obsessive personality, he would explore a theme over and over until they were both exhausted. José Pierre prefers to speak of "une poésie de paroxysme" focusing on love, eroticism, and scatology.[59] Entitled "Brochure bercée" ("Booklet Rocked in a Cradle"), the third poem chosen by Breton was published the following year in a mysterious journal called *Cradlet Pamphlet, Contemporary Poetry and Prose*.

> Brochure perdure
> tout en déclinant injustement
> une tasse
> une tasse portugaise quelconque
> qu'on fabrique aujourd'hui
> dans une usine de vaisselle
> car une tasse
> ressemble par sa forme
> à une douce antinomie municipale arabe
> montée au bout de l'alentour
> comme le regard de ma belle Gala
> le regard de ma belle Gala
> odeur de litre
> comme le tissu épithélial de ma belle Gala

son tissu épithélial bouffon et lampiste
oui je le répéterai mille fois

(Durable booklet while unjustly refusing a cup some sort of Portuguese
cup that they manufacture today in a crockery factory for a cup's
form resembles a sweet municipal Arab antinomy mounted at the
end of the neighbourhood like the gaze of my beautiful Gala the gaze
of my beautiful Gala odor of liter like my beautiful Gala's epithelial
tissue her farcical and scapegoat epithelial tissue yes I will repeat it a
thousand times).

Like Dalí's poetry in general, this strange little composition is
unabashedly eccentric. Not only does the title make no sense, for
example, but it also has nothing to do with the rest of the poem. In
general, Haim Finkelstein declares, "Dalí tends to fluctuate in his poetry
between the conceptual or abstract and the visual, with the visual often
taking the lead."[60] By and large, this description holds true for the
present poem as well. Following the first two lines, which are mixed,
"Brochure Bercée" devotes seven lines to the Portuguese cup, two lines
to abstractions, two lines to Gala, followed by a single abstraction, two
more lines to Gala, and finally Dalí's vow to repeat the poem a thousand
times. Because the discontinuity is so pronounced, meaningful relations
are simply impossible between the different sections. Contiguity is not
nearly enough to compensate for the brutal dislocations between one
part and the next. Furthermore, Dalí juxtaposes abstract and concrete
entities in a way that is highly disconcerting. How can a booklet refuse
anything, one wonders, since it is an inanimate object. Even more
annoying, the adverb "injustement" implies that such an action is
actually possible, when the reader knows good and well that it is not.
Nor is it possible for a cup's shape to resemble a term used in logic and
epistemology, no matter how sweet and municipal it is.

The disturbing juxtapositions continue unabated. How can a cup's
shape be mounted anywhere? In what way does an antinomy resemble
his wife's gaze or skin? The last six lines, which celebrate his recent
bride's beauty, are clearly intended to form a miniature love poem. Even

then, however, Dalí feels compelled to insert images that interrupt and undermine his praise. "Odeur de litre" is another one of his impossible constructions. Volumes obviously do not have odors and vice versa. Not only does Dalí use an unflattering term to refer to Gala's beautiful skin, but he also says it is "farcical" and "scapegoat"—whatever that means. As a result, his final promise to repeat this praise a thousand times falls a bit flat. As does the fact that he mimics his vow by repeating the poem once he has finished it. Nevertheless, since the work was designed to be read twice, Dalí had 499 readings to look forward to. Together with "Les Maîtres" and "Parle-moi," "Brochure bercée" signaled that Surrealism was alive and well in 1935. As the movement continued to expand, it attracted more and more members, who in turn influenced its future development.

Notes

1   See André Breton, *Manifeste du surréalisme in Oeuvres complètes*, Vol. 1, ed. Marguerite Bonnet, Philippe Bernier, Etienne-Alain Hubert, and José Pierre (Paris: Gallimard, 1988), pp. 322–3.

2   Ibid., p. 321.

3   Ibid., p. 319.

4   Pierre Reverdy, "L'Image," *Nord-Sud*, No. 13 (March 1918), p. 1.

5   Robert Champigny, "The S Device," *Dada/Surrealism*, No. 1 (1971), pp. 3–7.

6   L. C. Breunig, *The Cubist Poets in Paris: An Anthology* (Lincoln: University of Nebraska Press, 1995), p. 283.

7   Marcel Lecomte, "Tension de l'image chez Reverdy," *Le Journal des poètes*, August–September 1960, p. 6.

8   Pierre Reverdy, *Plupart du temps, poèmes 1915–1922* (Paris: Flammarion, 1967), pp. 61 and 243.

9   Stéphane Mallarmé, "Le Mystère dans les lettres," in *Oeuvres complètes*, ed. Henri Mondor and G. Jean-Aubry (Paris: Gallimard, 1965), p. 386.

10 Stéphane Mallarmé, "Crise de vers," in *Oeuvres complètes*, p. 366.

11 Jules Romains, "La Poésie immédiate," in *Vers et Prose*, October–November–December 1909. Repr. *Correspondance Jules Romains Guillaume Apollinaire*, ed. Claude Martin (Paris: Jean-Michel Place, 1994), p. 147.

12 Robert W. Greene, *The Poetic Theory of Pierre Reverdy* (Berkeley: University of California Press, 1967), pp. 17–18; Herbert S. Gershman, *The Surrealist Revolution in France* (Ann Arbor: University of Michigan Press, 1974), p. 122; and Gerald Mead, *The Surrealist Image: A Stylistic Study* (Berne: Peter Lang, 1978), pp. 14–22.

13 F. T. Marinetti, "Manifeste Technique de la Littérature Futuriste," in *Le Futurisme: Textes et manifestes 1909–1944*, ed. Giovanni Lista (Ceyzérieux: Champ Vallon, 2015), p. 393.

14 Georges Duhamel, "*Alcools* de Guillaume Apollinaire," *Mercure de France*, June 16, 1913, p. 801.

15 Dante Alighieri, *Paradiso*, Canto 33, verse 145. See also the *Inferno*, Canto 11.

16 Breton, *Manifeste du surréalisme*, p. 324.

17 Reverdy, *Plupart du temps*, pp. 125, 368, and 204.

18 Breton, *Manifeste du surréalisme*, pp. 337–8.

19 Marguerite Bonnet, *André Breton: Naissance de l'aventure surréaliste* (Paris: Corti, 1975), p. 363.

20 Anna Balakian, *Surrealism: The Road to the Absolute* (Chicago: University of Chicago Press, 1986), p. 149.

21 Léopold Peeters, "Critique de l'image surrealiste," *French Studies in Southern Africa*, No. 29 (2000), p. 70.

22 Saint-Pol-Roux, "Le Style C'est la Vie," in *De la Colombe au Corbeau par le Paon, Les Reposoirs*, Vol. 2 (Paris: Société du Mercure de France, 1904), p. 175.

23 Tristan Tzara, "Bilan," *SIC*, Nos. 49–50 (October 15–30, 1919), p. 385; reprinted in *De nos oiseaux* (1923) and retitled "Sels de minuit."

24 Gino Cantarelli, "Lumières de mercure," *SIC*, Nos. 21–22 (September–October, 1917), p. 159. Joan Salvat-Papasseit, *Arc-Voltaic*, No. 1 (February 1918). Guillermo de Torre, "Arco voltaico," *Grecia*, No. 34 (November 30, 1919), p. 3. Paul Morand, *Lampes à arc* (Paris: Au Sans Pareil, 1920).

25   Gershman, *The Surrealist Revolution*, p. 122.
26   Willard Bohn, *The Rise of Surrealism: Cubism, Dada, and the Pursuit of the Marvelous* (Albany: State University of New York Press, 2002), p. 161.
27   Breton, *Manifeste du surréalisme*, p. 338.
28   Ibid., p. 327.
29   Johnnie Gratton, "Poetics of the Surrealist Image," *Romanic Review*, Vol. 69, Nos. 1–2 (January–March 1978), p. 107.
30   Bonnet, *André Breton*, p. 362.
31   Mary Ann Caws, *André Breton* (New York: Twayne, 1971), p. 26.
32   Breton, *Manifeste du surréalisme*, p. 319.
33   J. H. Matthews, *Languages of Surrealism* (Columbia: University of Missouri Press, 1986), pp. 24–5.
34   Breton, *Les Pas perdus* in *Oeuvres complètes*, Vol. 2, p. 286.
35   Breton, *Les Vases communicants* in *Oeuvres completes*, Vol. 2, p. 181.
36   Bohn, *The Rise of Surrealism*, pp. 151–2. For an analysis of the various forces at work in the Surrealist image, see pp. 141–70.
37   Jacqueline Chénieux-Gendron, *Surrealism*, tr. Vivian Folkenflik (New York: Columbia University Press, 1990), p. 70.
38   Breton, *Manifeste*, p. 334.
39   Balakian, *Surrealism*, p. 143.
40   Breton, "Qu'est-ce que le surréalisme?" in *Oeuvres complètes*, Vol. 2, p. 250.
41   Breton, "Position politique du surréalisme," in *Oeuvres complètes*, Vol. 2, p. 485.
42   Paul Eluard, *Défense de savoir in Eluard, Oeuvres complètes*, Vol. 1, ed. Marcelle Dumas and Lucien Scheler (Paris: Gallimard 1968), p. 222.
43   Breton, "Position politique du surréalisme," pp. 486–8.
44   Riffaterre, *Text Production*, p. 51.
45   Richard Stamelman, "The Relational Structure of Surrealist Poetry," *Dada/Surrealism*, No. 6 (1976), p. 77.
46   Gershman, *The Surrealist Revolution*, p. 48.
47   J. H. Matthews, *Surrealism, Insanity, and Poetry* (Syracuse: Syracuse University Press, 1982), p. 58.
48   Robert Benayoun, "A plus d'un titre ...," in *Benjamin Péret, Le Grand Jeu*, ed. Benjamin Péret (Paris: Gallimard, 1969), p. 7.
49   Breton, *Anthologie de l'humour noir* in *Oeuvres Complètes*, Vol. 2, p. 1134.

50 Matthews, "Benjamin Péret: Marvelous Conjunction," in *About French Poetry from Dada to "Tel Quel": Text and Theory*, ed. Mary Ann Caws (Detroit: Wayne State University Press, 1974), p. 126.

51 Ibid., p. 131.

52 Benayoun, "A plus d'un titre," p. 13.

53 Benjamin Péret, "La Poésie est UNE et indivisible," *VVV*, No. 4 (February 1944), p. 10.

54 Roger Rothman, *Tiny Surrealism: Salvador Dalí and the Aesthetics of the Small* (Lincoln: University of Nebraska Press, 2012), p. 86.

55 Janine Mesaglio-Nevers, "Salvador Dalí peinture et poésie: de l'automatisme à la paranoia-critique," *Mélusine*, Vol. 7 (1985), p. 205.

56 See, for example, Matthews, *Surrealism, Insanity, and Poetry*, pp. 50–4.

57 W. L. Courshon, "Salvador Dalí's Expulsion from the Surrealist Group," *Dada/Surrealism*, No. 5 (1975), p.80.

58 Dawn Ades, *Dalí* (London: Thames and Hudson, 1990), p. 40.

59 José Pierre, "Salvador Dalí poète surréaliste," *Mélusine*, No. 12 (1991), p. 186.

60 Haim Finkelstein, *Salvador Dalí's Art and Writing 1927–1942: The Metamorphosis of Narcissus* (Cambridge: Cambridge University Press, 1996), p. 61.

3

Paul Eluard and Surrealist Love

One of the original "Four Musketeers" who founded the Surrealist movement, Paul Eluard is by far the most popular poet for reasons that are not hard to discover. Not only is he the author of a large number of love poems, but also, as J. H. Matthews observes, he appears to many readers to be the most accessible of the French Surrealists. His special contribution to Surrealism, the same critic adds, is "the apparent ease with which he reduced the Surrealist message to emotions directly communicable, in a form stripped of the linguistic sophistication which some find to be the stumbling block of Surrealist poetry."[1] The fact that most of Eluard's poems are short makes them even more attractive to some readers, who are put off by lengthy compositions. Some poems have no more than two or three lines, like this lovely example from *L'Amour la poésie*: "Le sommeil a pris ton empreinte/ Et la colore de tes yeux" ("Sleep has taken your impression/And the color of your eyes").[2] However, as this work demonstrates, the illusion of easy access is just that—an illusion. Any attempt to approach the poem head on—to impose a literal interpretation, for example—is doomed to failure. Eluard works by insinuation, intimation, and implication. Ironically, he turns out to be one of the hardest Surrealist poets to decipher rather than the easiest.

Composed in 1918, "Pour vivre ici" ("To Live Here") illustrates Eluard's poetry at the beginning of his Surrealist career, when it was still impregnated with Symbolism.[3] One of his most popular compositions, it is frequently anthologized:

Je fis un feu, l'azur m'ayant abandonné,
Un feu pour être son ami,

Un feu pour m'introduire dans la nuit d'hiver,
Un feu pour vivre mieux.

Je lui donnai ce que le jour m'avait donné:
Les forêts, les buissons, les champs de blé, les vignes,
Les nids et leurs oiseaux, les maisons et leurs clés,
Les insectes, les fleurs, les fourures, les fêtes.

Je vécus au seul bruit des flammes crépitantes,
Au seul parfum de leur chaleur;
J'étais comme un bateau coulant dans l'eau fermée,
Comme un mort je n'avais qu'un unique élément.

(I built a fire, the azure having abandoned me,
A fire to be its friend,
A fire to enter into the winter night,
A fire to live better.

I gave it what the day had given me:
Forests, bushes, fields of wheat, vines,
Nests and their birds, houses and their keys,
Insects, flowers, furs, feasts.

I lived with nothing but the noise of crackling flames,
With nothing but the perfume of their heat;
I was like a boat sinking in closed water,
Like a dead man I had only a single element.)

Despite its status as an early Surrealist composition, "Pour vivre ici"
looks very much like a traditional poem. Although it is written in free
verse, the three stanzas are all the same length, and most of the lines
are alexandrines. On one level, the poem tells the story of someone
who, caught out in the open on a cold winter night, builds a fire to
keep from freezing to death. Since it is written in the first person and
adopts a confidential tone, that person appears to be Eluard—at least
within the fictional parameters adopted by the poem. The reference in
the alliterative first line to "l'azur" is puzzling until one realizes that it
refers to the sky, which before night fell was perfectly blue. Since the
next three lines begin with the same word: "feu," technically they are

examples of anaphora. Paralleling each other, they emphasize the fire's importance and employ a common rhetorical strategy: repetition. As Richard Stamelman declares, "elaboration and repetition are the two structures by which a Surrealist poem weaves itself and unfolds through linguistic time and space."[4] He distinguishes between metaphoric elaboration, on the one hand, and metonymic elaboration on the other. Since the statements in the initial stanza are related by similarity, they exemplify the first principle. Since the objects in the second stanza are related by contiguity, they illustrate the second principle. Besides providing the poet with vital warmth, there are two more reasons why he chooses to build the fire. In addition to presenting a physical barrier to the darkness and cold, he confides, the flames create a psychological barrier. Having been abandoned earlier by "l'azur," he feels essentially as if he has found a new friend. Reassured by the crackling flames, he manages to impose his presence on the surrounding darkness as a general sense of well-being invades his body.

So pleased is Eluard by these recent developments that, according to the second stanza, he bestows all his possessions on his new companion. The fact that he originally received them from "le jour" makes little sense until one realizes that the stanza continues the binary oppositions introduced previously between day and night, light and darkness, and life and death, each of which can be superimposed on the two others. At this point, the stanza activates the third opposition. In the current context, "le jour" clearly represents life, while death is reserved for the next stanza. Thus Eluard is invoking his own personal experience, all the things in life that he has learned to treasure. The catalogue of his impressive presents, which also serves to advance the poem, falls into two categories: natural and man-made. The first two gifts in each of the three lines belong to the first group, while the last two gifts belong to the second. How Eluard managed to accomplish this impressive transfer of wealth is not immediately clear. Although it is tempting to conclude that he simply threw everything on the fire, that would have been physically impossible. In retrospect, his statement appears to mean that he shared his appreciation of life with his fiery friend.

Whereas the first stanza describes Eluard's plans to combat the cold, and the second lists the things that are the most important to him, the last stanza evokes his personal experience. No sooner does he sit down next to the fire than the sounds, the smells, and the warmth begin to hypnotize him. Before long, he is so completely immersed in this seductive experience that he is oblivious to everything else. That "seul" occurs twice in the space of only two lines emphasizes how intensely personal the incident is. To illustrate Eluard's unusual condition, the poem concludes with two equally unusual similes. Like a sinking boat surrounded by water or a dead man surrounded by earth, he is totally consumed by "un unique élément," which in this case is the fire.

On another level, as various critics have noted, it is possible to treat "Pour vivre ici" as an allegory. Observing that the poem was written in 1918, for example, a number of writers have sought to connect it with the horrors of the First World War. Thus Daniel Lefèvre suggests that Eluard's fire may have been suggested by "le feu de son bivouac" ("his army campfire").[5] Other authors, such as Nicolas Le Roux, view the poem as a survival manual for the modern age.[6] As the title proclaims, it includes a list of requirements that need to be satisfied in order to live a rewarding life. It seems more likely, however, that Eluard is writing about his experience with poetry, which, according to the title, he needs in order to survive. Seen from this angle, the poem describes what happened to him when he could no longer count on "l'azur" to help him out. Even Mallarmé, who popularized the term to begin with, could never explain exactly what it meant. However, as Robert Greer Cohn concludes, "l'azur" seems to have been roughly the equivalent of "heaven."[7] Thus the first line appears to chronicle Eluard's loss of faith and his subsequent discovery of poetry—symbolized by the fire—not as a source of passive enjoyment but rather as a quasi-divine activity. The next three lines describe poetry as a source of comfort, well-being, and protection against "la nuit d'hiver" which, activating one of the binary oppositions discussed previously, would seem to be death. As before, the second stanza enumerates the vast array of experiences that Eluard poured into his project, while the third stanza describes how poetry completely absorbed him. That poetry is symbolized by a blazing fire to begin with testifies to its tremendous power. Each of the subsequent lines confirms that power and justifies Eluard's passionate devotion. It is evident from the poem's complexity, finally, that the rhetoric of Surrealist poetry exceeds the metaphoric model proposed by the First Manifesto. While Surrealist images are an essential ingredient, rhetorical structures play an equally important role.

Like "Le Sommeil a pris ton empreinte," the next poem, which has no title, comes from *L'Amour la poésie* (1929) and illustrates his mature style. The title of the volume refers to Eluard's two central themes: the simple joys of love and the magical art of poetry.

Je te l'ai dit pour les nuages
Je te l'ai dit pour l'arbre de la mer
Pour chaque vague pour les oiseaux dans les feuilles
Pour les cailloux du bruit
Pour les mains familières
Pour l'oeil qui devient visage ou paysage
Et le sommeil lui rend le ciel de sa couleur
Pour toute la nuit bue
Pour la grille des routes
Pour la fenêtre ouverte pour un front découvert
Je te l'ai dit pour tes pensées pour tes paroles
Toute caresse toute confiance se survivent.[8]

(I have told you for the clouds
I have told you for the tree by the sea
For each wave for the birds in the leaves
For the stones of the sound
For the familiar hands
For the eye become face or countryside
And sleep gives it the sky of its color
For the whole night long
For the railings of the roads
For the open window for a bare forehead

I have told you for your thoughts for your words
Every caress every confidence outlives itself).

This composition illustrates why Eluard is the most lyrical Surrealist poet of all. The key to his broad appeal lies in the simplicity of his approach and the fervor with which he sings about subjects that matter to him. No poet before him, Pieyre de Mandiargues argues, has known how to "parler aux hommes le langage de tous les hommes et leur parler cependant un langage neuf, infiniment precieux et simple pourtant comme le pain de la vie quotidienne" ("speak the language of all the people to the people and yet speak a new language, infinitely precious and simple like their daily bread").[9] Although Eluard employs simple words, the ways in which he combines them are anything but simple. Therein, of course, lies much of the poetry's interest. How he manages to wring so much feeling from such meager materials is amazing. The present work is a case in point. While repetition occupies a single stanza in "Pour vivre ici," it occupies all but two lines of the present composition. "Je te l'ai dit" doesn't resemble a poem so much as a shopping list. Wary of being overly repetitive, Eluard varies the lines by alternating the initial preposition "pour" with "je" and "et." Similarly, several lines contain two prepositional phrases instead of a single phrase, and in one line the object of the initial preposition is followed by a relative clause.

Despite its apparent transparency, the poem is anything but clear. The first line alone contains four indeterminate references that need to be resolved before the reader can proceed. Even if we assume that the speaker is Eluard, that leaves the direct object pronoun, the indirect object pronoun, and the preposition "pour" to disentangle. Fortunately, a little detective work reveals that *L'Amour la poésie* is dedicated to the poet's first wife Gala, whom he met while they both were convalescing at a sanatorium in Switzerland. However, we still have no idea what it is that he wants to tell her. Eluard deliberately saves that piece of information for the very last line. Whatever it is, one gathers initially that it is something he wishes to share with her—something that he considers to be important. But how can it possibly be "*pour* les nuages"? Not only is the sentence grammatically incorrect, but it makes no sense. In the last analysis, however, since Eluard appears to be constructing another catalogue, it makes no difference whether the sentence is coherent or not. All that matters is the column of nouns on the right. There are thus two solutions to the problem posed by "pour." Readers can either substitute another word mentally, such as "des" ("about") or "à propos des" ("concerning"), or they can ignore it altogether.

The present situation is basically the same as that in "Pour vivre ici." Eluard lists a number of things that he personally considers precious. Interestingly, there is practically no duplication between the two lists. Birds are the only item that is mentioned twice. Whereas two-thirds of the objects in the first catalogue are associated with nature, the proportion is down to 50 percent in the second. Eluard introduces several words instead that apply to human beings: "mains," "oeil," "visage," "front," "pensées," and "paroles." While some of the lines are perfectly straight-foreword, others are more problematic, such as "Pour les cailloux du bruit." Consciously or unconsciously, the poet has reversed the original two nouns to create a surreal image. The same process occurs in the seventh line, where "le ciel de sa couleur" represents a similar reversal. The sixth line is in a class by itself: "Pour l'oeil qui devient visage ou paysage." The fact that the last two nouns rhyme probably indicates that the first one generated the second. (The same mechanism seems to be at work in the tenth line: "Pour la fenêtre ouverte pour un front découvert.") However, the metamorphosis of the eye into a face and/or a landscape is thoroughly surreal. The image resembles one of Salvador Dalí's paranoiac-critical paintings in which one object dissolves into another one. Like the Catalan artist, Eluard likes to play with perspectives.

The poem's last two lines focus on Gala, whose words and thoughts, he implies, are as precious as any of the preceding items. More importantly, the final line answers a question that has been hanging over the text from the very beginning: the identity of the direct object pronoun. The importance of a tender caress or an intimate secret,

Eluard declares, far outlasts the act itself. Affection begets affection, instilling trust, confidence, and a zest for life like nothing else. The line is not intended to be a lesson, but rather a reaffirmation of his and Gala's love for each other. At the same time, nevertheless, it reveals an intimate secret that Eluard is happy to share with his readers.

Dedicated to Gala, "Ne plus partager" ("No More Sharing") was published in *La Révolution surréaliste* in 1925.[10] Divided into three stanzas and a single last line, it contains a thoughtful meditation on poetry's powerful ability to transform experience.

Au soir de la folie, nu et clair,
L'espace entre les choses a la forme de mes paroles,
La forme des paroles d'un inconnu,
D'un vagabond qui dénoue la ceinture de sa gorge
Et qui prend les échos au lasso.

Entre des arbres et des barrières,
Entre des murs et des mâchoires,
Entre ce grand oiseau tremblant
Et la colline qui l'accable,
L'espace a la forme de mes regards.

Mes yeux sont inutiles,
Le règne de la poussière est fini,
La chevelure de la route a mis son manteau rigide,
Elle ne fuit plus, je ne bouge plus,
Tous les ponts sont coupés, le ciel n'y passera plus,
Je peux bien n'y plus voir
Le monde se détache de mon univers
Et, tout au sommet des batailles,
Quand la saison du sang se fane dans mon cerveau,
Je distingue le jour de cette clarté d'homme
Qui est la mienne,
Je distingue le vertige de la liberté,
La mort de l'ivresse,
Le sommeil du rêve,
O reflets sur moi-même! ô mes reflets sanglants!

(On the night of madness, bare and clear,
The space between things has the shape of my words,
The shape of a stranger's words,
Of a vagabond who loosens the belt around his neck
And captures echoes with his lasso.

Between trees and gates,
Between walls and jaws,
Between this great trembling bird
And the hill that overwhelms it,
Space has the shape of my gaze.

My eyes are useless,
The reign of dust is over,
The road's hair has put on its rigid coat,
It no longer flees, I no longer budge,
All the bridges are cut, the sky can no longer pass,
I can no longer see it.
The world detaches itself from my universe
And, at the battles' very summit,
When the season of blood fades in my brain,
I distinguish daylight from the human brightness
That is mine,
I distinguish fear of heights from freedom,
Death from ecstasy,
Sleep from dream,

O reflections on myself! ô my bloody reflections!)

Like "Pour vivre ici," this is an allegorical composition albeit one that is considerably more sophisticated. As before, rhetorical constructions play an important role in establishing its basic surreality, which according to Stammelman is "founded primarily on a new notion of relation."[11] During the seven years that separated the creation of the two works, Eluard matured as a poet and honed his formidable skills. On one level, the poem was conceived as a hallucinatory vision. "The basis of the Surrealist image," Derek Harris observes, "is hallucination, both imagistic and linguistic ... The principal characteristic [it] presents is the arbitrary and incongruous juxtaposition of normally unrelated elements."[12]

On another level, however, the poem dramatizes Eluard's thoughts about the power of poetry and the role of the poet. The "folie" introduced in the first line refers not just to mental delusions, therefore, but also to *la folie poétique*—the divine gift of inspiration.[13] On the one hand, the image of the poet that emerges in the first two stanzas is thoroughly traditional. Eluard describes himself as an unknown vagabond stifled by society's rules who yearns to breathe free. On the other hand, he portrays himself simultaneously as a demi-god, as a powerful figure able to shape the world around him. His remarks apply not to the physical world, however, but to the realm of poetry, where the poet exerts absolute control over his creation.

Readers of Surrealist poetry often encounter references that don't appear to make much sense. Whenever the unconscious assumes control, for example, there is a good chance that the poem will contain at least one illogicality. The same thing is true of works that employ chance operations. Some references, like the title of the present poem, may be obscure but only temporarily so. Others suffer from a lack of context and never make any sense at all. Readers can either walk away or sit back and enjoy the imagery. This describes much of the third stanza, for example, which is only partially comprehensible. Unexpectedly, a sudden break occurs after the second stanza. The image of the poet that now emerges is of a solitary figure who lives an isolated life. As the title proclaims, he doesn't share anything with anyone. Although his eyes used to be extremely powerful, they have since become "inutiles." Eluard seems to be describing two diametrically opposed aspects of becoming a poet. As long as he restricts his life to the sphere of poetry, he is all knowing and all powerful. But as soon as he ventures into the real world, he loses whatever advantage he may have had. As he notes, the world distances itself from his personal universe. The bridges connecting the two are "coupés." The poem concludes with four binary oppositions that summarize the choices that are available to him. Daylight is opposed to human brightness, fear of heights to freedom, death to ecstasy, and sleep to dream. For a dedicated Surrealist, the choice was not a difficult one.

Ironically, one of Eluard's most famous poems has no title at all.[14] Published in *L'Amour la poésie* (1929), it comprises sixteen lines of free verse arranged to make two unequal stanzas.

La terre est bleue comme une orange
Jamais une erreur les mots ne mentent pas
Ils ne vous donnent plus à chanter
Au tour des baisers de s'entendre
Les fous et les amours
Elle sa bouche d'alliance
Tous les secrets tous les sourires
Et quels vêtements d'indulgence
A la croire toute nue.

Les guêpes fleurissent vert
L'aube se passe autour du cou
Un collier de fenêtres
Des ailes couvrent les feuilles
Tu as toutes les joies solaires
Tout le soleil sur la terre
Sur les chemins de ta beauté.

(The earth is blue like an orange
No question of error words do not lie
They no longer serve as blackmail
It's the kisses' turn to conspire
Madmen and love affairs
She her wedding ring mouth
All the secrets all the smiles
And what indulgent garments
To believe her stark naked.

The wasps blossom green
The dawn adorns her neck

With a necklace of windows
Wings cover the leaves
You have every solar joy
All the sun on earth
On the paths of your beauty.)

Over the years, critics have wasted gallons of ink trying to interpret the poem's first line, which is modeled on the implicit sentence: "La terre est *ronde* comme une orange" ("The earth is *round* like an orange"). By simply substituting "bleue" for "ronde," Eluard created a defective simile and a rhetorical nightmare. "At the level of mimesis," Michael Riffaterre comments, "both sides of the coin are wrong, the earth is not blue, nor is it orange."[15] As he notes, this has not prevented critics from proposing one desperate explanation after another. Some focus on the earth seen from space, others on the color blue, and others again on the concept of sphericity. Unfortunately, none of these interpretations have been the least bit convincing. In retrospect, one fact seems inescapable: the first line was deliberately intended to be absurd. This is why Eluard hurried to reassure his readers in the second line: "Jamais une erreur les mots ne mentent pas." And of course he was right—words don't lie, people do. Left to themselves, words mean what they say and say what they mean. Eluard merely wanted to shock his readers out of their complacency and get them thinking in other directions.

Introducing visitors to his paintings in 2016, the Syrian Surrealist Mohammad Zaza explained that Eluard's words represent "an invitation to set our minds free from all their inner limits." Paraphrasing the *Manifeste du surréalisme*, he added that "they reflect the idea that the poetic image is a pure creation of the mind, in which the unconscious travels beyond traditional borders" (see chapter 2).[16] In addition, since blue and orange are complementary colors, Eluard's words anticipate the *Second Manifeste du surréalisme*, published several months later, with its attack on "le caractère factice des vieilles antinomies" ("the artificial character of traditional oppositions").[17] "Tout porte à croire," Breton announced, "qu'il existe un certain point de l'esprit d'où la vie et la mort, le réel et l'imaginaire, le passé et le futur, le communicable et l'incommunicable, le haut et le bas cessent d'être perçus contradictoirement" ("Everything leads one to believe that a certain point exists in the brain where life and death, real and imaginary, past and future, communicable and incommunicable, up and down cease to be perceived as contradictions"). Since blue and orange cease to be perceived as opposites at this point, the original contradiction simply vanishes.

Satisfied that he has captured the reader's attention, Eluard turns from the subject of words to the subject of love—or at least sex. The poem is so fragmented that it is hard to be certain. Amid scattered references to lovers and kisses, a woman briefly appears with her mouth puckered up for a kiss. The fact that she has a mouth shaped like a wedding ring suggests she may be looking for a husband. Or perhaps that she is already married. She is so provocatively dressed at any rate that she appears nearly naked. The second stanza begins with a nonsensical sentence that is completely unrelated to anything else: "Les guêpes fleurissent vert." Because this statement is both abrupt and irrelevant, one suspects that Eluard's thought processes may have been momentarily interrupted. Discussing automatic writing in the *Manifeste du surréalisme*, Breton advised would-be practitioners to "[rompre] sans hésiter avec une ligne trop claire. A la suite ... posez une lettre quelconque, la lettre 'l' par exemple, ... et ramenez l'arbitraire en imposant cette lettre pour l'initiale du mot qui suivra" ("[delete] a line that is too clear without hesitation. Next ... pick any letter, the letter 'l' for example, ... and resume the arbitrary process by making it the initial letter of the next word").[18]

With green wasps buzzing all about, day dawns in the guise of the goddess Aurora, who wears a sparkling necklace of windows that reflect the rising sun. Like the first stanza, the second is purely descriptive until the reader reaches the last three lines. At this point, Eluard switches from the third person singular to the second person singular. Instead of referring to "elle," he suddenly addresses someone he calls "tu." Whether the pronouns refer to the same individual or to two different individuals is hard to say. All we know is that the women in both stanzas are beautiful. In addition, a third possibility exists that is definitely worth considering. Since the second woman is closely associated with the sun, there is an excellent chance that Eluard's words are addressed to Aurora, who appears earlier and who is the sister of Helios. The lover of several different mortals, she is usually depicted dressed in diaphanous robes and occasionally bare breasted.

Entitled "L'Amoureuse" ("Woman in Love"), the next poem was published in *Mourir de ne pas mourir* in 1924.[19] Like "Je te l'ai dit," it demonstrates Eluard's matchless skills as a poet of love. Unlike the latter poem, it depicts him and Gala as they experience an intimate moment.

> Elle est debout sur mes paupières
> Et ses cheveux sont dans les miens
> Elle a la forme de mes mains
> Elle a la couleur de mes yeux
> Elle s'engloutit dans mon ombre
> Comme une pierre sur le ciel.
>
> Elle a toujours les yeux ouverts
> Et ne me laisse pas dormir.
> Ses rêves en pleine lumière
> Font s'évaporer les soleils,
> Me font rire, pleurer et rire,
> Parler sans avoir rien à dire.
>
> (She is standing on my eyelids
> And her hair is in my hair.
> She has the shape of my hands,
> She has the color of my eyes,
> She is engulfed in my shadow
> Like a stone against the sky.
>
> She never closes her eyes
> Nor lets me sleep.
> Her dreams in broad daylight
> Make the suns evaporate
> Make me laugh, cry and laugh,
> Speak when I have nothing to say).

Written almost entirely in octosyllables, this much anthologized poem is basically unrhymed except for a final couplet that provides an excellent conclusion. As the title announces, the composition represents an intimate portrait of Gala, who is lying in bed next to Eluard after they have apparently made love. However, it is immediately evident from the first stanza that much more is involved than that. Although four of the first six lines begin with "Elle," five of the lines end with "mes," "mien," or "mon." Gala is the subject of the column on the left, but Eluard is the object of the column on the right. In reality, the poem is not about her so much as about the effect that she exerts on him. The subject of the first stanza is the incredible closeness that exists between them. She is pressed so firmly against him that their bodies are practically fused together. The fact that Gala is stroking Eluard's eyelids seems to indicate that he has his eyes closed, ready to drift off to sleep. Initially, therefore, he experiences her presence through his sense of touch. As he continues to hold her, he opens his eyes in line 4 and finds himself looking straight into her eyes, which are the same color as his own. Wrapping his arms around her, he completely envelops her so that she resembles a stone surrounded by the immensity of the sky.

In contrast to Eluard, whose exertions have made him sleepy, Gala has no trouble at all staying awake. While his eyelids continue to droop, she looks directly at him and showers him with loving comments. Her words are so powerful, he confides, that they cause the very stars in the sky to evaporate. Since stars are powered by nuclear fusion at a temperature of around 100,000,000 degrees Kelvin, that is an impressive feat, to say the least. Not surprisingly, Gala's words have a tremendous effect on Eluard, who is overcome with emotion. Delighted to see his love reciprocated so passionately, he laughs and cries and babbles incoherently. Thus the poem concludes on a joyous note while, having shared a moment of passion, the couple reaffirm their love for each other. If, as Mary Ann Caws declares, "the themes of purity, spontaneity, and intensity … pervade all the writings of Eluard," "L'Amoureuse" is one of the best examples.[20] Not only does it celebrate the purity of love, but it also possesses an extraordinary freshness of vision and is filled with intense emotion.

As Xavière Gauthier remarks in her groundbreaking study of Surrealist women, "La femme apparaît très fréquemment dans les oeuvres surréalistes comme objet passif du désir mâle" ("Woman appears frequently in Surrealist works as a passive object of male desire").[21] And yet, based on this fact alone, it would be wrong to conclude that the Surrealists regarded women as sex objects or that they preferred women whom they could easily dominate. There is a huge difference between a sexual fantasy and an actual woman. Although Surrealist men may have fantasized about docile women, their partners in real life were far from passive. For that matter, not all the women in Gauthier's list of Surrealist stereotypes are passive either.[22] Despite her arguments to the contrary, *la mante religieuse* ("the preying mantis"), *la femme fatale*, and *la sorcière* ("the sorceress") are active figures in Surrealist mythology. In addition, several types of Surrealist women appear to be missing from Gauthier's list. The following portrait, which has no title, was published in *La Révolution Surréaliste* in July 1925.[23]

> Sous la menace rouge d'une épée, défaisant sa chevelure qui guide des baisers, qui montre à quel endroit le baiser se repose, elle rit. L'ennui, sur son épaule, s'est endormi. L'ennui ne s'ennuie qu'avec elle qui rit, la témeraire, et d'un rire insensé, d'un rire de fin du jour semant sous tous les ponts des soileils rouges, des lunes bleues, fleurs fanées d'un bouquet désenchanté. Elle est comme une grande voiture de blé et ses mains germent et nous tirent la langue. Les routes qu'elle traîne derrière elle sont ses animaux domestiques et ses pas majestueux leur ferment les yeux.

> (Beneath a sword's red menace, undoing her hair that guides kisses, that indicates where the kiss lies, she laughs. Boredom has fallen asleep on her shoulder. Boredom only gets bored with her when she laughs, the reckless one, with an extravagant laugh, with an end-of- the-day laugh, sowing beneath all the bridges red suns, blue moons, wilted flowers from a disillusioned bouquet. She is like a large wagon of wheat, and her hands sprout and stick their tongues out at us. The roads she drags behind her are her pets and her majestic footsteps close their eyes.)

This Surrealist woman is certainly not submissive. She is daring, attractive, exciting, and earthy all at the same time. That she lives with a sword of Damocles hanging over her head testifies both to her boldness and to her courage. The fact that the sword is already stained with blood reinforces the initial impression of danger and emphasizes the fate that may lie in store for her. As the anonymous woman unwinds her beautiful long hair, her only response to this threat is laughter. Since she is clearly a vibrant character, she has nothing in common with Boredom, who loses interest as soon as she opens her mouth. The key to her personality is her irrepressible laughter, which defines her relationship to the rest of the world. On the one hand it represents defiance, on the other, assertiveness in the face of a long list of dehumanizing forces. More than anything, however, the woman represents a tremendous source of vitality. The fact that she sows cosmic seeds beneath the bridges suggests that she possesses some kind of supernatural power. Indeed, since shoots sprout from her hands, she appears to be an autochthonous deity. Because of her association with wheat in particular, one suspects that she is an avatar of the Greek goddess Demeter, known to the Romans as Ceres. As such, she constitutes another type of Surrealist woman to add to Gauthier's list.

In order to fully appreciate the previous woman's uniqueness, it is instructive to examine another female portrait by Eluard, which also has no title. Published in *L'Amour la poésie* four years later, it depicts the antithesis of the ideal Surrealist woman.[24]

Ni crime de plomb
Ni justice de plume
Ni vivante d'amour
Ni morte de désir.

Elle est tranquille indifférante
Elle est fière d'être facile
Les grimaces sont dans les yeux
Des autres ceux qui la remuent.

Elle ne peut pas être seule
Elle se couronne d'oubli
Et sa beauté couvre les heures
Qu'il faut pour n'être plus personne.
Elle va partout fredonnant
Chanson monotone inutile
La forme de son visage.

(Neither crime of lead
Nor justice of pen
Nor living from love
Nor dead from desire.

She is quiet emotionless
She is proud of being pliable
The grimaces are in the eyes
Of others, those who move her.

She cannot stand to be alone
She crowns herself with forgetfulness
And her beauty covers the hours
That are necessary to keep her from being someone
She goes everywhere humming
Useless monotonous song
The shape of her face.

Once again, Eluard relies on repetition and parallel constructions to forward the action in the poem. As the reader soon discovers, the portrait of the woman above is far from flattering. Indeed, it joins a long history of deplorable women in French poetry that includes such illustrious examples as Verlaine's "Une Grande Dame" and Apollinaire's "1909." If concision is a virtue, the initial stanza is positively saintly. The first four lines are so concise that they are practically unintelligible. Not until the second stanza does the reader discover that they describe the woman in question, who turns out to be a total non-entity. Eluard begins accordingly by listing characteristics that do *not* describe her rather than some that do. Although the phrase "crime de plomb" is intriguing, it is also rather puzzling. It could describe a crime committed with a gun, for example, but also one committed with a pencil. The remaining phrases speak more or less for themselves. All we know about the woman initially is that she is neither a criminal nor a judge, neither happy in love nor unhappy in love.

Although the second stanza provides more information about her, it contains two words that are difficult to pin down: "indifférente" and "facile." The first term can mean many different things, ranging from "indifferent" or "unconcerned" to "apathetic," "insensible," and "emotionless." While each translation has a different nuance, they all agree on one thing: that she is seriously repressed. "Facile" is another adjective with multiple meanings. It probably does not signify that she is sexually promiscuous. Other possibilities include "easy," "pliable," "weak," and "frail." Unlike the previous woman, who is full of life, she seems to have no personality. The word "wishy-washy" comes to mind. This conclusion is confirmed by the reaction of those around her, whom she likes but who don't much like her. Ironically, the third stanza informs us, she cannot stand to be alone but is oblivious to the impression she makes on other people. Much of her time appears to be spent in the boudoir making up her face instead of trying to accomplish something worthwhile. And when she does go out, she keeps humming the same stupid song over and over. In Eluard's opinion, the song matches her face. Both are not only monotonous but thoroughly useless as well. Interestingly, the poem constitutes an excellent blueprint for anyone seeking to become an ideal Surrealist woman. To succeed, candidates need to be the exact opposite of the woman it describes.

Published in *Disque Vert* in 1925, the final text, like so many others, has no title.[25] Written in prose and divided into five sections, it is concerned with the perpetual war of the sexes.

> Dans la brume où des verres d'eau s'entrechoquent, où les serpents cherchent du lait, un monument de laine et de soie disparaît. C'est là que, la nuit dernière, apportant leur faiblesse, toutes les femmes entrèrent. Le monde n'était pas fait pour leurs promenades incessantes,

pour leur démarche languissante, pour leur recherche de l'amour. Grand pays de bronze de la belle époque, par tes chemins en pente douce, l'inquiéude a déserté.

Il faudra se passer des gestes plus doux que l'odeur, des yeux plus clairs que la puissance, il y aura des cris, des pleurs, des jurons et des grincements de dents.

(In the mist where glasses of water clink together, where serpents search for milk, a monument of wool and silk disappears. It was there, last night, that the women all entered bearing their weakness. The world wasn't made for their ceaseless strolls, for their languid steps, for their search for love. Great bronze Belle Epoque nation, anxiety deserted via your gently sloping paths.

You will need to dispense with gestures milder than smells, eyes brighter than power, there will be cries, tears, curses, and the gnashing of teeth.)

Unexpectedly, the first sentence introduces the reader to the fascinating world of folklore. Viewed in this context, the eerie mist that sweeps over everything at the beginning probably represents the mist of time. The first folkloric reference involves a common superstition about clinking glasses of water. According to Jess Lander, for example, "Clinking glasses with water is looked down upon across many cultures. It's believed that the act brings bad luck or even death upon the recipient, and in some cases, death upon yourself."[26] That snakes are fond of milk is another widespread superstition, despite the fact that they can't digest dairy products. As Chris Stewart explains, snakes will supposedly steal the milk of goats and cows by winding themselves around a back leg to get at their udder.[27] However, the third item in the sentence is frankly puzzling. That a monument constructed of wool and silk could appear and disappear boggles the mind. Fortunately, the fact that it is made of those two fibers narrows the possibilities considerably. The unknown object must either be a rug, a fabric, or a garment. In addition, it must be associated with a superstition or fanciful story. Given these requirements, there is an excellent chance that it is a magic carpet.

Since the rest of the stanza reads like a misogynistic nightmare, one wonders who the speaker is. It cannot be Eluard who, if anything, loved women too much. Curiously, whoever is speaking knows exactly what is going to happen. Are we supposed to equate this figure with God the omniscient narrator? With Satan the betrayer of Eve and all her daughters? Without more information, it is impossible to say. As the women enter the mist, in any event, they bring all the things that the speaker associates with them including weakness, a penchant for strolling, leisurely steps, and an obsession with love. As soon as they disappear, a huge burden of anxiety is lifted from the nation, which at that point consists entirely of men. The second stanza begins with the speaker addressing the women directly. He instructs them to refrain from feminine gestures and eye makeup and predicts that they will be miserable. The second half of the sentence seems strangely familiar: "il y aura des cris, des pleurs, des jurons et des grincements de dents." Describing the torments of the damned in Hell, a similar phrase appears at least six times in the New Testament (Matthew 8:12, 13:42, 13:50, 22:13, 24:51, and 25:30). It is beginning to look more and more like the narrator is God after all.

> Les hommes qui se coucheront ne seront plus désormais que les pères de l'oubli. A leurs pieds le désespoir aura la belle allure des victoires sans lendemain, des auréoles sous le beau ciel bleu dont nous étions parés.
>
> Un jour, ils en seront las, un jour ils seront en colère, aiguilles de feu, masques de pois et de moutarde, et la femme se lèvera, avec des mains dangereuses, avec des yeux de perdition, avec un corps dévasté, rayonnant à toute heure.
>
> Et le soleil refleurira, comme le mimosa.

> (Henceforth, men who retire to bed will be no more than fathers of oblivion. At their feet, despair will have the handsome bearing of short-lived victories, of the halos beneath the beautiful blue sky with which we were adorned.
>
> One day, they will grow tired of it, one day they will be angry, needles of fire, masks of pitch and mustard, and woman will rise up

with dangerous hands, with eyes of perdition, with a devastated body, perpetually radiating light.

And the sun will blossom again, like the mimosa.)

At this point, the speaker focuses his attention on the men who have been left behind. Whether they are happy or sad to see the women go, one thing is clear: there will be no more sex. They will be fathers not of children but of oblivion. In addition, their short-lived victories will be soon forgotten, leaving them to silently despair. The mention of "auréoles ... dont nous étions parés" is surprising, to say the least. It brings us back to the vexed question of the speaker's identity, which the previous stanza appeared to answer. The fact is that halos are reserved exclusively for Jesus, the Virgin Mary, the angels, and the saints. Unfortunately, this means that the speaker cannot be God after all. Nevertheless, the phrase includes a piece of information that finally allows us to track him down: the pronoun "nous." The speaker confides that he belonged to a group of men who were also adorned with halos. All of a sudden, everything falls into place. The narrator is one of Christ's apostles, and, judging from the first two stanzas, he can only be St. Paul. Eluard is thinking of the following verse from the New Testament:

> In like manner also, that women adorn themselves in modest apparel, with shamefacedness and sobriety; not with braided hair, or gold, or pearls, or costly array (1Timothy2:9).

The fact that St. Paul was reputed to be a prophet explains how he knows everything that will happen in the future. Unfortunately, the next to last stanza is not exactly crystal clear. One day, Paul predicts, when the men grow angry and fall to fighting, the women will rise from the grave like zombies and vanquish them. Although the description makes it clear that the women are dangerous adversaries, the fact that each is surrounded by a perpetual aura signifies that they are also God's representatives. The final one-line stanza transforms the image of the aura into the image of the sun and then the mimosa flower, both of which are round and yellow. Applied to the sun, the verb *refleurir* emphasizes their similarity as well. An example of *le merveilleux*, the sun's miraculous recovery reflects the women's victory but also serves as a sign that now everything will `be all right. Conceived as a Surrealist allegory from the beginning, the text concludes with the triumph of the Surrealist woman. Like the woman in "Sous la menace rouge," she is both formidable and a source of vitality. Unlike the former, who loves to laugh, she is deadly serious.

Notes

1   J. H. Matthews, *Surrealist Poetry in France* (Syracuse: Syracuse University Press, 1969), p. 103.

2   Paul Eluard, *Oeuvres complètes*, Vol. 1, ed. Marcelle Dumas and Lucien Scheler (Paris: Gallimard, 1968), p. 235.

3   Ibid., pp. 1032–3.

4   Richard Stamelman, "The Relational Structure of Surrealist Poetry," *Dada/Surrealism*, No. 6 (1976), p. 73.

5   https://www.poesie-daniel-lefevre.fr/Eluard-PourVivreIci.pdg

6   https://www.lalanguefrancaise.com/litterature/pour-vivre-ici-paul-eluard/

7   Robert Greet Cohn, *Toward the Poems of Mallarmé*, rev. ed. (Berkeley: University of California Press, 1980), p. 300.

8   Eluard, *Oeuvres complètes*, Vol. 1, pp. 230–1.

9   Pieyre de Mandiargues, *"Préface" to Paul Eluard, Capitale de la douleur suivie de L'Amour la poésie* (Paris: Gallimard, 1966), p. 7.

10 Eluard, *Oeuvres complètes*, Vol. 1, p. 175.

11 Stammelman, "The Relational Structure," p. 63.

12 Derek Harris, *Metal Butterflies and Poisonous Lights: The Language of Surrealism in Lorca, Alberti, Cernuda, and Aleixandre* (Arnecroach, Scotland: La Sirena, 1998), p. 56.

13 See, for instance, Alain Billault, "La Folie poétique: remarques sur les conceptions grecques de l'inspiration," *Bulletin de l'Association Guillaume Budé: Lettres d'Humanité*, No. 61 (December 2002), pp. 18–35.

14 Eluard, *Oeuvres complètes*, Vol. 1, p. 232.

15 Michael Riffaterre, *Semiotics of Poetry* (Bloomington: Indiana University Press, 1978), p. 61.

16 "Mohammad Zaza—The earth is blue like an orange." Catalogue to his exhibition at the Depo Gallery in Istanbul, April 21 to May 18, 2016. See http://www.depoistanbul.net/en/event/exhibition-mohammad-zaza-the-earth-is-blue-like-an-orange/

17 André Breton, *Seconde Manifeste du surréalisme in Breton, Oeuvres complètes*, Vol. 1, ed. Marguerite Bonnet et al. (Paris: Gallimard, 1988), p. 781. First published in *La Révolution Surréaliste*, No. 12 (December 15, 1929), pp. 1–17.

18 Breton, *Manifeste du surréalisme in Breton, Oeuvres complètes*, Vol. 1, p. 332.

19 Eluard, *Oeuvres complètes*, Vol. 1, p. 378.

20 Mary Ann Caws, *The Poetry of Dada and Surrealism: Aragon, Breton, Tzara, Eluard, and Desnos* (Princeton: Princeton University Press, 1970), p. 136.

21 Xavière Gauthier, *Surréalisme et sexualité* (Paris: Gallimard, 1971), p. 191.

22 Ibid., pp. 98–189.

23 Eluard, *Oeuvres complètes*, Vol. 1, p. 179.

24 Ibid., p. 251.

25 Eluard, *Oeuvres complètes*, Vol. 1, p. 192.

26 Jess Lander, "Say Cheers. Five Unique Toasting Traditions from Around the World," https://www.winecountry.com/blog/say-cheers-5-unique-toasting-traditions-from-around-the-world/

27 " Eight Myths about Snakes," https://museumsvictoria.com.au/article/8-myths-about-snakes/ and Chris Stewart, "Watch out for Snakes. They Steal Mothers' Milk You know," https://www.telegraph.co.uk/expat/expatlife/9535237/Watch-out-for-snakes.-They-steal-mothers-milk-you-know ... html

4

Surrealism and the Poetic Act

This chapter is devoted to Surrealist metapoetry, that is, to concepts of poetry (and the poet) that are embodied in specific poems. In theory, the Surrealists' image of themselves should be confirmed by Surrealist practice and vice versa. It is time also to widen the present examination of Surrealism to include poets writing in other languages—especially Spanish. For reasons that would be interesting to go into, Spanish speakers have been awarded three Nobel prizes for poetry, while French speakers have received no recognition whatsoever from the Nobel committee. This despite the fact that Surrealism was invented in France. In choosing texts to discuss in this chapter, I was surprised to discover that the French Surrealists have almost never written poetry about their craft. By contrast, their Spanish-speaking colleagues have published a number of very fine poems. One of the reasons for this discrepancy may be related to the creation of the Surrealist movement itself. At the very beginning, André Breton envisioned a poetry that would be completely free from conscious interference. Surrealism was basically conceived as a purely automatic technique involving the unconscious dictation of thought.[1] Words were supposed to tell the poet what to say instead of the other way around. Inspired perhaps by Guillaume Apollinaire's conversation poems, "où le poète au centre de la vie enregistre ... le lyrisme ambiant" ("where the poet at the center of life records ... the ambiant lyricism"), Breton insisted that he and his colleagues were merely "sourds réceptacles" ("mute receptacles") and "appareils enregistreurs" ("tape recorders").[2] In the absence of any conscious control, poets were simply expected to record what their unconscious dictated. With their conscious role seriously devalued, the French poets never quite regained the importance they had once enjoyed.

Robert Desnos

Although Robert Desnos was perhaps the most interesting of the early French Surrealists, he is far from well known today. From time to time, some of his love poems surface in an anthology. But between 1922, when he arrived in Paris, and 1930, when he left the Surrealist group, Desnos enjoyed an almost legendary status among his colleagues. This was the period when the Surrealists were experimenting with hypnosis, which they hoped would open a door to the unconscious. While in a deep hypnotic sleep, Jean-Louis Bédouin explains, Desnos "parl[ait], écri[vait] et dessin[ait] avec une prodigieuse aisance" ("was able to speak, write, and draw with prodigious facility").[3] In fact, Breton was so impressed by his ability that he complimented him in the *Manifeste*. Desnos, he wrote, was "celui d'entre nous qui, peut-être, s'est le plus approché de la vérité surréaliste, celui qui ... a justifié pleinement l'espoir que je plaçais dans le surréalisme" ("the one of us who has perhaps gotten the closest to Surrealist truth, the one of us who ... has fully justified the hope that I have placed in Surrealism"). Adding that he looked forward to more of his splendid discourses in the future, Breton announced: "Aujourd'hui Desnos *parle surréaliste* à volonté" ("Today Desnos *speaks Surrealist* whenever he wants").[4]

Besides being the most successful Surrealist to tap into his unconscious, Desnos was arguably the most experimental as well. Published in 1930, for example, *Corps et biens* (*Bodies and Goods*) contains numerous verbal acrobatics and visual effects. Mary Ann Caws attributes Desnos's insistence on novelty to the emphasis he places on "the changing instant" in his works.[5] To this I would add that he obviously enjoyed playing with language. He was especially fond of *jeux de mots* ("wordplay"), which assume all sorts of guises in his poetry. Thus a section punningly entitled "Rrose c'est la vie" ("Eros/Rose that's life"), whose title acknowledges Marcel Duchamp's influence, contains no fewer than one hundred and fifty *contrepets* (spoonerisms) that Desnos created himself. Breton even quotes one of them in the *Manifeste*: "Dans le sommeil de Rrose Sélavy il y a un nain sorti d'un puits qui vient manger son pain la nuit" ("In Rrose Sélavy's sleep, there is a dwarf who has emerged from a well who comes to eat her bread at night").[6] The sentence's humor derives from two separate sources, one phonetic and the other visual. The section following "Rrose Sélavy" is divided into two rhyming halves that are exactly the same length (nine syllables). The fact that they rhyme in two different places creates a humorous effect that is reinforced by the phonetic reversal *nain/puits* → *pain/nuit*. The two vowels and both the initial consonants are reversed. At the same time, this operation generates an amusing mental picture. One imagines Happy, Sleepy, or Dopey dressed in the appropriate costume, sitting on the edge of a well, and eating a slice of bread. Created via linguistic manipulation, the image exemplifies the concept of *le hasard objectif* ("objective chance").

For the present purposes, however, one of the more interesting poems in *Corps et biens* is entitled "P'Oasis."[7] Conceived as an investigation into the complex workings of language and the imagination, the first half is concerned with *poesis*—with creativity and the creative act. Since the second half appears to be a separate poem, it is excluded from the following analysis. Whereas traditional poetry is constructed stanza by stanza, like a wall being built brick by brick, Desnos focuses on its structural elements, which follow a different pattern. As the title implies, "P'Oasis" is preoccupied with the creative act. In particular, it continues the dialogue between word and thought introduced in an earlier poem beginning "Notre paire quiète, ô yeux" ("Our quietist pair, O eyes").[8] Beginning with an amusing parody of the Lord's Prayer, the latter portrays syllables and words as prisons that restrict freedom of thought. As we will see, the situation is quite different in the present poem.

Nous sommes les pensées arborescentes qui fleurissent sur les chemins des jardins cérébraux.
— Soeur Anne, ma Sainte Anne, ne vois-tu rien venir … vers Sainte-Anne?
— Je vois les pensées odorer les mots.

— Nous sommes les mots arborescents qui fleurissent sur les chemins
   des jardins cérébraux.
De nous naissent les pensées.
— Nous sommes les pensées arborescentes qui fleurissent sur les
   chemins des jardins cérébraux.
Les mots sont nos esclaves.
— Nous sommes
— Nous sommes
— Nous sommes les lettres arborescentes qui fleurissent sur les
   chemins des jardins cérébraux.
Nous n'avons pas d'esclaves.
— Soeur Anne, ma soeur Anne, que vois-tu venir vers Saint-Anne?
— Je vois les Pan C
— Je vois les crânes KC
— Je vois les mains DCD
— Je les M
— Je vois les pensés BC et les femmes ME et les poumons qui en ont
   AC de l'RLO poumons noyés des ponts NMI.
Mais la minute précédente est déjà trop AG.
— Nous sommes les arborescences qui fleurissent sur les déserts des
   jardins cérébraux.

(We are arborescent thoughts blooming on cerebral garden paths.
— Sister Anne, my Blessed Anne, don't you see anybody coming …
   toward Saint-Anne?
— I see thoughts that are odoring words.
— We are arborescent words blooming on cerebral garden paths.
From us thoughts are born.
— We are arborescent thoughts blooming on cerebral garden paths.
Words are our slaves.
— We are
— We are
— We are arborescent letters blooming on cerebral garden paths.
We have no slaves.
— Sister Anne, my sister Anne, what do you see coming toward
   Sainte-Anne?
— I see words

— I see broken skulls
— I see deceased hands
— I love them
— I see thoughts that have been kissed and women who are loved and
   lungs that have had enough air and water drowned lungs of enemy
   bridges.
But the previous minute is already too old.
— We are arborescences blooming on cerebral garden deserts).

Upon reflection, the poem does not seem to be a dialogue so much as an argument about precedence and status. Reflecting the metaphorical garden setting representing the brain, one group of speakers represents flowery thoughts, while another represents flowery words. Thus the central scene revolves about an extended metaphor. Although it is never voiced, the implicit question that haunts the participants is which group is the most important. The first group claims priority because words are necessary in order to formulate thoughts. The second group replies that the situation is actually the reverse. Thoughts are more important because they organize words into meaningful sentences. Thus the poem resembles a drawing by M. C. Escher. One perspective is encompassed by a second perspective that, in turn, encompasses the first perspective. In other words, both statements are correct. It depends on which perspective one adopts.

This debate is well known to specialists in linguistics and other areas that involve speech. Some scholars argue that language precedes thought, while others believe that thought precedes language. Like Tristan Tzara, who proclaimed that "la pensée se fait dans la bouche" ("thoughts are made in the mouth"), the Surrealists believed that by liberating words they would revolutionize our way of thinking.[9] After trying twice to make themselves heard, a third group representing the letters of the alphabet intervenes in the dispute. Unlike the first two groups, which believe that the other group is inferior, they have no slaves. Since nobody is below them, they occupy the bottom rung on the linguistic ladder. They freely admit that they are inferior. And yet, paradoxically, the other two groups could not exist without them. Since letters are the basic building blocks of language, and possibly thought, they actually outrank the first two groups. As in so many instances, appearances turn out to be deceiving.

In order to arrive at the previous interpretation, we have had to neglect other features of the cerebral garden, such as neologisms ("odorer") and wordplay, that essentially serve as camouflage. By continually distracting the reader, they make it difficult to follow the main line of development. The biggest impediment is a network of references superimposed on the central dispute between language and thought. Introduced by playful allusions to different Annes, it is framed initially as a question: "Soeur Anne, ma Sainte Anne, ne vois-tu rien venir ... vers Saint-Anne?" The first Anne is a famous character in "La Barbe bleue" ("Bluebeard"), one of the tales in Charles Perrault's *Contes de ma mère l'oye* (*Stories of My Mother the Goose*) (1697). Married to a horrible man (Bluebeard) who has murdered his previous wives, his current wife discovers their disgusting remains in a room she has been forbidden to enter. While her husband prepares to execute her, she asks for a few minutes to pray and sends her sister Anne to the top of the tower to see if her brothers will arrive in time to save her. The refrain "Soeur Anne, ne vois-tu rien venir?" is taken directly from the tale. Instead of Anne's actual reply (which is essentially "not yet"), Desnos inserts a line that dovetails with the linguistic garden theme: "Je vois les pensées odorer les mots." The second Anne mentioned by Desnos may be the saint who, according to Christian legend, was the Virgin Mary's mother, or she may be someone Desnos loved. The third Anne (Sainte-Anne) may be the well-known psychiatric hospital in Paris, or it may be the rue Sainte-Anne, also in the French capital.

Two-thirds of the way through the poem the reader encounters the same question directed, once again, at Soeur Anne. This time the replies are even more unexpected. As Desnos demonstrates, letters can be used not only to create words but also to replace them—proof once more of their superiority. While the first response echoes the previous one, the next four are frankly appalling. The speaker, who as before seems to be Soeur Anne, describes the horrible scene she encounters when she opens the secret chamber. Smashed skulls, internal organs, and various body parts of Bluebeard's former wives are strewn all over the bloody room. Even more disturbing, the speaker appears to actually like what she sees ("Je les M"). However, since the scene changes abruptly, we will never know why she says such a horrible thing. Before she can respond, Desnos suddenly disappears, leaving the arborescent words, thoughts, and letters to repeat the initial sentence—with one difference. The cerebral garden inhabited by thoughts, words, and letters turns out to be a desert garden. More precisely, as the title indicates, it is an oasis surrounded by miles and miles of sand. Representing the human brain first and foremost, the oasis also makes an excellent metaphor for poetry itself. Like a desert garden, poetry is both a place of refuge and a source of beauty—an island in the midst of turbulent waters.

Vicente Aleixandre

Born in Seville but raised in Málaga, Vicente Aleixandre arrived in Madrid in 1909, where he remained for the rest of his life. Although he was trained as a lawyer, he devoted himself entirely to poetry from an early age. Always in poor health, he remained in Madrid during the Spanish Civil War but retained his political independence. For this reason, his works were banned in Spain from 1936 to1944 by the Franco regime. Nevertheless, as Anthony L. Geist remarks, Aleixandre is "one of the most important poets to have written in Spanish in [the twentieth] century."[10] Despite governmental disapproval, he continued to write brilliant poetry and received the Nobel Prize in Literature in 1977. When *Sombra del paraíso* (*Shadow of Paradise*) appeared in 1944, Andrew P. Debicki notes, he was "one of only three established poets of his generation left in Spain."[11] Assuming the role of an elder literary statesman, he served as a mentor and a guide to younger Spanish writers.

With the publication of *La distrucción o el amor* (*Destruction or love*) in 1935, Aleixandre's style had begun to mellow. By 1944, the tortured imagery, anguished eroticism, and relentless fragmentation of his previous poetry were gone. His new style was more lyrical, more open, and more communicative. He himself was older as well—more experienced and more confident in his view of life. The first of forty-four poems included in *Sombra del paraíso*, "El poeta" is a monologue written in free verse and divided into eight unequal stanzas.[12] The first three stanzas are occupied by a single sentence that winds its way down the page line by line. Thereafter, most stanzas contain a single sentence. Filled with visionary images, the sentences utilize conjunctions, prepositions, adjective clauses, and relative clauses to achieve their considerable length. As the lines accumulate one after the other, they advance according to a stately rhythm. Unexpectedly—especially for a Surrealist work—they lend the poem dignity.

> Para ti, que conoces cómo la piedra canta,
> y cuya delicada pupila sabe ya del peso de una montaña sobre un
>   ojo dulce,
> y cómo el resonante clamor de los bosques se aduerme suave un día
>   en nuestras venas;
>
> para ti, poeta, que sentiste en tu aliento
> la embestida brutal de las aves celestes,
> y en cuyas palabras tan pronto vuelan las poderosas alas de las águilas
> como se ve brillar el lomo de los calientes peces sin sonido:
>
> oye este libro que a tus manos envío
> con ademán de selva,
> pero donde de repente una gota tresquisima de rocío brilla sobre
>   una rosa,
> o se ve batir el deseo del mundo,
> la tristeza que como pápardo doloroso
> cierra el poniente y oculta el sol como una lágrima oscurecida,
> mientras la inmensa frente fatigada
> siente un beso sin luz, un beso largo,
> unas palabras mudas que habla el mundo finando.

Sí, poeta: el amor y el dolor son tu reino.
Carne mortal la tuya, que, arrebatada por el espíritu,
arde en la noche o se eleva en el medodía poderoso,
inmensa lengua profética que lamiendo los cielos
ilumina palabras que dan muerte a los hombres.

(For you, who know how the stone sings,
and whose delicate pupil knows a mountain's weight on a
loving eye, and how the forest's resounding echoes softly
fall asleep in our veins one day;

for you, poet, whose breath felt
the celestial birds' brutal assault,
and whose words are traversed by the eagle's powerful wings
silently like the hot fishes' gleaming spine:

listen to this book conveyed by my hands
with jungle gestures,
but where a fresh dewdrop suddenly glistens on a rose,
or where the world's desire can be seen beating,
sadness that closes the west like a sorrowful eyelid
and conceals the sun like a hidden tear,
while an enormous exhausted forehead
feels a kiss without light, a long kiss,
a few mute words spoken by the dying world.

Yes, poet: love and pain are your kingdom.
Carried away by the spirit, your mortal flesh
blazes in the night or rises in the midday sun,
immense prophetic tongue licking the heavens
illuminating words that doom men to death.)

Despite Aleixandre's use of normal syntax, which smooths the reader's path, "El poeta" is far from easy to understand. "The relations created by the Surrealist poem are non-mimetic," Richard Stammelman explains. "It is this literal *making* of new realities that is the truly creative aspect of the Surrealist poem."[13] As Carolina Cayuela González has demonstrated, "El poeta" is structured around a series of binary oppositions.[14] Or rather, it is structured around the dialectic that exists between them. The constant tension between opposing principles is what brings the poem to life. The first binary opposition, that between darkness and light, is illustrated by the collection's title: *Sombra del paraíso*. Additional oppositions exist between spirituality and materiality and between pain and love. To which I would add three more: artifice versus nature, bad versus good, and sadness versus joy. The first two stanzas are addressed to an anonymous poet about whom we know absolutely nothing. Assuming that the speaker is Aleixandre, according to a common convention, three scenarios are possible. The author may be speaking to another poet, to an idealized poet, or, as Cayuela believes, to himself. As she points out, the first stanza praises the unknown poet for his impressive body of knowledge—knowledge about the natural world. He is one of those rare individuals who are so close to nature that they can hear stones sing, judge a mountain's weight simply from its appearance, and be lulled to sleep by forest sounds.

The second stanza continues to emphasize the poet's closeness to nature. According to Cayuela, it praises him for his "perceptibilidad," but it hardly requires much perceptiveness to withstand an attack by an eagle. A truly perceptive person would have seen the eagle coming and taken precautions. Judging from the poem's description, nevertheless, it seems to have been a very close encounter. Aleixandre compares the eagle's powerful attack to the spine of a cooked fish, which pierces the succulent flesh from head to tail like a spear. One wonders, however, why the eagle attacked the poet in the first place. Why was he, the persistent friend of nature, perceived as a threat? The answer seems to be that the eagle attacked the poet's *words* rather than the poet himself. As incredible as it sounds, poetry appears to be the real enemy.

The third stanza begins with the gift of a book of poetry by the speaker, who instructs the unknown poet to "listen" to it. Perhaps that means he should read its contents out loud. Despite the speaker's awkward gestures, he reassures him that the book contains many beautiful images. The conjunction "pero" ("but") heightens the contrast between the speaker's dubious appearance and the book's treasures. Juxtaposed with the themes of desire and beauty, "la tristeza" ("sadness") in the fifth line introduces an additional contrast, which occupies the rest of the stanza. Aleixandre suddenly imposes the theme but provides no explanation. The brutal transition between lines 4 and 5 is not only surprising but also grammatically awkward. In particular, one wonders why the second line begins in medias res. The answer, when it eventually comes, seems to be that line 5 is meant to be read in apposition to the four preceding lines. More precisely, "la tristeza" describes "el libro." Once again, poetry finds itself under attack.

Since the stanza's fourth line evokes a beating heart ("o se ve batir el deseo del mundo"), the reader is prepared to encounter other body parts as well. The two similes in lines 5 and 6 involve tearful eyes. Referring to the setting sun, which is traditionally associated with death, both images exemplify the theme of sadness. Previously a source of light, the sun plunges the scene into darkness as soon as it sets, prompting the reference to a "mundo finando." Although the fourth stanza occupies only five lines, it contains four binary oppositions, each of which complements the other in various ways. The first example describes the poet's destiny. Although love will always be followed by pain, it implies, pain will always be followed by love. The remaining oppositions are between spirit and flesh, light and darkness, and joy and sadness. The stanza ends with a visionary image of the poet being consumed by apocalyptic flames while apparently explaining the purpose of death.

La juventud de tu corazón no es una playa
donde la mar embiste con sus espumas rotas,
dientes de amor que mordiendo los bordes de la tierra,
braman dulce a los seres.

No es ese rayo velador que súbitamente te amenaza,
iluminando un instante tu frente disnuda,

para hundirse en tus ojos e incendiarte, abrasando
los espacios con tu vida que de amor se consume.

No. Esa luz que en el mundo
no es ceniza última,
luz que nunca se abate como polvo en los labios,
eres tú, poeta, cuya mano y no luna
yo vi en los cielo una noche brillando.

Un pecho robusto que reposa atravesado por el mar
respira como la inmensa marea celeste
y abre sus brazos yacentes y toca, acaricia
los extremos límites de la tierra.
¿Entonces?
Sí. poeta; arroja este libro que pretende encerrar en sus
páginas un destello del sol,
y mira a la luz cara a cara, apoyada la cabeza en la roca,
mientras tus pies remotísimos sienten el beso postrero del poniente
y tus manos alzadas tocan dulce la luna,
y tu cabellera colgante deja estela en los astros.

(Your heart's youthfulness is not a beach
where the sea charges with its foaming breakers,
love teeth biting the earth's edges,
softly bellowing at various beings.

And it is not the vigilant lightning that suddenly threatens you,
briefly illuminating your bare forehead,
sinking into your eyes and incinerating you, consuming
space and your life burning itself out from love.

No. This light that is not the
the world's final ashes,
light that never loses heart like dust on someone's lips
is you, poet, whose hand and not the moon
I saw shining in the heavens one night.

A robust chest covered by the sea
breathes like the immense celestial tide

and opens its inert arms to touch, to caress
the earth's furthest frontiers.

And so?
Yes, poet, throw away this book whose pages pretend to
enclose a flash of sunlight,
and look in the light face to face, with your head against a rock,
while your remote feet feel the sun's last kiss
and your uplifted hands gently touch the moon,
and your long hair leaves a trail among the stars.)

After singing the poet's praises and listing his virtues at the beginning of "El poeta," the speaker devotes the fifth, sixth, and seventh stanzas to telling him what he is not. What keeps your heart young, he declares in stanza 5, is not the beach, where the waves slam into the sand in a sexual frenzy. Nor is it lightning, he adds in stanza 6, which enters your body through your eyes and incinerates you from within. The eternal, unfailing light, he insists in stanza 7, emanates not from the world in flames but from the poet himself, whose hand he saw shining in the sky one night instead of the moon. This astonishing development changes everything. That the poet's luminescent hand is able to replace the moon is a sign that he has cosmic connections. He appears to be a natural phenomenon like the moon and the stars. The next stanza, which depicts the poet bathing in the sea, confirms this impression. Not only is he one with nature, with the "la inmensa marea celeste," but he embraces the entire universe as well. Although the speaker originally gave him the book of poetry, now he advises him to throw it away. The problem with poetry and language in general, Posuelo explains, is that it prevents the poet from fusing with the universe. The real sunlight is not to be found in books but rather in nature, where its existence is authentic. For this reason, the speaker advises the poet to step outdoors and enjoy the sun before it sets. With the onset of night, he touches the rising moon, the stars come out, and he prepares to merge with the cosmos. As the poem concludes, we glimpse him flying through the air with his long hair streaming behind him, "deja estela en los astros." One of several visionary images that appear in the last stanza, the final sentence depicts the poet as a comet. Since the latter term derives from the ancient Greek word for long hair (*kometes*), the allusion is unmistakable.

Pablo Neruda

Born and raised in Chile, Pablo Neruda published his first book of poetry in 1921, followed by many more works in the years to come. In *Residencia en la tierra* (*Residence on Earth*), whose three volumes were published in 1933, 1935, and 1947, he employed Surrealist techniques to explore his turbulent unconscious. In particular, Enrique Anderson-Imbert explains, Neruda wanted to "ensnare profound life, show its spontaneous fluidity, bring to light the irrepressible movements of the subconscious."[15] Nevertheless, like several other poets included in this volume, he approached Surrealism with a mixture of admiration and antagonism. Like them, he rejected the Surrealist label and insisted on maintaining his poetic independence. Beginning in 1927, Neruda assumed a series of Chilean diplomatic and consular posts all over the world. From 1934 to 1936, he was Consul General to the Spanish Republic, where he met and fraternized with many of the Spanish Surrealists. When the Republic fell, he was sent to France to help with the refugees who were pouring in from Spain. Eventually becoming Consul General in Paris, he was awarded the Nobel Prize in Literature in 1971.

Neruda was at the height of his creative powers when he wrote *Residencia en la tierra*, which would influence several generations of Latin American writers. He had previously experimented with two other poetic styles, but during his years in Asia he felt the urge to experiment with Surrealist techniques. With the publication of *Residencia* after he returned from the Orient, Neruda finally came into his own. Here at last was a style that granted him unrestricted freedom, allowed him to express his unconscious impulses, and reflected his frustrations, insecurities, and desires. Reserved for the exact center of the first volume, "Arte Poética" is perfectly situated to comment on the other poems and to speculate about the nature of poetry.[16] The only problem is that it is completely inscrutable, which, nevertheless, describes a lot of Surrealist poetry. The critics all agree with Dominic Moran that it is an "opaque and enigmatic poem."[17] "While the title promises to reveal the hermetic mission of the poet," Maryalice Ryan-Kobler explains, "the text retains its secrets in its impenetrable syntax."[18] Hoping to find the key to its hidden meaning, the critics have tried every conceivable approach. The fact that the original manuscript is lacking complicates their task even more.

Among the more interesting interpretations, Emir Rodríguez Monegal believes that "Arte poética" charts Neruda's flight from Rangoon to Calcutta to escape his lover Josie Bliss, Moran that it represents Neruda's attempts to readjust upon arriving in Calcutta, David Lagmanovich that it describes Neruda's awakening to a new poetic voice, Stephen Roberts that it represents an aesthetic guide to *Residencia en la tierra*, and Ryan-Kobler that it is an analogical model of the human body.[19] In 1940, Amado Alonso subjected the poem to such a detailed analysis that it is still considered to be the authoritative text today. After rejecting all the interpretive frameworks available, he concluded that the poem essentially had no form, that the images were arranged randomly.[20] Like most Surrealists, who avoid rigid frameworks like the plague, Neruda preferred to work without a net. Among other things, this means that there is no hidden key that will unlock the composition. It is not a secret allegory but rather a living and breathing creation. From all appearances, Neruda began with a few ideas and let the poem evolve according to unconscious cues, pausing to intervene from time to time.

Like "El poeta," examined earlier, "Arte poética" is a lengthy monologue written in free verse. Unexpectedly, its twenty-one interlocking lines comprise a single, meandering sentence. Neruda utilizes repetition, conjunctions, and parallel constructions to link the different sections together. In only twenty-one lines, moreover, he employs twenty-seven commas. Except for a brief interjection in line 15, there is nothing to slow the sentence down. As Lagmanovich notes, "el poema corre irremisiblemente hacia los versos finales" ("the poem flows irretrievably toward the final verses").[21]

> Entre sombra y espacio, entre guarniciones y doncellas,
> dotado de corazón singular y sueños funestos,
> precipitadamente pálido, marchito en la frente
> y con luto de viudo furioso por cada día de vida,
> ay, para cada agua invisible que bebo soñolientamente
> y de todo sonido que acojo temblando,
> tengo la misma sed ausente y la misma fiebre fría,
> un oído que nace, una angustia indirecta,
> como si llegaran ladrones o fantasmas,
> y en una cáscara de extensión fija y profunda,
> como un camarero humilliado, como una campana un poco ronca,
> como un espejo viejo, como un olor de casa sola
> en la que los huéspedes entran de noche perdidamente ebrios,
> y hay un olor de ropa tirada al suelo, y una ausencia de flores,—
> posiblemente de otro modo aún menos melancólico—
> pero, la verdad, de pronto, el viento que azota mi pecho,
> las noches de substancia infinita caídas en mi dormitorio,
> el ruido de un día que arde con sacrificio
> me piden lo profético que hay en mí, con melancolía,
> y un golpe de objetos que llaman sin ser respondidos
> hay, y un movimiento sin tregua, y un hombre confuso.
>
> (Between shadow and space, between frills and maidens,
> endowed with a singular heart and ill-fated dreams,
> precipitously pale, with a withered brow
> and a furious widower's mourning for each day of life,
> oh, for each invisible water that I drink drowsily
> and from each sound that I welcome trembling,
> I have the same absent thirst and the same cold fever,
> a nascent ear, an indirect anguish,

as if thieves or ghosts were arriving,
and in a shell of constant and profound size,
like a humiliated waiter, like a slightly hoarse bell,
like an old mirror, like the smell of an empty house
with guests returning at night hopelessly drunk,
and with the odor of clothes thrown on the floor and no flowers,
—or else possibly even less melancholy—
but suddenly the truth, the wind that lashes my chest,
the nights of infinite importance fallen in my bedroom,
the noise of a day that burns with sacrifice,
ask me sadly what prophecy there is in me,
and there are a bunch of objects that call with no reply
and ceaseless movement, and a confused man).

One of the things that frustrate critics is the number of private allusions that populate "Arte poética." Another, despite the numerous conjunctions that ostensibly hold the poem together, is Neruda's widespread use of hypotaxis. The conjunctions link various words and images together but not necessarily in a meaningful way. Or rather, as Stammelman insists, "they create relations which on the level of syntax are logical but on the level of meaning illogical."[22] As Alonso insisted, the work is basically composed of isolated phrases and floating signifiers. The most fruitful approach accordingly is to concentrate on the imagery and the themes, which speak for themselves. Even so, the first four lines are left hanging for some time until the subject they modify—a disembodied "I"—appears in lines 5, 6, and 7. Since the poem is about poetry, one assumes that the speaker is Neruda, or rather, since this is a Surrealist poem, that it is Neruda's unconscious speaking. Indeed, because the logic is so peculiar and the imagery so strange, the whole work seems to have been dictated by his unconscious. Already the portrait of the poet that emerges from the first lines is an unhappy one. Although he has a big heart, his dreams have clearly not worked out. There are multiple suggestions, in addition, that he is suffering from poor health. One of the "doncellas" in the first line is undoubtedly Josie, who represents one of his ill-fated dreams and, since she is no longer with him, has left him a "viudo." That Neruda mourns for each day of life may mean that he mourns for each wonderful day he spent with her or, conversely, that he regrets the time he wasted with her.

Despite their obvious difficulty, which is primarily referential, the beginning (lines 1–4) and the end (lines 16–21) of "Arte poética" are relatively clear. By contrast, the middle section contains a number of vexing problems. Not only is the syntax confusing, for example but the prepositions "para" and "de" don't seem to make any sense. Is line 5 merely the second in a series, one wonders, or is it meant to introduce the following section? Should the lines read "con luto de viudo furioso por cada día de vida,/para cada agua invisible que bebo." or should line 4 end with a period and line 5 begin with a capital? Since "Ay" seems in fact to function as a period, the second option is undoubtedly the best course. In addition, "agua invisible" anticipates "sed ausente" two lines later, just as "sonido" looks forward to "oído" two lines later. It is important to realize that Neruda suddenly decides to alternate lines here. Line 5 is juxtaposed not with line 6 but with line 7 and line 6 with line 8. While other references continue to be as opaque as before, the middle section contains three challenging oxymorons: "agua invisible," "sed ausente," and "fiebre fría." Defined as a "condensed paradox," the oxymoron defies the reader to resolve the impasse between its two contradictory elements.[23] One of the Surrealists' favorite rhetorical figures, it is closely related to the concept of *le point suprême* introduced in the Second Surrealist Manifesto (1930).[24]

The oxymorons in "Arte poética" can actually be resolved fairly easily. That the glass of water is "invisible" may signify that it is transparent or that, like the speaker's thirst, it is temporarily missing. Similarly, the cold fever that suddenly envelops him probably indicates that he is covered in a cold sweat. During the transition from "sonido" to "oído" and from "temblando" to "angustia," Neruda thinks he hears unwanted visitors arriving and quickly panics. Why the visitors are not welcome and what they might do to him are never made clear. Nevertheless, his sudden fear generates four comparisons between himself and people or objects that have been compromised, that have lost their original purity. The humiliated waiter has lost his self-respect, the bell its pure tone, the mirror its silver backing, and the empty house its friendly smell. The clothes thrown on the floor by drunken guests simply add to this melancholy portrait.

On a slightly more cheerful note, Neruda could still redeem himself if he chose to. If he decided to face the truth about himself, he could regain his respect and his dignity. That is the implicit message that the symbolic wind, night, and day convey to him at the very end. "Arte poética" has had a double focus from the very beginning: on Neruda's miserable personal circumstances and on his equally miserable poetic situation. As Moran observes, the picture that the opening lines paint is of "a lonely, world-weary poet drained of all inspiration."[25] The invisible water for which he thirsts but cannot find, the fever that has diminished to the point of no return both symbolize his poetic failure. The anguish that pervades the poem stems from his failure as a man but also as a poet. The fact that he does not answer the multiple calls to rescue himself finally does not bode well. As Neruda himself admits, he is "un hombre confuso."

The three previous poems are so different from each other that it is impossible to generalize. Desnos ignores the poet altogether and focuses on the nature of poetry, which he portrays as a perpetual (but fruitful) competition between words, thoughts, and occasionally letters. It is primarily the mechanics of poetry that interest him as the poet struggles to find the right thoughts and the right words. Nevertheless, poetry itself is conceived as a source of beauty and as a refuge from the harsh realities of the world. Individual poems grow like plants or trees but need privacy to mature. Both Aleixandre and Neruda believe that poetry is a form of prophecy. For Aleixandre, the poet is a cosmic figure who embraces nature and has a superior knowledge of natural forces. Like life itself, poetry is conceived as a series of oppositions involving fundamental dichotomies, like those between the spirit and the flesh. The power of poetry pales, however, before the actual experience, which is far superior. Because Neruda's poem is autobiographical, its vision of the poet is severely limited. Nevertheless, it is clear that poets need inspiration—however one chooses to define that—in order to become successful. Poetry itself is conceived as a deliberately chaotic, apparently random, operation. Generated by the poet's unconscious, a series of images are linked together in ways that are not immediately discernible. As these three works demonstrate, Surrealist poetry assumes a number of different guises. So too does the role of the unconscious, which varies from barely noticeable to prominent to all-consuming.

Notes

1   André Breton, *Manifeste du surréalisme in Breton, Oeuvres complètes*, Vol. 1, ed. Marguerite Bonnet et al. (Paris: Gallimard, 1988), p. 328.

2   Guillaume Apollinaire, "Simultanisme-Librettisme," in Apollinaire, *Oeuvres en prose complètes*, Vol. 2, ed. Pierre Caizergues and Michel Décaudin (Paris: Gallimard, 1991), p. 976. Breton, *Manifeste*, p. 330.

3   Jean-Louis Bédouin, *La Poésie surréaliste: anthologie*, rev. ed. (Paris: Seghers, 1977), p. 279.

4   Breton, *Manifeste*, p. 331.

5   Mary Ann Caws, *The Poetry of Dada and Surrealism: Aragon, Breton, Tzara, Eluard & Desnos* (Princeton: Princeton University Press, 1970), p. 173.

6   Robert Desnos, *Corps et biens*, in Desnos, *Oeuvres*, ed. Marie-Claire Dumas (Paris: Gallimard, 1999), p. 504. Quoted in Breton, *Manifeste*, p. 339. For a detailed analysis of this spoonerism, see Willard Bohn, *The Rise of Surrealism: Cubism, Dada, and the Pursuit of the Marvelous* (Albany: State University of New York Press, 2002), p. 152.

7   Desnos, *Oeuvres*, pp. 525–6.

8   Ibid., pp. 515–16.

9   Tristan Tzara, "Dada manifeste sur l'amour faible et l'amour amer," in Tzara, *Oeuvres complètes*, Vol. 1, ed. Henri Béhar (Paris: Flammarion, 1975), p. 379.

10 Anthony L. Geist, "'Esas fronteras deshechas': Sexuality, Textuality, and Ideology inVicente Aleixandre's *Espadas como labios*," in *The Surrealist Adventure in Spain*, ed. C. Brian Morris (Ottawa: Dovehouse, 1991), p. 181.

11 Andrew P. Debicki, *Spanish Poetry of the Twentieth Century: Modernity and Beyond* (Lexington: University Press of Kentucky, 1994), p. 63.

12 Vicente Aleixandre, "El poeta," in Aleixandre, *Poesía completa*, ed. Alejandro Sanz (Barcelona: Lumen, 2017), pp. 389–90.

13 Richard Stammelman, "The Relational Structure of Surrealist Poetry," *Dada/Surrealism*, No. 6 (1976), p. 61.

14 Carolina Cayuela González, "Metapoesía y pragmática en 'El Poeta' de Vicente Aleixandre," *Espéculo: Revista de estudios literarios*, No. 34 (November 2006–February 2007). http://www.ucm.es/info/especulo/numero34/metaalei.html

15 Enrique Anderson-Imbert, *Spanish-American Literature: A History* (Detroit, MI: Wayne State University Press, 1969), Vol. 2 p. 604.

16 Pablo Neruda, "Arte poética," in *Obras completas*, Vol. 1, ed. Hernán Loyola and Saúl Yurkievich (Barcelona: Galaxia Gutenberg, 1999), p. 274.

17 Dominic Moran, "Neruda's 'Arte poética': Some Further Thoughts," *Bulletin of Spanish Studies*, Vol. 88, Nos. 249–271 (2011), p. 249.

18 Maryalice Ryan-Kobler, "Pablo Neruda's 'Arte Poética': At the Prophetic Crossroads," *Revista Hispánica Moderna*, Vol. 53, No. 2 (December 2000), p. 439.

19 Emir Rodríguez Monegal, *El viajero inmóvil. Introducción a Pablo Neruda* (Buenos Aires: Losada, 1966), p.62. Moran, "Neruda's 'Arte Poética,'" p. 252. David Lagmanovich, "Las 'Artes poéticas' de Pablo Neruda, *Espéculo: Revista de estudios literarios*, No. 28 (November 2004), n. p.. Stephen Roberts, "The Self-Adjusting Sonnet: Pablo Neruda's 'Arte poética,'" in *The Kate Elder Lecture* (London: Department of Hispanic Studies, Queen Mary University, 2002). Ryan-Kobler, "Pablo Neruda's 'Arte Poética," pp. 439–48.

20 Amado Alonso, *Poesía y estilo de Pablo Neruda; Interpretación de una poesía hermética* (Buenos Aires: Losada, 1940), pp. 56–7.

21 Lagmanovich, "Las 'Artes poéticas,'" n. p.

22 Stammelman, "The Relational Structure of Surrealist Poetry," p. 72.

23 Roland Greene et al., *The Princeton Encyclopedia of Poetry and Poetics*, 4th ed. (Princeton: Princeton University Press, 2012), p. 988.

24 André Breton, *Second Manifeste du surréalisme* in Breton, *Oeuvres complètes*, Vol. 1, (1946), p. 781.

25 Moran, "Neruda's 'Arte poetica,'" p. 258.

5

José María Hinojosa and Early
Spanish Surrealism

The Spanish Surrealists were somewhat younger than their French colleagues. Although some of them began publishing in the mid-1920s, as Andrew P. Debicki observes, overtly Surrealist texts were few and far between before 1929.[1] Most writers waited until the 1930s to experiment with the daring new style. By that time, Surrealism was well established, automatic writing had become semi-automatic writing, and numerous French examples were available for them to study. Several Spanish Surrealists even spent time in France, where they fraternized with their French counterparts. For those in Spain who were not able to read French, C. B. Morris has identified eighteen texts that were translated and published in Spanish magazines between 1918 and 1936. Another ten works were translated into Catalan and published in Catalonia.[2] In addition, Louis Aragon lectured at the Residencia de Estudiantes in Madrid in 1925 and André Breton in Santa Cruz de Tenerife in 1935. Although the Spanish poets enjoyed socializing with each other at weekly or even daily *tertulias*, they never created an official group with rules and regulations as the French did. More importantly, they were never controlled by a central authority who could banish them if they got out of line. Since they were only loosely organized, poets like Vicente Aleixandre, Rafael Alberti, Vicente Aleixandre, and Luis Cernuda were free to do whatever they liked. Whether they decided to implement Breton's guidelines, to partially implement them, or to ignore them altogether was strictly their decision. Unlike the French Surrealists, who insisted initially that they were simply "appareils enregistreurs" ("recording devices"), the Spaniards regarded poetry as a craft and themselves as authors.[3] Accordingly, they tended to assume a more conscious role in its creation than their French colleagues.

Ironically, although José María Hinojosa is practically unknown, he was the first person to import Surrealism into Spain (excluding Catalonia). For this reason, Manuel Durán has called him the Christopher Columbus of Surrealism.[4] Born near Málaga, Hinojosa studied law in Granada and then in Madrid, where he participated in literary gatherings at the Café Gijon. Through Emilio Prados he met other members of the Generation of '27 at the Residencia de los Estudiantes. In 1924, barely two months after the *Manifeste du surréalisme* appeared, Hinojosa wrote a poem entitled "Sueños" "by duplicating the physical and mental state prescribed by Breton to release the world of dreams."[5] In July 1925, he traveled to Paris, where he met a number of French Surrealists at the café La Rotonde located in Montparnasse.[6] After nine months in Paris, during which he published a book of poetry entitled *Poesía de perfil*, (*Profile Poetry*), he returned home full of enthusiasm for the French movement.[7] "Il rapportait de ses voyages à Paris des documents en grand nombre," according to Lucie Personneaux-Conesa, "et un enthousiasme fou pour ce nouvel idéal" ("From his trips to Paris, he brought back a great many documents and an enormous passion for this new ideal").[8] As soon as Hinojosa returned to Spain, he attempted to convert his friends in Madrid to Surrealism but without much success. Nevertheless, he managed to convince Emilio Prados in Málaga, who founded a Surrealist group that was active for some time thereafter.

The Dream Narratives

Following the appearance of *La Rosa de los vientos* (*The Compass Card*) in 1927, Hinojosa published *La flor de California* (*The Flower of California*) in 1928, *Orillas de la luz* (*Shores of Light*) the same year, and *La sangre en libertad* (*Blood at liberty*) in 1931, all of which were inspired by Surrealism. However, the second book was destined to become the most successful, eliciting widespread praise from his colleagues in Madrid and elsewhere. It cannot be mere chance, Julio Neira remarks, that Hinojosa's friends actively embraced Surrealism after that, including Rafael Alberti, Vicente Aleixandre, Federico García Lorca, and Luis Cernuda.[9] Containing seven dream narratives and seven oneiric texts, *La flor de California* charts Hinojosa's painful search for his identity amid several motifs and techniques borrowed from the French Surrealists. In particular, Morris points out, the texts not only share the French passion for freedom and chance but also contain "rich and mobile fantasies."[10] Conceived as a dream narrative, "Diez palomas" ("Ten Doves") typifies the genre.[11]

> Salieron diez palomas blancas, mensajeras, de cada uno de mis dedos y llevando cada uno de ellas en el pico la rama de olivo post-diluviano fueron a posarse sobre los sexos de nácar de la mujeres que constantemente repiqueteaban con sus nudillos en el tambor que hicieron los pupúes con el pellejo del Sol. Tenían la piel tan fina que con solo el aliento de las palomas quedaron fecundadas aquellas mujeres y de sus sexos brotaron azucenas en tal cantidad que jamás volverán a faltarle azucenas frescas, como sucedió en año 1904 a San José para su mano izquierda.
>
> En la carola de una azucena apareció el busto de una mujer rubia, con sus pechos de miel, rodeado de pétalos. Por delante del busto saltaban los peces que trazaban estelas elípticas verdosas para ocultar aquella aparición a los ojos de los profanos con una malla de agua del estanque romántico lleno de algas donde iban todas las mañanas a mojar su pico las palomas mensajeras.
>
> Ya solo podíamos ver el busto, reflejado en las aguas olvidadas de toda fuerza extraña, las palomas y yo, cuando de mi boca comenzó a salir un enjambre yendo a posarse las abejas para chupar de ellos sobre los pechos dorados del busto de la mujer rubia.
>
> (Ten white homing pigeons emerged from each of my fingers carrying the post-diluvian olive branch in their beaks, landing on the mother-of-pearl vaginas of the women whose knuckles were constantly beating the drum fashioned out of the sun's skin by their navels. Their skin was

so delicate that they were impregnated by the pigeons' breath alone, and so many Madonna lilies sprouted from their vaginas that they would never lack for fresh lilies again, as happened in San José in 1904 for their left hands.

The bust of a blond woman appeared in a lily's corolla, with breasts of honey and surrounded by petals. Fish were jumping before the bust, drawing greenish elliptical stars to hide the apparition from profane eyes with a net of water from the romantic algae-filled lake, where the homing pigeons dipped their beaks every morning.

The pigeons and I were looking at the bust, reflected in the forgotten waters by a strange force, when a swarm of bees emerged from my mouth and flew toward the golden breasts of the blonde woman's bust in order to suck them.)

Bursting upon the scene in the mid-nineteenth century, the prose poem soon became a popular choice for avant-garde poetry. "With its oxymoronic title and its form based on contradiction," Mary Ann Caws explains, "[it] is suitable to an extraordinary range of perception and expression."[12] Indeed, André Breton was so struck by the hybrid genre's possibilities that he chose it for his first attempts at automatic poetry (see Chapter 1). Although Surrealist prose poems look different from Surrealist poems, they function in very much the same manner. As Laurent Jenny declares, "le principe structural du récit surréaliste est un principe essentiellement poétique" ("the structural principle of the Surrealist narrative is essentially poetic").[13] Form is meaning, he adds, and play is meaning. From which we can deduce that form is play and vice versa. Since the playful elements in a poem constitute both its form and its basic meaning, they are far from incidental. Nevertheless, as we will see in Chapter 7, there are Surrealist narratives and then again there are Surrealist narratives.

As Jacqueline Rattray observes, "the dream narrative gives the poet a means to express his transgressive thoughts and also allows the reader into the bizarre and labyrinthine workings of the subconscious."[14] If proof were needed, it would be hard to find a better example than

Hinojosa's first sentence in which ten *palomas* emerge from the tips of his fingers carrying olive branches in their beaks. Although we don't know how many women are present—at least ten—we learn immediately that they have mother-of-pearl vaginas. Indeed, breasts and vaginas play an active role throughout the text to the point of becoming an obsession. For that reason, Antonio A. Gómez Yebra calls it an "alegoría erótico."[15] The fact that the birds are white and carry olive branches seems to indicate that they were initially doves. Hinojosa repeated a common error going back at least to St. Augustine, who believed that, according to the *Bible*, Noah's dove returned to the Ark with an olive branch (*De doctrina christiana*). In actuality, however, the dove returned with an olive *leaf* (*Genesis* 8.11). Signifying peace today, the olive branch was borrowed from ancient Greece, where it signified victory or surrender.

At some point, and for unknown reasons, Hinojosa decided to transform his doves into *palomas mensajeras*, which means they are really pigeons. As soon as the latter take flight, they land on the vaginas of a group of naked women who are performing a mysterious ritual with a solar drum. The story gets even more bizarre as it evolves, involving bestiality, like the tale of Leda and the Swan, and inter-kingdom parturition. The pigeons have chosen their mother-of-pearl destinations for a good reason: to impregnate the women with their breath—who immediately give birth to large numbers of Madonna lilies (*Lilium candidum*). A majestic flower with large white trumpets and a lovely fragrance, the latter is ironically a symbol of purity. According to Hinojosa, a similar episode supposedly occurred in 1904 in San José, a seaside village on the Costa de Almería. However, Gómez Yebra believes that the phrase refers to the custom of leaving lilies before an image of San José on his name day.[16] Investigating one of the flowers more closely, Hinojosa discovers that the petals enclose the bust of a naked blonde woman with "pechos de miel." Like Alice vanishing down the rabbit hole, he suddenly finds himself in an erotic Wonderland. The scene opens out before him to reveal the bust of the blonde woman beside a lake where fish are jumping and drawing pictures of mysterious stars. Representing Hinojosa's licentious thoughts, a swarm of bees erupts from his mouth and flies toward the woman to suck her breasts. At this point, her nude statue gradually begins to acquire human characteristics.

Yo, José María Hinojosa, estaba tendido en el césped, junto al borde del estanque, los brazos en cruz, la luna en la frente y con un dolmen distanciado a tres metros, cubierto de musgo, preparado para servir de pedestal a mi exhibición de gala, mientras las abejas endulzaban mi boca con la miel traída de la mujer rubia y edificaban un panal alrededor de mi cabeza; y ellas, las palomas, cogidas de sus alas mostraban la nieve cristalizada de su cuerpo derritiendose con lentitud sobre el estanque de un verde inútil y cogían con sus picos las abejas que perdían su ruta atraídas por el rugido de los leones del desierto. Ya el panal construído y envuelta mi cabeza por completo fué un manantial de tantas salidas como celdillas tenía, de las que manaba leche purísima que resbalando por mi cuerpo dejábalo blanco y alimentaba mis entrañas con su tibieza. Mis labios caían y se posaban sobre mujeres distantes que desaparicián de mi presencia, violentemente despedidas, por los ángulos superiores de mi retina. Mis labios dejaban sus huellas sobre el dolmen recubierto de musgo y del estanque se elevó una tromba que sorbió todo mi interior dejándome hueco, quedando mi cuerpo en condiciones de poderse llenar, como asi sucedió, con la miel extraída de los pechos de la mujer rubia, con la miel y la leche purísima de las palomas que volaban en torno mío.

Cuando llegó la Primavera mi cuerpo de leche y miel esperó ausente de recuerdos a que bajasen, una a una, las diez palomas, para dejar sobre mi rostro una caricia velada, de hoja recién brotado, capaz de reavivar en mí la savia adormecida de castaño que corre por mis venas. Mil veces esperé estas caricias sin llegar siquiera a rozarme las diez palomas que revoloteaban a mi presencia.

El dolmen deseaba fuertemente verse hollado por mis plantas pero yo permanecía quieto mientras patinaban por mi carne las miradas escurridizas de todas las mujeres distantes que me rodeaban y mis miradas languedecían a cada despedida, a cada adiós dado para siempre sobre la piel apetecida para cubrir mis labios, quedándome encerrado en un anillo negro imposible de romper, mas espeso y blindado a cada nueva despedida.

(I, José María Hinojosa, was stretched out on the lawn by the edge of the lake with my arms forming a cross, the moon on my forehead, and a dolmen nine feet away covered with moss, ready to serve as a pedestal at my gala exhibition, while the bees sweetened my mouth with the honey sucked from the blonde woman and built a honeycomb around my head; suspended by their wings, the pigeons revealed their bodies covered with crystallized snow, slowly melting over the useless green lake, and snatched disoriented bees attracted by the roaring of the desert lions. Now the new honeycomb completely enveloping my head was a spring with numerous cell-like holes from which fresh milk flowed, splashing my body, painting it white, and feeding my bowels with its tepidness. My lips lowered and pressed themselves against distant women who disappeared from my presence, violently ejected by the upper corner of my retina. My lips left their prints on the moss-covered dolmen, and a waterspout arose on the lake that sucked out all my insides, leaving me hollow and ready to be refilled, as actually happened, with honey extracted from the blonde woman's breasts, with honey and fresh milk from the pigeons flying around me.

When spring arrived, my milk and honey body waited, in the absence of memories, for the ten pigeons to fly down one by one, lightly caressing my face like a newly sprouted leaf, and able to revive the chestnut's dormant sap that runs through my veins. I waited for those caresses a thousand times without ever receiving one from the ten pigeons fluttering around me.

The dolmen strongly wished to see itself trampled by my plants, but I remained quiet while the distant women's glances skated across my flesh—the elusive glances of all the distant women who surrounded me—and my glances languished at each farewell, each eternal goodbye kiss bestowed forever upon the desired skin in order to cover my lips, leaving me enclosed in a black ring that was impossible to break, thicker and armored at every new farewell.)

Stretched out on the lawn next to the lake, Hinojosa is juxtaposed with three suggestive but enigmatic symbols. To be sure, the cross he

creates by extending his arms symbolizes Christianity, but it is difficult
to see how it would fit into the present scenario. Similarly, the moon
and the dolmen have numerous symbolic possibilities, but none of
them seem to work here. All Hinojosa can figure out to do with the
dolmen, for example, is to use it for a table. And although he finally gets
to taste honey from the blonde woman's breasts it is only at second hand,
brought to him by bees constructing a honeycomb around his head as
if he were the queen bee. While he is brushing snow from the pigeon's
breasts, however, the honeycomb springs numerous leaks, revealing
that it is actually filled with milk. As milky streams flow all over his
body, Hinojosa experiences an unpleasant baptism. Unwittingly (and
comically), he finds himself in the Land of Milk and Honey prophesied
in the *Bible* (*Exodus* 3), which turns out not to be so great after all.
Instead of being reborn, he undergoes a series of frustrating experiences.
Rejected by some distant women he wants to kiss, he kisses the dolmen
instead and loses his insides to a passing waterspout. An empty vessel
again, Hinojosa waits for the pigeons to bring him more milk and
honey. With the arrival of spring, he waits unsuccessfully for them to
show him a sign of affection. His lack of success with the pigeons and
the distant women finally leaves him feeling imprisoned.

> Ya solo podía percibir el aire levantado por las palomas sobre mi rostro
> y de mis ojos no manaba más que sangre cuando me encontré rodeado
> de fieras del desierto. Entre rugidos y zarpazos la sangre se extendía,
> dibujando mi cuerpo, por el césped en que estaba recostado. Las fieras
> del desierto clavaban con ahínco sus garras en mis pupilas vacías y un
> martirio quedaba reflejado en el estanque romántico con un rictus de
> dolor y ungido de esperanza por verse libertada de aquél aislamiento.
> Un leve toque sobre mi carne, dado por una paloma mensajera, sería
> capaz de hacer revivir en mí toda la flora del continente americano.
>
> Las diez palomas pusieronse de parte mía y así formamos un grupo
> lo bastante fuerte para luchar contra todo aquéllo que se nos opusiese a
> nuestra llegada a la otra ribera donde aguardaba con suspies ocultos en
> la arena, la mujer rubia que tuvo la atención de dirigirme mi primera y
> única sonrisa de toda la jornada.

El aire seco que venía de tierra hacía vibrar mi cuerpo arrancando de él sonidos de bordón y las ondas sonoras repercutían en el sexo de la mujer rubia. Sus brazos desunidos del cuerpo venían a mí y acariciaban mi garganta mientras ella ponía sus miradas lejanas al alcance de mis ojos.

Despues de atravesar selvas y pantanas, valles y montañas llegué, extenuado, a dar vista a la otra ribera; podía tocarla con las manos pero no con los pies. Estaba tan cerca que, a pesar del cansancio, me era imposible resistir la tentación de cubrir este último trecho para dar cima a mi propósito de unirme a la mujer rubia.

Comencéa mover lentamente mis pesados pies llenos de distancia y fueron sumerigiéndose en el agua que separaba una orilla de la otra. El agua iba cubriendo paulatinamente mi cuerpo y ya llegaba a mi garganta y aún faltaba mucho espacio para conseguir mi deseo. Llegó un momento que me fué imposible avanzar y era arrastrado por la corriente. Todo esfuerzo resultaba inútil y cuando ya había perdido la esperanza de llegar a la otra orilla y creía perdidos todos mis afanes vinieron en mi ayuda las diez palomas que separando mi cabeza del tronco la transportaron a la ribera donde me esperaba la mujer rubia y la pusieron a sus pies en el preciso instante de poder recoger un último beso exhalado sobre mis labios.

(I alone could feel the air the pigeons fanned in my face, and only blood flowed from my eyes when I found myself surrounded by desert beasts. Between roars and clawings the blood spread, outlining my body on the lawn where I was lying. The desert beasts eagerly sank their claws into my empty pupils, and a martyrdom remained reflected in the romantic lake with a grin of pain and anointed with the hope of seeing itself freed from that isolation. A homing pigeon's light touch on my skin could revive in me all the flora of the American continent. The ten pigeons turned toward me, and we formed a group strong enough to fight everything that opposed our arrival on the other bank, where the blonde woman was waiting with her feet in the sand who was kind enough to flash me her first and only smile of the day.

The dry air coming from the ground made my body vibrate, extracting buzzing sounds, and the sound waves resounded in the blonde woman's vagina. Separated from her body, her arms came to me and caressed my throat while she put her distant glances within reach of my eyes.

After crossing jungles and marshes, valleys and mountains, I managed to glimpse the other bank; I could touch it with my hands but not with my feet. I was so near that, despite my fatigue, I could not resist the temptation to cover this last distance to achieve my plan to unite with the blonde woman.

I slowly began to move my heavy feet full of distance, and they submerged themselves in the water separating one shore from the other. The water slowly covered my body and came up to my throat, leaving little space to obtain my desire. A moment came when it was impossible to advance, and I was swept away by the current. All my strength was useless, and when I had lost all hope of reaching the other bank, and thought my efforts lost, the ten pigeons came to my rescue who, separating my head from my body, transported it to the bank where the blonde woman was waiting for me, and they lifted her to her feet at the precise moment that I experienced one last breathless kiss on my lips.)

So far Hinojosa has simply found life to be frustrating, but a darker theme invades the text as the story progresses. As a number of critics have noted, the Spanish Surrealists were attracted to "acts of savagery"—to blood, mutilation, blindness, and disembodied limbs.[17] Without warning Hinojosa suddenly finds himself bleeding from the eyes and surrounded by "fieras del desierto," which sink their claws into his pupils. As the nightmare scenario continues, blood streams down his face and accumulates in pools on the lawn where he is lying. Then, as if the attack had never happened, the animals are suddenly gone, and Hinojosa is making plans to fight his way to the opposite side of the river, where the blonde woman is now waiting for him. Detached from her body, as if she were a mannequin, her two arms come to greet him and bestow the caresses that he has been longing for. When he attempts to cross the river to join her, however, he is swept away by the current and nearly drowns. Fortunately, the ten pigeons who are accompanying Hinojosa come to his rescue and devise a novel plan. Transporting his decapitated head across the river, they arrive just in time for the blonde woman to bestow a breathless kiss before he expires. Presumably, he dies with a smile on his face. Once again, another Surrealist hero has been attracted to a femme fatale like a moth to the flame.

The Oneiric Texts

The difference between Hinojosa's dream narratives and his oneiric texts is one of degree rather than kind. If anything, the former tend to be slightly more coherent than the latter, which more closely resemble automatic writing. However, the difference between dreams and automatic texts is hard to quantify. Both procedures seek to express unconscious impulses via familiar mechanisms—words or visual images. The Surrealists utilized both approaches to glean as much information as they could about the unconscious. But since poetry ultimately translates pictures into their verbal equivalents, the difference between words and images practically vanishes. As Morris declares, the *textos oníricos* are "an eloquent and ambitious attempt to emulate the free flow and imaginative freedom of much Surrealist writing."[18] Indeed, during the period preceding their publication, a number of French examples appeared in *La Révolution Surréaliste*, which Hinojosa almost certainly saw. Whereas the previous text demonstrated his penchant for eroticism, "Texto onírico no. 2" displays his fondness for blasphemy.[19]

Envuelto en un rumor de olas atajo en mi cerebro todos los pensamientos que pretenden escaparse por la escotilla y mientras apoyo mi mano sobre el testuz de Napoleon cae rodando mi cabeza por las cataratas de Niágara. Jamas he pretendido ser un saltimbanqui para apoyar mi cuerpo sobre el dedo del corazón y aunque lo afirmasen todos los horóscopos yo podría negarlo aún con solo dar una pincelada de azul cobalto sobre la estatua de la Libertad. Siempre podría negarlo y la negación seria infinita convirtiendose en un punto negro enorme, lo suficiente para ecllipsar el Sol y con esto me bastaría para bañarme tranquilamente a la luz de la Luna sin que las aguas mojasen mi cuerpo

envuelto en el original de "La espístola a los Corintios." Yo soy la
epístola náufrago entre almas desvencijadas de ateos comulgaré todas
las mañanas con almendras amargas.

Y soy la epístola, corintios, tomad y comed porque mi cuerpo va
detrás de mi cabezo por las cataratas del Niágara y mi alma está entre
vuestras almas hecha epístola. ¡tomad y comed porque mi cuerpo
va detrás de mi cabeza por los cataratas del Niágara y mi alma está
entre vuestras almas hecha epístola. ¡Tomad y bebed agua del Niágara
porque es sangre de mi sangre! Vuestros disparos no me hieren porque
mi cuerpo es blanco y se confunde con las nubes y con la cal; con la
espuma y con la sal. La nieve no me sirve para ocultarme, mi cuerpo
ensangrentado la teñíria de rojo y los corintios se verían defraudados
al encontrar mi rastro. ¡Oh! si la gran negación se transformase en
este pez que llevo in la mano quizás se escurriría de entre mis dedos
y caería al mar para dar la vuelta al mundo a través de las aguas pero
la negación está firmemente entrelazada a mis dedos y tendría que
sumergirlos en azufre para dejarlos en libertad.

¡Tomad y comed! ¡Tomad y bebed! Que el dedo del corazón
entrara a rosca en la cúspide de la pirámide Cheops y quedara mi
cuerpo flotando en el aire en espera de la resurreción de la carne y de
la apertura de las primaveras y para ello no necesitaré la partida de
nacimiento ni la bendición de Su Santidad.

Entonces, corintios, haciendo de mi cuerpo un arco y de mi alma
una flecha me dispararé en las cuatro direcciones de los puntos
cardinales y caerá sobre todo el globo terrrestre una capa de ceniza
roja hecha con la cremación de mi carne.

(Enveloped in the sound of waves, I intercept my thoughts trying to
escape through the hatchway, and while I place my hand on Napoleon's
forehead my head rolls over Niagara Falls. I have never claimed to be
an acrobat in order to balance my body on my middle finger, and even
though all the horoscopes agree, I could still deny it by simply dabbing
some cobalt blue on the Statue of Liberty. I could always deny it, and
this denial would be infinite, transforming itself into an enormous
black dot, large enough to eclipse the Sun, and with this I could
bathe myself quietly by the light of the moon without wetting my
body wrapped in the original copy of the "Epistle to the Corinthians."

I am the epistle and castaway; among atheists' dilapidated souls I will receive the sacrament every morning with bitter almonds.

I am the epistle, Corinthians, eat and drink because my body passes behind my head over Niagara Falls, and my soul is made epistle among your souls. Take and drink water from Niagara Falls because it is the blood of my blood! Your shots do not wound me because my body is white and blends with the clouds and with the lime; with the foam and with the salt. The snow would not serve to hide me, my blood-stained body would dye it red, and the Corinthians would see themselves defrauded on encountering my face. Oh, if the great denial were transformed into this fish that I am carrying in my hand, perhaps it would slip from my fingers and fall into the sea in order to overturn the world across the waters, but denial is firmly intertwined with my fingers, and I would have to submerge them in sulphur to free them.

Eat and drink! Eat and drink! My middle finger will trace a spiral on the summit of the Cheops pyramid, and my body will remain suspended in the air hoping for the resurrection of the flesh and the beginning of spring, and in this case neither a birth certificate nor His Holiness' blessing will be necessary.

Thus, Corinthians, making my body into a bow and my soul into an arrow, I will shoot myself in the four cardinal directions, and a cloak of red ash from my flesh's cremation will cover the entire terrestrial globe.)

Conceived essentially as an address to a community of disciples, "Texto onírico no. 2" is divided into four parts, each one of which is shorter than its predecessor. Much, if not all, of the text takes place in the United States—in the state of New York to be precise. When the reader first encounters Hinojosa, he is leaving a boat that is docked on the Niagara River. Placing his hand on a statue of Napoleon to steady himself, he suddenly loses his head—literally—which is unfortunately swept over Niagara Falls, into the river below and eventually into Lake Ontario. Except for the surreal element, this episode was probably inspired by newsreels of the era, which included footage of numerous individuals going over the Falls in a barrel. The reference to Napoleon is harder to pin down. There are statues to Nicola Tesla, who built the hydroelectric plant, on both sides of the Falls but none to the French emperor. One of the people who made Niagara Falls a popular honeymoon destination, however, was Napoleon's younger brother Jerome, who in 1804 honeymooned there with his American bride. It is just possible that Hinojosa was aware of this fact.

Fortunately, since Hinojosa survived to write about it, his dangerous experience was obviously not fatal. As a result, however, everyone— even his horoscope—assumes that he must be an acrobat, which he vehemently denies. Acrobatic tricks, such as balancing himself on one finger, do not interest him at all. The fact that the finger is the middle one, nevertheless, is the first sign of his persistent anticlericalism. Without seeming to do so, Hinojosa succeeds in giving the Catholic Church the finger. The insulting symbolism is universal and unmistakable. Still insisting that he is not an acrobat, he evokes three hypothetical acts he could perform to support this claim, including dabbing some paint on the Statue of Liberty. Eventually acquiring an infinite dimension— apparently through sheer persistence—his denial would somehow be transformed into a huge black dot. Eclipsing the sun, the latter would allow him to bathe by moonlight without becoming wet. This is just as well, since he would be wearing the original copy of the "Epistle to the Corinthians," which shouldn't get wet either. As preserved in Books Seven and Eight of the New Testament, the latter actually consists of two letters written by St. Paul to the Christian community in Corinth, which he had previously founded. Written between 53 and 55 AD, they discuss church business and proper Christian conduct. At this point, Hinojosa appears to take on St. Paul's persona. Announcing that he is the epistle himself, he outlines his plans to go among the atheists and take the Eucharist every morning with bitter almonds. Since the latter are not only unpleasant to taste but potentially lethal, his purpose is unclear. Perhaps he is atoning for a previous sin.

The second section juxtaposes references to Niagara Falls, the Letter to the Corinthians, and the Last Supper. Perhaps not coincidentally, the oldest biblical account of the Last Supper is contained in the First Epistle to the Corinthians. Urging the latter to eat and drink, Hinojosa adopts a mocking tone and assumes the persona of Jesus. Parodying the latter's speech to his disciples, he instructs them to drink water from Niagara Falls during the Eucharist, instead of wine, because "es sangre de mi sangre." Jacqueline Rattray believes Hinojosa is presiding over "a type of satirical mass and preach[ing] to the Corinthian congregation."[20] However, it is by no means certain that he has left New York or that he needs to. On the contrary, since he insists repeatedly that he is the Epistle himself, most, if not all, of the text seems to be a letter that, like St. Paul before him, he is sending to the Corinthians. Since the next reference to the latter is in the conditional ("los corintios se verían defraudados"), he is clearly not in Corinth himself.

Following Hinojosa's words to his disciples, which are modeled on those of Jesus, he is attacked by people with guns, rather than by Roman soldiers, who manage to wound him. Although he insists that he is not wounded, his body is stained with blood. Since he is surrounded by snow, the season seems to be winter. Returning to the theme of denial, introduced in the first section, Hinojosa wishes it would slip away like the fish he suddenly finds himself holding in his hand. The amount of attention given to this theme suggests, on the one hand, that it is a paranoid fantasy and, on the other, that it is highly symbolic. In the present context, the first example that comes to mind is St. Peter's triple denial of Jesus, which is usually interpreted as a betrayal. Although Hinojosa merely denied that he was an acrobat originally, his gesture has been magnified all out of proportion. In particular, he claims, it could wreak serious havoc on Europe.

Inviting the Corinthians to eat and drink again in the third section, Hinojosa gives the Catholic Church the finger one last time. For unknown reasons, he plans to use his middle digit to draw a spiral on the Great Pyramid of Giza while he hangs suspended in the air. From that vantage point, he confides, he will wait for nature—and the dead— to be resurrected in the spring. Looking forward to both events, he jokes that they will not need the blessing of civil servants or the Church. The fourth section ends not with a whimper but a bang. Addressing the Corinthians again, Hinojosa announces that he plans to fashion a bow and arrow made from his body and soul. Shooting himself in the four cardinal directions—and thus making the sign of the cross—he plans to cover the entire world with his cremated ashes.

"Texto onírico no. 3" differs considerably from the previous composition. Although it begins somewhere near the Vatican, it contains no obvious attacks on Christianity or the Church. While Hinojosa paints a humorous portrait of the Pope, he does not ridicule him or engage in invective. On the contrary, the main differences between the two texts are structural and thematic. Whereas most of the first work is structured around the "Epistle to the Corinthians," which it parodies, the second work has no fixed structure. Unlike the former, which is relatively coherent, the latter meanders all over the place.[21]

Atormentado por los luces desconfié desde entonces de su buena intención y rehuía su encuentro cuando desbocado buscaba los acuarios escondidos en los pliegues de la madrugada. No pude dar alcance a mi buena intención y rodeado mi cuerpo de aristas que engranaban en las esquinas fui recorriendo la ciudad con una marcha a la deriva mientras se desperezaban los árboles despertados por un grito que brotaba en espiral del cielo y venía a clavarse en el sexo de la Tierra dejándola embarazada de ecos. El aire áspero que refrescaba mis pupilas pedía con insistencia la transfiguración de la carne. La niebla deshojaba las perspectivas con un rumor desorientado y mi cansancio llegó al límite al verme rodeado de ardillas que con sus ardides me impedían asomarme a los balcones de la calle empinada con dirección al Vaticano. El Papa me recibió en pyjama y santificó todas las fiestas algo extrañado de ver mi piel rosada. ¿Qué de particular tenía mi piel rosada? ¿Es que la araña se descuelga del cielo y pica en cualquier parte? Perdido en este bosque de ángulos rectos tropecé con la visectriz olvidada que me condujo entre voces amigas a la cumber del Mont Blanc desde donde volaron mis cabezas en varias direcciones disfrazadas de buenas palabras para convencer a los murciélagos de la conveniencia de que hablasen el esperanto o cualquier otra lengua parecida. La ciudad disparó sus calles en el vacío en apoteosis final mienen el vacío en apoteosis final mientras dos verdaderos enamorados se cobijaban bajo la parra muscatel unidos por un beso condensado en éxtasis. Los enamorados transcribían exactamente las palpitaciones lunares y siempre que comenzaban a contar no pasaban del uno. Aquella mañana de bramidos encandiló mis oídos que se rindieron a la menor indicación del silencio a la muerte.

(Tormented by the dawn's light I distrusted its good intentions thenceforth and avoided its accidental encounter when I hurriedly looked for aquariums hidden in the folds of the early morning. I could not live up to my good intentions and my body surrounded by ridges which interlocked at the street corners I drifted through the town with an informal procession while the trees stretched their branches awoken by a shout that spiraled down from the sky and finally penetrated the Earth's vagina leaving it pregnant with echoes. The raw air refreshing my pupils repeatedly demanded the transfiguration of the flesh. The mist stripped the perspectives of their leaves with a confused rustling and my exhaustion reached its limit upon finding myself surrounded by squirrels whose trickery prevented me from looking out of the steep street's balconies toward the Vatican. The Pope received me in his pajamas and blessed every feast a little surprised to see my pink skin. What in particular made my skin pink? Did a spider descend from the sky and bite you somewhere? Lost in this forest of right angles I stumbled upon the forgotten bisector that led me toward friendly voices at the top of Mont Blanc where my heads flew off in different directions disguised as good words convince the bats of the convenience of speaking Esperanto or a similar language. The town fired its streets into space in its grand finale while two ardent lovers united by an ecstatic concentrated kiss took shelter beneath the muscatel grapevine. The lovers transcribed the lunar throbbing precisely but every time they began to count they never got past "one." The bellowing morning dazzled my ears which surrendered to death at the least indication of silence.)

In contrast to the previous work, which is centered around a biblical epistle, the present text has no story line whatsoever. It resembles a miniature version of *The Odyssey*, except that Odysseus was actually trying to get somewhere. The reader basically follows the speaker as he encounters one example of *le merveilleux* after another. Something amazing and completely different happens in every sentence—often two or three things. As a result, the text not only proceeds at a faster pace but possesses a much quicker rhythm. Rather than linear, its structure is accumulative and episodic. Although many people love the dawn because it is so quiet and peaceful, Hinojosa is clearly an exception. For some reason, he finds the early light absolutely unbearable. In which case, one wonders why he got up so early in the first place. The answer seems to be that he is looking for aquariums, but that raises more questions than it answers. Why does he need more than one, for instance? Is he a tropical fish fancier? Why is he looking so early in the morning, before the stores have opened? Since the stores are closed, where on earth does he plan to look? In the city dump? And most of all, why are the aquariums "escondidos"? Who is hiding them from whom?

After building a protective barrier around his body, Hinojosa ventures out into the city, which is later revealed to be Rome, and either joins or accompanies a ragtag procession that has sprung up. Not only are the trees endowed with peculiarly human qualities, such as sleeping, stretching, and shouting, but they also possess phallic voices, which impregnate the equally anthropomorphic earth with future voices. Interestingly, the cool morning air also possesses the ability to talk, but what it asks for defies belief: that Jesus appear and reveal himself to be the son of God as he did in the episode related in the Bible. Continuing for another nine verses, the account in the King James version begins as follows: "And after six days Jesus taketh Peter, James, and John his brother and bringeth them up into a high mountain apart, and was transfigured before them, and his face did shine like the sun, and his raiment was white as the light" (*Matthew* 17. 1–2). After some time, it dawns on the reader that the reference is meant to be humorous. Tired of shivering in the "aire áspero," Hinojosa jokes that it would be nice if Jesus were to appear and warm the place up.

Amid swirling leaves generated by a sudden wind, Hinojosa, who by this time is extremely tired, finds himself surrounded by a band of nefarious squirrels. Somehow they manage to prevent him from getting a look at the Vatican up the street. Refusing to be thwarted by the spiteful rodents, he obtains an audience with the Pope, who greets him in an undignified manner. For some reason, he has forgotten to get dressed. Following a conversation concerning Hinojosa's pink skin, the latter takes his leave, loses himself in a geometrical maze, and winds up on top of Mont Blanc. At this point, despite the friendly voices surrounding him, he suffers a bizarre accident. As in the two previous texts, he literally loses his head. More precisely, he loses four heads. This is the first indication we have had that the poet is a biological oddity, but that doesn't stop him—or rather his heads—from trying to persuade the bats to speak Esperanto. Having apparently retrieved his errant heads somehow, Hinojosa next observes two lovers sheltering beneath a huge grapevine. Again and again they try to record the number of pulsations the moon is emitting, but, since they can't stop kissing, never manage to get past "one." According to the final sentence, all of the foregoing events have taken place during the space of a single morning. The dawn quietly slipped away hours ago, and now the clock is about to strike twelve. The peaceful early hours have given way to a "mañana de bramidos" that dazzle Hinojosa's ears. Once again, his reaction to events taking place around him is contrary to what one would normally expect. As he says himself, he would rather die than be exposed to silence, the slightest hint of which fills him with dread. For some unknown reason, Hinojosa prefers intensity to subtlety and blatancy to nuance. An experienced traveler, he is much happier when the light is strong and the noise around him is loud. Perhaps that explains why he adapts so quickly to different circumstances.

White Hearts and Fields of Grain

A later example of a dream narrative, "Su corazón no era más que una espiga" ("Her Heart Was Simply an Ear of Wheat") was published in *Litoral* in 1929.[22] Since dreams are unconscious attempts to resolve a repressed conflict, according to Freud, this one is frankly erotic.

> Nuestras manos entrelazadas se fundían con los pámpanos a orillas de aquel río que tenía su lecho lleno de chinas en forma de corazones blancos a media noche cuando los enamorados pierden su sangre por

la única herida abierta en el amor durante el sueño. Y nuestra sangre blanca se evaporaba durante el sueño antes que la vigilia formase con ella estatuas de mármol o iceberg flotantes en estas aguas turbias pobladas de trozos de esqueletos y de sonrisas largas de pieles rojas. Entonces el amor se fundió con el fuego sagrado de tu lengua en llamas y todos los pájaros asistían en silencio a aquell aurora boreal con el mismo respeto que los fieles presencían el Sacrificio Divino. Pero tu piel era transparente y en la conciencia ocultabas una raís cúbica amarilla que se resolvía en maragaritas a las primeras lluvias, siendo imposible que llegases al fin del itinerario sin el menor desfallecimiento. Estaba cierto de esto y también tenía la certeza de que una margarita entre tus manos originaría une copiosa nevada. Mis palabras flotaban en torno tuyo, en torno tu piel transparente sin atreverse a lanzarse por el torrente de tu pecho para disolver el nudo en las aguas profundas de estos dos pozos abiertos en las cuencas de mis ojos. A pesar de todo, yo sabía que en el verano nacían espigas de tu carne, pero nadie, ni mis dientes siquiera, supieron romper la blancura almidonada de tus cabellos sin el menor remordimiento, con la conciencia en alas de los pájaros. Tus manos en un tiempo me traían la sombra de los caminos a los labios mientras escapaban por las rendijas los últimos restos de aquel gran exército de corazones blancos para zambullirse en el río despues de haber cantado tu canción favorita. Y oías cómo las espigas crujíian a nuestros besos cuando mis ojos se derramaban sobre tu carne y era posible el vuelo de las mariposas alrededor de tu sexo, de tu ombligo, de tus pechos, tu boca entreabierta por donde salían nubes blancas que humedecían con sus lluvias nuestros dos corazones. Mis manos huyeron de mí y fueron a perderse tras el horizonte de aquella llanura amarilla. Cuando vuelvan traerán entre ellas una espiga dorada que puede ser tu corazón.

(Our interlaced hands merged with the leaves beside the river whose bed was filled with Chinese shaped like white hearts at midnight when lovers lose their blood through the only open wound during love making and dreaming. And our white blood evaporated during the dream until the evening made marble statues or floating icebergs out of it in the turbid waters with skeleton parts and redskins' broad smiles. Then love merged with the sacred fire of your flaming tongue and the birds all watched the northern lights silently with the same respect that the faithful witness the Divine Sacrifice. But your skin was transparent and you deliberately concealed a yellow cube root that dissolved into daisies during the first rains, making it impossible for you to arrive at the end of your trip without the slightest fatigue. I was sure of that and also I was sure that a daisy in your hands would produce a copious snowfall. My words floated around you, around your transparent skin, without daring to throw themselves upon the torrent of your breast in order to dissolve the knot in the deep waters of my eye sockets' two open wells. Nevertheless, I knew that in summer ears of wheat were born from your flesh, but no one, not even my teeth, knew how to break the starched whiteness of your hair without the least remorse, with the consciousness of bird wings. Your hands used to bring the paths' shade to my lips while the remains of that great army of white hearts escaped through the cracks in order to plunge into the river after singing your favorite song. And you heard how the ears of wheat crunched with our kisses when my eyes overflowed onto your flesh and butterflies were flying around your vagina, your navel, your breasts, your half-open mouth from which issued white clouds dampening our two hearts with their rain. My hands escaped from me and fled headlong across the yellow plain's horizon. When they return, they will bring a golden ear of wheat that can be your heart.)

Although the Surrealists wrote a great many poems about love, the subject of this text is not passionate attraction (*l'amour fou*) but rather passionate sex. While the two can certainly coexist, "Su corazón no era más que une espiga" celebrates both the primal drive and the erotic impulse. The Surrealists, who were mostly healthy young men, were well aware of Eros's power from the very beginning. The problem was that any mention of sex—let alone its importance—was frowned upon by polite society. Since the Surrealists sought to free humanity from its numerous bonds, including sexual repression, they naturally made sexual liberation a cornerstone of their program. Writing many years later, Breton called the Marquis de Sade, Sigmund Freud, and Charles Fourier "les trois grands émancipateurs du désir" ("the three great emancipators of desire").[23] All three strove to free humanity from its traditional chains—sexual, conscious, and societal respectively. Breton celebrated Sade's role in particular in a poem addressed to his second wife Jacqueline Lamba. Thanks to the Marquis de Sade, he wrote, who ignored the traditional moral code, he was able to love her "comme le premier homme aima la premiére femme/En toute liberté" ("like the first man loved the first woman/In complete freedom").[24]

Not surprisingly, perhaps, Hinojosa's prose poem contains a number of sex symbols, sex acts, and sexual references. The first sentence describes the poet and his imaginary lover holding hands on a river bank somewhere. Although the river turns out to be dry, the river basin makes a convenient container for hundreds of Chinese, who have appeared out of nowhere and are patiently awaiting their fate—whatever that is. Perhaps they have come to work the land like *campesinos*, or perhaps they have been detained for unknown reasons. As if that were not weird enough, the Chinese resemble hearts for some reason rather than human beings. Perhaps, they have been transformed into hearts by a powerful wizard or an evil witch. Even stranger, the hearts are all white as if they were carved out of marble. One wonders whether they are shaped like Valentine's Day sugar candies or whether they resemble human hearts. The reason they are associated with midnight, in any event, is because that is the witching hour when supernatural events occur. According to the speaker, who is presumably Hinojosa, that is also when menstruation, sex, and dreaming can take place simultaneously. Little by little, it becomes clear that the text itself is a dream, which is why it defies ordinary logic. The second sentence confirms this impression and reveals that the lovers' blood is white, like the Chinese hearts encountered earlier. After their blood evaporates, moreover, it is fashioned into statues and icebergs floating in murky waters filled with skeletons and smiles.

At this point, the sexual references become more pointed. As Hinojosa and his lover are passionately kissing, they watch the northern lights and then begin to engage in sex. Since her skin is transparent, he confides, he can observe himself penetrating her and ultimately his flowery climax. The symbolism of the yellow root dissolving into daisies is all too clear. The fact that *raíz cúbica* is actually a mathematical term injects a little humor into the proceedings as well. As the symbolic drama continues, however, Hinojosa's partner is not able to reach a climax because he is *hors de combat*. Instead of helping her finish in the next sentence, he invites her to masturbate him ("una margarita entre tus manos" etc.), which apparently brings him to a second climax. The fact that ears of wheat sprout from his lover's body in summer reveals that, like the subject of Eluard's "Sous la menace rouge" (see Chapter 3), she is some sort of earth goddess. That she is somehow able to transfer shade (or shadow) to his lips confirms this impression. The last four sentences echo the very first sentence in the text. Disguised as white hearts, the Chinese—who are revealed to be soldiers—escape from the dry river bed, which miraculously fills with water, and then dive back into the river. That they are singing the woman's favorite song is also miraculous. For his finale, Hinojosa recalls how he and his naked lover once had sex in a wheat field surrounded by swarms of butterflies. Although his hands absconded and fled across the wheat field, he adds, they will return with a special ear of wheat to replace his lover's heart. The last statement makes no sense until we remember that she is an earth goddess. From all appearances, in fact, she seems to be Ceres, who presides over cereals in general and wheat in particular. Thus the final sentence brings Hinojosa's text full circle. At the very last moment, it finally explains the poem's title: "Su corazón no era más que una espiga."

From the previous texts, it is clear that Hinojosa had good teachers in Paris and that he learned his lesson well. The key to writing automatic poetry, they undoubtedly told him, is to disconnect yourself from the conscious world while simultaneously cultivating a state of half sleep in which images gradually emerge from the unconscious. Although some of these are invariably memories, others are expressions of unconscious desire that may assume any number of unsuspected forms. As Breton declares, "les profondeurs de notre esprit recèlent d'étranges forces" ("the depths of our minds harbor strange forces").[25] Where Hinojosa excels is in his ability to conjure up marvelous images while weaving them effortlessly into his narrative fabric. If James Joyce is an expert at stream of consciousness, Hinojosa is an expert at stream of unconsciousness. A drum made from the sun's skin, a honeycomb dripping milk, a woman with transparent skin—these and other Surrealist images defy the conscious imagination.

Notes

1 Andrew P. Debicki, *Spanish Poetry of the Twentieth Century: Modernity and Beyond* (Lexington: University Press of Kentucky, 1994), p. 39.

2 C. B. Morris, *Surrealism and Spain: 1920–1936* (Cambridge: Cambridge University Press, 1972), pp. 190–211.

3 André Breton, *Manifeste du surréalisme in Breton, Oeuvres complètes*, Vol. 1, ed. Marguerite Bonnet et al. (Paris: Gallimard, 1988), p. 330.

4 Manuel Durán Gili, *El superrealismo en la poesía española contemporanea* (Mexico City: Universidad Autónoma de México, 1950), p.20.

5 Julio Neira, "Surrealism and Spain: The Case of Hinojosa," tr. C. Brian Morris, *The Surrealist Adventure in Spain*, ed. C. Brian Morris (Ottawa: Dovehouse, 1991), p. 109. See also Neira, "José María Hinojosa y el primer poema surrealista español," *Insula*, Nos. 452–453, (July–August 1984), p. 17.

6 Julio Neira, *Viajero de soledades: estudios sobre José María Hinojosa* (Seville: Fundación Genesian, 1999), p. 207.

7 Julio Neira, "El surrealismo en José María Hinojosa (Esbozo)," in *El surrealismo*, ed. Victor García de la Concha (Madrid: Taurus, 1982), p. 275.

8 Lucie Personneaux-Conesa, "Histoire et historiographie du surréalisme espagnol," *Mélusine*, No. 11 (1990), p. 137.

9 Neira, "Surrealism and Spain," p. 111.

10 Morris, *Surrealism and Spain*, p. 23.

11 José María Hinojosa, *La flor de California*, ed. José Antonio Mesa Toré (Madrid: Huerga y Fierro, 2004), pp. 67–73.

12 Mary Ann Caws, "Prose Poem," in *The Princeton Encyclopedia of Poetry and Poetics*, ed. Roland Greene et al., 4th ed. (Princeton: Princeton University Press, 2012), p. 1112.

13 Laurent Jenny, "La Surréalité et ses signes narratifs," *Poétique*, No. 16 (1973), p. 512.

14 Jacqueline Rattray, "Celebrating Transgression: Blasphemy and Lust in the Work of the Spanish Surrealist José María Hinojosa," *Romance Studies*, Vol. 16, No. 2 (1998), p. 48.

15 Antonio A. Gómez Yebra, "Mujer y erotismo en *La Flor de California*," *Monographic Review/Revista Monográfica*, Vol. 7, p. 118. The same author detects a sexual scenario in which the birds represent ejaculation, the fingers phallic symbols, and the olive branches spermatazoa.

16 Ibid., p. 123, n. 9.

17 For an instructive overview, see Morris, *Surrealism and Spain*, pp. 111–30.

18 Morris, *Surrealism and Spain*, p. 23.

19 Hinojosa, *La Flor de California*, pp. 67–73. See Rattray, "Celebrating Transgression," pp. 45–55.

20 Rattray, "Celebrating Transgression," p. 48.

21 Hinojosa, *La flor de California*, pp. 105–7.

22 José María Hinojosa, "Su corazón no era más que una espiga," published with another poem under the title "Estos dos corazones," *Litoral*, No. 9 (June 1929), pp. 10–13.

23 André Breton, *Entretiens (1913–1952)*, ed. André Parinaud, rev. ed. (Paris: Gallimard, 1969), p. 270.

24 André Breton, *L'Air de l'eau in Breton Oeuvres complètes*, ed. Marguerite Bonnet et al., Vol. 2 (Paris: Gallimard, 1992), p. 399.

25 Breton, *Manifeste du surréalisme*, p. 316.

6

Federico García Lorca

Although the Spanish Surrealists are relatively unknown outside their home country, three prominent exceptions come immediately to mind: Salvador Dalí, Luís Buñuel, and Federico García Lorca. Each has made outstanding contributions to the particular medium in which he works, and each enjoys a worldwide reputation. Although Lorca's folkloric poetry, flamenco compositions, and gypsy ballads have attracted widespread attention, fewer readers are familiar with the poetry written in New York. While the discussion continues as to whether Lorca was a doctrinaire Surrealist, we know that he was introduced to the movement by Buñuel and Dalí and that his style changed radically thereafter. Suffering from intense depression, Lorca was persuaded by friends and family to spend a year in New York studying English at Columbia University. According to Andrew A. Anderson, "all or almost all" of the poems in *Poeta en Nueva York* were written in America between August 1929 and June 1930.[1] "Aunque Lorca permaneció independiente del surrealismo 'oficial,'" Virginia Higginbotham declares, "es imposible ignorar su afinidad con las actitudes y técnicas surrealistas" ("Even though Lorca remained independent from 'official' Surrealism, it is impossible to ignore his affinity with Surrealist attitudes and techniques").[2] While admitting that Lorca's poetics do not perfectly match those of his French models, Carlos Marcial de Onis identifies three principles they share: (1) the elimination of conscious control, (2) the escape from reality, and (3) the importance of instinct and inspiration.[3]

Recent commentators have detected additional Surrealist influence while downplaying the role of Surrealism itself. Where they differ is with regard to the extent of that influence. Anderson concludes that the poems of *Poeta en Nueva York* merely "share some surface similarities with Surrealist works."[4] Derek Harris deduces from the manuscripts, however, that Lorca was "well acquainted with some Surrealist writing practices"— especially automatism—with which he seems to have experimented.[5] Even so, he continues, "Lorca's vision of New York comes [primarily] from within him through the distorting prism produced by his personal crisis."[6] The poet's sense of moral outrage is so intense that Pietro Menarini calls *Poeta en Nueva York* "uno de los textos más deconcertantes de la literatura espanola y europea del siglo XX" ("one of the most disturbing works in twentieth-century Spanish and European literature").[7] What offsets the sense of despair that would otherwise overwhelm the volume, Miguel García-Posada points out, is "la revuelta … la denuncia lúcida e implacable de todas las fuerzas enemigas de la vida" ("the revolt … the lucid and relentless denunciation of all the enemy forces in life").[8]

The third poem in *Poeta en Nuevo York*, "La Aurora" ("Dawn") typifies Lorca's hallucinatory approach to language:[9]

La aurora de Nueva York tiene
cuatro columnas de cieno
y un huracán de negras palomas
que chapotean las aguas podridas.
La aurora de Nueva York gime
por las inmensas escaleras
buscando entre las aristas
nardos de angustia dibujada.

La aurora llega y nadie la recibe en su boca
porque allí no hay mañana ni esperanza posible.
A veces las monedas en enjambres furiosos
taladran y devoran abandonados niños.
Los primeros que salen comprenden con sus huesos
que no habrá paraíso ni amores deshojados;
saben que van al cieno de números y leyes,
a los juegos sin arte, a sudores sin fruto.
La luz es sepultada por cadenas y ruidos
en impúdico reto de ciencia sin raíces.

Por los barrios hay gentes que vacilan insombes
como recién salidas de un naufragio de sangre.

(Dawn in New York has
four pillars of muck
and a hurricane of black pigeons
splashing in the putrid waters.

Dawn in New York moans
on the immense staircases,
searching between the cracks
for spikenards of drawn anguish.

Dawn arrives, and no one receives it in his mouth
because neither morning nor hope are possible:
at times furiously swarming coins
perforate and devour abandoned children.

The first to arise know in their bones
there will be neither paradise nor leafless loves:
they know the muck of numbers and laws awaits them,
of simple-minded games, of fruitless labor.

The light is buried by chains and noises
in a shameless challenge to rootless science.
Insomniacs stagger around in each district
like refugees from a shipwreck of blood.)

As one soon discovers, the poetic discourse in *Poeta en Nueva York* varies not only from one poem to the next but also within a single poem. Anderson distinguishes three levels of imagistic language: (1) straight-forward, (2) difficult but ultimately decipherable, and (3) totally enigmatic.[10] Consisting of five four-line stanzas written in free verse, "La aurora" clearly belongs to the second category. As day dawns, the poem focuses on an area in New York City that has standing water. Whereas the sunrise is traditionally associated with beauty, epitomized by the Roman goddess Aurora, dawn in New York is spectacularly unattractive, even repulsive. The first stanza contains three negative markers that repeatedly drive that message home. The four skyscrapers are not just described as pillars but rather as pillars of *muck*. Whereas pillars are normally made of sturdy materials, these offer little or no support and will collapse at the first opportunity. Harris speculates that the image may have been suggested by the Standard Oil Building, which Lorca would have seen as soon as his ocean liner docked.[11] Similarly, although pigeons come in several different colors, the flock in the poem is *black*, a color traditionally associated with mourning. Perhaps the birds actually have black feathers, or perhaps they are simply back-lit against the morning sky. That they are all the same color intensifies their visual effect, as does the fact that they constitute a restless "huracán." There seem to be a lot of pigeons vying for a chance to bathe in the *putrid* water.

That the reader's first impression of New York is of a city overwhelmed by filth, death, and pollution is no accident. Lorca was appalled by what he personally witnessed, much of which is recorded in his poetry. To make things worse, the stock market crashed while he was there, plunging the world into the Great Depression. Anderson provides an excellent summary of how the city is portrayed in *Poeta en Nueva York*. It is "a place of inhuman buildings," he writes, "relentless commerce, runaway consumption and polluting industry, of avarice, superficiality, footlessness, alienation and (hypocritical) organized religion; poverty and exploitation are all around."[12] Although Onis basically concurs with this assessment, he comes to a different conclusion than most critics, who condemn New York for its numerous shortcomings. On the contrary, he argues that the city symbolizes the spiritual state of the modern world. "La visión lorquiana," he explains, "es la idea de que sólo a través del amor por lo elemental y lo puro, por lo espontáneo de la vida, es posible la salvación del mundo moderno" ("Lorca's vision is the idea that only through love for the elemental and the pure, for the spontaneity of life, is the salvation of the modern world possible").[13]

The next stanza is more difficult to decipher. Not only is New York a dirty place to live, but we learn that it is also overcome with anguish. While it is moaning for some reason, the dawn sun insists on looking for spikenards (*Nardostachys jatamansi*) at the same time. An aromatic herb from the Himalayas, the latter has been used as a perfume, a medicine and in various religious contexts. Since it is related to valerian, perhaps it will help calm New York's anguish. It is generally agreed that the "inmensas escaleras" are exterior fire escapes, which zigzag up and down the buildings. Because of their height, they are the first to receive the sun's light in the morning, which explains what the sun is doing there. Although fire escapes could be found elsewhere, they were mainly attached to tenement buildings. Rising five to seven stories, eighty thousand tenements had been built in New York City by 1900, housing a good two-thirds of the city's population.[14] Since by law fire escapes had to be attached to the front of the buildings, the ones in "La aurora" are situated either on the western side of the avenues or on the southern side of the streets, where they receive the morning sun.

As Menarini points out, Lorca employs symbols more often than metaphors in *Poeta en Nueva York*.[15] One thinks of the columns of muck and the black pigeons, for example, that inhabit the first stanza. Whereas a metaphor refers to an identifiable antecedent, a symbol has no such responsibility. It draws its power either from the wider culture or from a set of conventions created by the author and used repeatedly, i.e., a symbolic grammar. As a result, symbols can be harder to recognize than metaphors. Because the first symbol in stanza 3 is never actually identified, it is merely implicit. Nevertheless, it is perfectly clear to anyone who has ever been in a Christian Church that Lorca is referring to a communion wafer. The context alone is enough to make the symbol explicit. Since the wafer is generally round and white, it makes a perfect substitute for the rising sun and vice versa. The poet sees the dawn sun through the mist as a pale white circle; hence as it rises aloft he relates it to a priest elevating the host during Mass. However, everyone's situation in New York is so hopeless that no one wants to participate in the Christian ritual. They are completely cut off from any kind of spirituality. Moving from one circular shape to another, hordes of cannibalistic coins arrive, like swarms of bees or wasps, ready to devour abandoned children. This is Lorca at his most surreal. Since coins don't have mouths, the scene is virtually impossible to visualize. Despite this drawback, the pieces of gold and silver make excellent symbols. Like iron, Menarini insists, they are "metales de la alienación" and participate in a larger competition between civilization and nature.[16] More to the point, as Harris points out, they are also symbols of the capitalist world.[17] Men who value money over human beings have no scruples about sacrificing innocent children to get their way.

The fourth stanza addresses the serious imbalance that exists between the poor and the rich. Those who rise early in the morning in order to perform a variety of menial jobs know full well that they will never get ahead in the world. "Amores deshojados" is simply a picturesque synonym for "paraíso," a time of prelapsarian innocence when Adam and Eve did not need to cover their nakedness with leaves. Not only is this goal permanently out of reach for the poor, but they know exactly what fate awaits them: to engage in the "ciéno" of fruitless labor while the bankers and the lawyers profit from their efforts. Indeed, the latter's offices are probably housed in the "columnos de ciéno" encountered the first stanza.

The final stanza is filled with symbols, not all of which are possible to decipher. On the surface level, the light mentioned in the first line comes from the rising sun. Juxtaposed with the chains, however, it acquires a symbolic meaning. As Menarini notes, "la polaridad del binomio *luz / cadenas* puede considerarse como una de los constantes estructurales de toda la colección" ("the polarity of the binomial *light / chains* can be considered as one of the structural constants of the whole collection").[18] Each term—or rather what it symbolizes—is opposed to the other: light to darkness and chains to freedom. In view of the previous discussion, the chains are clearly those imposed by social institutions, which penalize poor people. However, the initial paradigm can be extended indefinitely to encompass additional binary oppositions. For example, good can be contrasted with evil, knowledge with ignorance, and amateur science with professional science. Unfortunately, the fact that the left side of the chain of oppositions is "sepultada" means that the forces of light, etc. have already been defeated. The poem concludes on this dismal note with a group of insomniacs staggering around as if they were drunk. Like the survivors of a shipwreck, they are exhausted and totally disoriented.

Entitled "Norma y paraíso de los Negros" ("Norms and Paradise of the Blacks"), the next poem belongs to Anderson's third category— it appears at first to be totally enigmatic. Not surprisingly, therefore, critics generally find the poem frustrating. It responds reluctantly at best to traditional attempts at critical analysis. Whatever meaning the poem possesses is apparently buried securely beneath the surface. In theory, the title should prepare readers for the task ahead and point them in the right direction. However, the text is neither an ethnography of the Negro race, as the title suggests, nor a sociological study of Black life in New York. And the paradise it refers to, as Derek Harris points out, is a nightclub in Harlem called "Small's Paradise" that Lorca used to frequent.[19] Owned and operated by Ed Smalls, an African American who opened the club's doors on October 26, 1925, it was the only one of the well-known Harlem night spots where Blacks and Whites could mingle freely. Although most of the Harlem clubs closed between 3 and 4 am, it was open all night and featured a breakfast dance with a full floor show beginning at 6 am. Divided into seven four-line stanzas, "Norma y paraíso de los negros" looks perfectly normal but turns out to be extremely adventuresome.[20] Curiously, the first two stanzas focus on what the Blacks detest rather than on what they love.

Odian la sombra del pájaro
sobre el pleamar de la blanca mejilla
y el conflicto de luz y viento
en el salón de la nieve fría.

Odian la flecha sin cuerpo,
el pañuelo exacto de la despedida,
la aguja que mantiene presión y rosa
en el gramíneo rubor de la sonrisa.

(They hate the bird's shadow
on the white cheek's high water
and the struggle between light and wind
in the cold snow's great hall.

They hate the incorporeal arrow
the farewell's faithful handkerchief,
the needle that maintains pressure and rosiness
in the smile's grassy blushing.)

Seeking a meaningful pattern in the first two stanzas, Richard L. Predmore claims that the Blacks are characterized "como seres que odian lo abstracto, lo formal, lo reglamentado y que aman lo natural, lo espontáneo, lo sensual" ("as beings who hate abstraction, formality, and regulation and who love naturalness, spontaneity, and sensuality").[21] In reality, however, there is only one abstraction: "la flecha sin cuerpo" which, as we will see, turns out to be a concrete image after all. By contrast, García-Posada is convinced that the first stanza represents an allegory. In his opinion, "los negros ... odian que lo natural, el pájaro, pueda tener alguna relación con la opulencia ('pleamar') de los blancos, una opulencia puramente artificial" ("the Blacks ... hate the idea that a representative of nature, the bird, can have a relationship with the Whites' opulence ('high water'), which is purely artificial").[22] Unfortunately, while *pleamar* connotes a great many things, opulence is not one of them. And although the poem is structured around several binary oppositions, none of them are between nature and opulence.

Discussing *Poeta en Nueva York* in general and the role of the Blacks in particular, Menarini calls attention to two central oppositions: "la relación antagónica *civilización / naturaleza*" and "el binomio *blanco / negro*, que funciona como contrapunto" ("the antagonistic relationship *civilization / nature* and the binomial *white / black*, which functions as counterpoint").[23] Like the rest of the poem, which appears to have been inspired by French experiments with Surrealism, the first stanza presents a number of problems. Just to name a few, one wonders where the bird came from, how a cheek can have high water, and what kind of struggle involves light and wind. To a certain extent, the answers to these questions do not matter because they are peripheral issues. What does matter is the pattern of black and white identified by Menarini, which is simultaneously superimposed on, and generated by, the poem's words. The bird's dark shadow contrasts not only with the white cheek but also with the white snow. In this way, Lorca introduces the theme of black and white, which reflects the composition of the crowd in Small's Paradise. Or rather, the theme originated the other way around. The racially mixed crowd in the nightclub, apparently the only club in Harlem that was integrated, generated the black and white theme. Existing photographs show a cavernous interior filled with round tables covered with linen tablecloths, which was able to accommodate a great many people. In practice, the tables were pushed to the sides to expose a large dance floor. Judging from the poem, Lorca seems to have visited the club—presented here as "el salón de la nieve fría"—at least once when it was snowing outside.

The second stanza poses a whole new set of problems. The "flecha sin cuerpo" is puzzling initially but probably refers to an arrow painted on the wall. Since the "pañuelo" is associated with departure, it most likely belongs to someone waving goodbye. Although the "sonrisa" clearly belongs to a pretty woman, the references to "la aguja que mantiene presión y rosa" and "el gramíneo rubor de la sonrisa" make very little sense—for completely different reasons. While an *aguja de presión* is a pressure gauge, there is no such thing as an *aguja de rosa*.

In general, the text is organized methodically, proceeding line by line and stanza by stanza. Each line contributes a discrete piece of information that is expressed in a complete sentence, a dependent clause, or a prepositional phrase. This describes the first stanza, for example, which contains all three. Other stanzas, such as the one under discussion, consist of a series of noun phrases that basically constitute a list. In both cases, the poem's structure is essentially additive. Problems arise when the relationship between two or more lines is unclear or when that between two words is impossible. The first case is illustrated by every line in stanza 2, the second by the expression "el gramíneo rubor." In the first instance, the lines suffer from a lack of context that would connect them in some meaningful way. In the second instance, the words suffer from semantic incompatibility. Since Surrealism relies heavily on hallucination and random juxtaposition, its practitioners would probably not agree that this represents a problem at all. Surrealist texts are filled with floating signifiers, unmotivated juxtapositions, phonetic pairings, and hybrid constructions of all kinds. Viewed in this perspective, the incorporeal arrow, the faithful handkerchief, and the grassy smile simply reflect the continual search for *le merveilleux*. They represent attempts to create magic sparks like those described by André Breton in The First Manifesto (see Chapter 2).

Having dedicated the first two stanzas to things the Blacks supposedly detest, Lorca devotes the remaining stanzas to things they supposedly love.

> Aman el azul desierto,
> las vacilantes expresiones bovinas,
> la mentirosa luna de los polos,
> la danza curva del agua en la orilla.

> (They love the desert blue,
> the hesitant bovine expressions,
> The poles' deceitful moon,
> the water's curved dance on the shore.)

The third stanza is slightly more accessible than the previous ones. Lines 1 and 3 pose serious questions, but lines 2 and 4 seem perfectly clear. The first problem that confronts the reader is the meaning of the adjective "desierto," which can be translated in numerous ways—for example, as "deserted," "bleak," "desolate," "unihabited," "empty," "wild," or "desert." Coupled with "blue," however, the combination that appears to make the most sense is "desert blue," which is confirmed by subsequent events in the poem. At this point, the scene in Small's Paradise gradually starts to dissolve into an imaginary African Paradise. Or rather, the two scenes overlap to form an imaginary montage. Although Harris believes that "el azul desierto" refers to the empty sky, another scene is equally possible.[24] Lorca could have been thinking of *los hombres azules*, the famous Tourareg people who inhabit the Sahara Desert. Because they wear robes dyed with indigo, their skin is perpetually stained blue. This particular tribe, which could conceivably have a bovine appearance, would need to live either near the ocean or in an oasis with a big pool of water. The reference to the "mentirosa luna de los polos" is initially rather puzzling. Why is the moon deceitful? How can both the North Pole and the South Pole have the same moon? Eventually one realizes what must have happened. The primitive, purely mental phrase was probably something like "los mentirosos polos de la luna." Consciously or unconsciously, Lorca reversed the two nouns at some point, a procedure that occurs fairly frequently in Surrealist texts. As Harris has shown and expertly analyzed, the line was subjected to four more transformations before it reached its final form.[25] Interestingly, Lorca's method of working resembles that of many of the French Surrealists, including André Breton. After initially choosing a theme, he apparently created an automatic text according to the instructions given in The First Manifesto. Thereafter, he seems to have revised the text consciously and conscientiously until he was satisfied.

For better or worse, the fourth stanza is almost completely impenetrable:

> Con la ciencia del tronco y el rastro
> llenan de nervios luminosos la arcilla
> y patinan lúbricos por aguas y arenas
> gustando la amarga frescura de su milenaria saliva.

> (Familiar with the trunk and the trail
> they fill the clay with luminous nerves
> and skate lubriciously on water and sand
> tasting their millennial saliva's bitter coolness.)

Although the image of luminous nerves has interesting possibilities, we have no idea why the blacks are packing them into the clay. Similarly, the magic skates that can skate on sand as well as on water are interesting to contemplate. Harris speculates that they could allude to roller skating or ice skating in Central Park.[26] In either case, nevertheless, one wonders why the Blacks are skating "lubriciously." Some sort of context is drastically needed to put these words into proper perspective. Because the two paradises are still blending with each other, one suspects that this is a reference to Small's Paradise, where the waiters often wore roller skates and danced the Charleston (though not at the same time). In addition to regular floor shows every night, the club used to sponsor dancing contests that attracted large crowds. Many of the female dancers were scantily dressed so they could move without being restricted by heavy clothing.

The concluding sequence juxtaposes the two versions of paradise—the American and the African—for the very last time:

Es por el azul crujiente,
azul sin un gusano ni una huella dormida,
donde los huevos de avestruz quedan eternos
y deambulan intactas las lluvias bailarinas.
Es por el azul sin historia
azul de una noche sin temor de día,
azul donde el desnudo del viento va quebrando
los camellos sonámbulos de las nubes vacías.
Es allí donde sueñan los torsos bajo la gula de la hierba.
Allí los corales empapan la desesperación de la tinta,
los durmientes borran sus perfiles bajo la madeja de los caracoles
y queda el hueco de la danza sobre las últimas cenizas.

(It is through the crisp blue,
blue with neither worm nor sleepy footstep,
where ostrich eggs remain forever
and the dancing rains stroll intact.
It is through the ahistorical blue
the blue of a night with no fear of day,
blue where the wind's nudity is breaking up
the empty clouds become sleepwalking camels.
It is there where torsos dream beneath the grass's gluttony.

There the corals absorb the ink's desperation,
beneath the seashells' skein sleepers erase their profiles
and a hole remains from the dance on the last ashes.)

Evoking the Blacks' original homeland, which is presented retrospectively as a lost paradise, each of the last three stanzas refers to some sort of African animal. Indestructible ostrich eggs and sleepwalking camels give way to a vivid underwater scene involving corals and seashells. The eggs are apparently "eternos" because they have thick shells that are impossible to break. The camels seem to be "sonámbulos" because of the slow, deliberate way the members of a camel train plod along, one behind the other. The ink absorbed by the corals appears to have come from a frightened octopus escaping from a predator. The comparison of a snail shell to a skein of wool, García-Posada explains, is justified by "la forma ovillada del caracol" ("the curled up shape of the snail").[27] Interestingly, the last three stanzas contain no fewer than five references to the color blue. Although blue could still refer to the Touareg people, the sudden accumulation suggests that something else is involved here. Paralleling the successive references to Africa, Lorca evokes the blues music that the band used to play at Small's. The Charlie Johnson Paradise Orchestra included some of the biggest names in the music business, and other musicians would drop by after hours to jam with them. Since white audiences had only recently discovered the blues (and jazz), Lorca describes the latter as "crujiente" and "sin historia."

As mentioned previously, Small's Paradise also featured popular dance competitions, and the Charleston was all the rage. According to one historian, "the solo Charleston was, more than anything else, the signature dance of the flapper: a dance for a liberated woman to say "Look at me! I'm free, beautiful and sexy!"[28] Foreshadowed by the anthropomorphic metaphor "lluvias bailarinas" in the penultimate stanza, the final line evokes a female dancer performing at the club during just such a competition. She was so incredibly hot, the poet jokes, that she burned a hole right through the floor. The poem ends not "en una parálisis total" ("in total paralysis"), as García-Posada asserts, but in an exuberant burst of energy.[29] "Norma y paraíso de los negros" provides a welcome respite from some of the harsher poems in the volume. Although Lorca found most of New York City depressing, he could always count on enjoying himself when he came to Harlem.

Unlike the previous poem which, despite our initial impression, turned out to be decipherable after all, "Panorama ciego de Nueva York" ("Blind Panorama of New York") is virtually impenetrable.

> Si no son los pájaros
> cubiertos de ceniza,
> si no son los gemidos que golpean las ventanas de la boda,
> serán las delicadas criaturas del aire
> que manan la sangre nueva por la oscuridad inextinguible.
> Pero no, no son los pájaros,
> porque los pájaros están a punto de ser bueyes.
> Pueden ser rocas blancas con la ayuda de la luna
> y son siempre muchachos heridos
> antes de que los jueces levanten la tela.

> (If it isn't the birds
> covered in ashes,
> if it isn't moaning sounds beating against the wedding windows
> it must be the delicate creatures of the air
> whose new blood flows through the perpetual darkness.
> But no, it isn't the birds,
> because the birds are about to become oxen.
> They can be white rocks with the moon's help
> and they are always wounded boys
> before the judges lift the cloth.)

The first stumbling block lying in wait for the unwary reader is the poem's title, which appears to be patently absurd. Since a panorama is a sweeping view or visual representation, how can a blind person possibly experience it? Thus the title appears to be a contradiction in terms.

As such, it provides a model for a number of contradictory statements and/or images that are sprinkled throughout the poem. Although most of them are impossible to resolve, one eventually perceives that the title is structured around a paradox. The poem was conceived as an *imaginary* portrait of New York, one that is largely symbolic. Leaving aside the question of whether blind people can perceive mental images (some can, some can't), the panorama turns out to be entirely fictitious. As in "Norma y paraíso de los negros," Lorca's style is essentially additive. Each line tends to contribute a discrete thought or to contain a significant piece of information. Instead of "thoughts," Onis prefers to speak of "visions," which is perhaps closer to the truth. In *Poeta en Nueva York*, he declares, "las visiones constituyen la imagen principal, que lo domina todo" ("visions constitute the principal images, which dominate everything").[30] In his opinion, they are one of the basic characteristics of the Surrealist imagination.

Like "La Aurora," which opens with the image of pigeons splashing in the dirty water, "Panorama ciego de Nueva York" begins with birds covered in ashes. Although birds are normally positive symbols, they are defiled in both cases by their filthy surroundings, which reflect the city as a whole. The fact that the first and third lines employ parallel constructions suggests to Harris that the "gemidos" beating against the windows are a conscious or unconscious substitution for birds, which for some reason are excluded from the wedding celebration inside.[31] Thus happiness is contrasted with unhappiness and joy with sadness. The reader is free to imagine any number of possible explanations. Perhaps the moans come from a former lover, for example, who has been changed into a bird-like King Charming in Madame d'Aulnoy's "L'Oiseau bleu" ("The Bluebird").

The first five lines of Lorca's blind panorama are structured around a familiar grammatical model: *si* / *entonces* ("if" / "then"). A hypothetical clause is followed by a result clause that fulfills the original condition. However, Lorca deliberately complicates things by introducing two *si* clauses and making them both negative. The resulting statement is not only confusing but also contradictory. There are three possibilities. Either the birds or the moans or the delicate creatures are responsible for the mysterious bloodshed mentioned in line 5. Two of the candidates need to be eliminated somehow before a winner can be chosen. Unexpectedly, the situation turns out to be even more complicated than before. Upon closer inspection, two of the candidates appear to be identical: the "pájaros" and the "delicadas criaturas del aire." This time the birds are portrayed in a positive light. However, the discovery that they appear in both a hypothetical clause and the result clause creates an impossible situation. "Si no son los pájaros," the poem effectively declares, "serán [los pájaros]." Before the hapless reader can begin to digest this information, Lorca contradicts himself again in line 6, where he announces "Pero no, no son los pájaros." Incredibly, this leaves the moaning sounds as the source of the new blood. Or rather, the latter would seem to have resulted from the same injury that produced the former.

The reason the birds are not responsible for the blood, Lorca adds rather illogically, is because they are about to be transformed into oxen. The poetic world of *Poeta en Nueva York*, Onis explains, is a dynamic world. "Las cosas … encierran en sí la potencialidad de transformarse en otras cosas" ("Things … possess the potential to transform themselves into other things").[32] This is especially true of the present poem, in which objects undergo a continual metamorphosis. Not only can the birds become oxen, for instance, but with the moon's aid they can also be transformed into white rocks. Given the general tone of the poem, Harris is undoubtedly right that these are all negative symbols.[33] As he points out, the oxen are castrated, the moon is a symbol of death, and the white rocks resemble tombstones. Since all of them are associated with "pained and damaged innocence," he adds, they are encompassed by the penultimate image of the birds transformed into wounded youths, which, in view of Lorca's homosexuality, possesses a special significance. In retrospect, moreover, the "muchachos heridos" would seem to be the source of the moans and blood encountered earlier. How they were injured, why, and by whom remains a permanent mystery. In view of the wounds' symbolic role, however, the answers can probably be found in Lorca's psycho-sexual history. As Harris has shown, the last line combines two set phrases to create the image of judges lifting or raising a cloth.[34] In the first case they would resemble pathologists preparing for an autopsy, in the second case stagehands raising a theater curtain.

Todos comprenden el dolor que se relaciona con la muerte,
pero el verdadero dolor no está presente en el espíritu.
No está en el aire, ni en nuestra vida,
ni en estas terrazas llenas de humo.
El verdadero dolor que mantiene despiertas las cosas
es una pequeña quemadura infinita
en los ojos inocentes de los otros sistemas.
Un traje abandonado pesa tanto en los hombros
que muchas veces el cielo los agrupa en ásperas manadas;
y las que mueren de parto saben en la última hora
que todo rumor será piedra y toda huella latido.
Nosotros ignoramos que el pensamiento tiene arrabales
donde el filósofo es devorado por los chinos y las orugas
y algunos niños idiotas han encontrado por las cocinas
pequeñas golondrinas con muletas
que sabían pronunciar la palabra amor.

(Everyone understands the pain associated with death,
but true pain is not present in the mind.
It isn't in the air or in our lives,
or in these terraces full of smoke.
True pain that keeps things awake
is a small infinite burn
in other systems' innocent eyes.
An abandoned suit weighs so much on the shoulders
that the sky often gathers them in rugged herds;
and women who die in childbirth know during their final hour
that every murmur will be a stone and every footprint a heartbeat.
We ignore the fact that thought has slums
where philosophers are devoured by Chinese and caterpillars
and kitchens where idiot children have found tiny swallows
on crutches that knew how to say the word "love.")

Although Lorca adopts a more traditional style for the remainder of the poem, he inserts Surrealist touches whenever the spirit moves him. The four remaining stanzas are loosely organized around the theme: "el dolor que se relaciona con la muerte." Although *dolor* can signify many different things, including "grief," "sorrow," "anguish," "heartache," and " misery"—just to name a few—its primary sense is "pain." The latter term is broad enough to encompass all these meanings and many more. While the first line refers to the physical pain a dying person experiences, it also evokes the emotional pain that others feel at the death of a loved one. The definition of *true* pain in the second stanza is puzzling to say the least. As we have seen, *Poeta en Nueva York* is filled with references to physical and psychological pain. Much of the previous stanza, for example, revolves around recent wounds that leave a trail of blood behind them. And yet Lorca refuses to acknowledge that these incidents are truly painful. Unfortunately, his description of the latter condition as a small infinite burn is not particularly helpful nor is his reference to "otros sistemas."

Lorca drops the subject at this point and returns to his experiments with Surrealist tropes in the following stanza. Why an old suit should weigh more than a new one is hard to say, unless the former owner left a heavy object in one of the pockets. Assuming that the suit is made out of cashmere (from goats) or wool (from sheep), however, one can see where the poet got the idea of creating a whole herd of them. Centered around women who die in childbirth, the next attempt at a Surrealist trope is unsuccessful, but the final attempt works nicely. Lorca compares thought first to a city and then to a house. Like a metropolitan town, he claims, philosophy has areas that are dilapidated and dangerous to explore. Exemplifying the Surrealist concept of *le merveilleux*, the houses contain kitchens inhabited by swallows that use crutches and are able to talk. The fact that they value love so highly partially offsets the risk of encountering the Chinese cannibals.

No, no son los pájaros.
No es un pájaro el que expresa la turbia fiebre de laguna,

ni el ansia de asesinato que nos oprime cada momento,
ni el metálico rumor de suicidio que nos anima cada madrugada;
es una cápsula de aire donde nos duele todo el mundo,
es un pequeño espacio vivo al loco unisón de la luz,
es una escala indefinible donde las nubes y rosas olvidan
el griterío chino que bulle por el desembarcadero de la sangre.
Yo muchas veces me he perdido
para buscar la quemadura que mantiene despiertas las cosas
y sólo he encontrado marineros echados sobre las barandillas
y pequeñas criaturas del cielo enterradas bajo la nieve.
Pero el verdadero dolor estaba en otras plazas
donde los peces cristalizados agonisaban dentro de los troncos;
plazas del cielo extraño para las antiguas estatuas ilesas
y para la tierna intimidad de los volcanes.

(No, it isn't the birds.
It isn't a bird that expresses the lagoon's turbid fever,
nor the fear of murder that oppresses us at every moment,
nor suicide's metallic sound that wakes us every morning:
it's an air bubble where everybody wants to hurt us,
it's a small lively space in the light's crazy unison,
it's an indefinable station where the clouds and roses forget
the Chinese uproar down on the bloody dock.
Many times I have lost myself
searching for the burn that keeps things awake
and I have only found sailors leaning over the railings
and little celestial creatures buried in the snow.
But true pain was in other plazas
where crystallized fish were dying inside tree trunks;
plazas in the strange sky for ancient pristine statues
and for the volcanoes' tender intimacy.)

The third stanza begins in much the same way as the first, except that there are no "si" clauses. Quietly, and without specifically announcing it, Lorca and several others have set out to find true pain. What he intends to do when and if he succeeds is anybody's guess. Ironically, most people spend their lives trying to *avoid* pain. After insisting that the birds are in no way to blame, Lorca adds a series of parallel statements that summarize their current situation. Although the three negative statements are meant to be reassuring, they are actually a mixed blessing. On the one hand, it is good to learn that the problems they are experiencing are not caused by a bird, the fear of murder, or the sound of suicide. On the other hand, we discover that they are suffering from fever, a sense of oppression, and insufficient sleep. Not only are they confined to a tight space, according to the three positive statements, but everybody wants to harm them. Lorca's quest for true pain is beginning to look like a mountaineering expedition, his oppressors like hostile natives, and the "pequeño espacio" like a nylon tent. Ironically, the pain always seems to be located in another space where, surrounded by volcanoes, preserved fish exist side by side with ancient statues.

> No hay dolor en la voz. Sólo existen los dientes,
> pero dientes que callarán aislados por el raso negro.
> No hay dolor en la voz. Aquí sólo existe la Tierra.
> La Tierra con sus puertas de siempre que llevan al rubor de los frutos.

> (There is no pain in my voice. Only my teeth exist,
> but teeth that will fall silent isolated by black satin.
> There is no pain in my voice. Here only the Earth exists.
> The Earth with its eternal doors leading to blushing fruits.)

The last stanza is brief and to the point. When the curtain rises, we discover Lorca lying in a coffin lined with black satin but able to utter a few sentences before he expires. Although the details are lacking, his search for true pain—whatever that is—has finally ended with his own death. He may have been mortally injured during his last expedition, he may have committed suicide, or he may even have died of old age. In any event, the poem opens and closes with the theme of death, which this time at least is painless. Speaking from the grave, Lorca focuses on the earth around him as he descends to his final resting place. As he disappears from sight, he extols the Earth's endless fertility and welcomes the new door that is opening before him.

As Richard Stammelman has demonstrated, Surrealist poetry is governed by the principle of structured discontinuity. "A poem's images ... are often irrational and incomprehensible," he explains, "while a poem's form is often ordered."[35] A high degree of semantic disorder exists within a formal rhetorical framework. Indeed, the text's illogicality is precisely what signals that it is a Surrealist composition. Lorca utilizes repetition and parallel constructions (especially anaphora) to drive his poetry forward, whereas Hinojosa simply proceeds sentence by sentence. Since his poetry is dictated by the unconscious, he chooses the simplest, most direct form possible. While Lorca and Hinojosa both employ a hallucinatory approach to poetry, the one conscious and the other unconscious, they differ with regard to how they choose to exploit marvelous imagery (see Chapter 2). To be sure, Lorca's poetry contains some striking images—such as the tiny swallows on crutches or the crystallized fish in tree trunks. However, these are relatively infrequent and tend to be embedded in a larger matrix. Many stanzas contain no examples at all. By contrast, marvelous images are much more common in Hinojosa's compositions and are often strung together, two or three to a paragraph. While the conscious mind thinks in words, the unconscious mind thinks in terms of images. Pictures play a much greater role in dreams than words.

Notes

1   Andrew A. Anderson, "García Lorca's *Poemas en prosa* and *Poeta en Nueva York*: Dalí, Gasch, Surrealism, and the Avant-Garde," in *A Companion to Spanish Surrealism*, ed. Robert Havard (Woodbridge: Tamesis, 2004), p. 168.

2   Virginia Higginbotham, "La iniciación de Lorca en el surrealismo," in *El Surrealismo*, ed. Victor García de la Concha (Madrid: Taurus, 1982), p. 240.

3   Carlos Marcial de Onis, *El surrealisimo y cuatro poetas de la generación del 27* (Marid: Porrúa Turanzas, 1974), p. 90.

4   Anderson, "García Lorca's *Poemas en prosa*," p. 183.

5   Derek Harris, *Metal Butterflies and Poisonous Lights: The Language of Surrealism in Lorca, Alberti, Cernuda, and Aleixandre* (Arncroach: La Sirena, 1998), pp. 113–14.

6   Ibid., p. 85.

7   Pietro Menarini, "Emblemas ideológicos de *Poeta en Nueva York*," in *El surrealismo*, ed. Victor García de la Concha (Madrid: Taurus, 1982), p. 255.

8   Miguel García-Posada, *Lorca: Interpretación de "Poeta en Nueva York"* (Madrid: Akal, 1981), p. 63.

9   Federico García Lorca, *Romancero gitano, Poeta en Nueva York, El Publico* ed. Derek Harris (Madrid: Taurus, 1993), pp. 133–4.

10   Anderson, "García Lorca's *Poemas en prosa*," pp. 177–8.

11   Harris, *Metal Butterflies*, pp. 91–2.

12   Anderson, "García Lorca's *Poemas en prosa*," p. 181.

13   Onis, *El surrealisimo*, p. 96.

14   https://www.theatlantic.com/technology/archive/2018/02/how-the-fire-escape-became-an-ornament/554174/

15   Menarini, "Emblemas ideológicos," p. 257.

16   Ibid., pp. 259–60.

17   Harris, *Metal Butterflies*, p. 92.

18   Menarini, "Emblemas ideológicos," p. 258.

19   Derek Harris, *Federico García Lorca: Poeta en Nueva York* (London: Grant and Cutler, 1978), p. 31.

20   Lorca, *Romancero gitano*, pp. 141–2.

21   Predmore, Richard L., *Los poemas neoyorquinas de Federico García Lorca* (Madrid: Taurus, 1985), p. 61.

22   García-Posada, *Lorca*, p. 93.

23   Menarini, "Emblemas ideológicos," pp. 262–3.

24   Harris, *Federico García Lorca*, p. 31.

25   Harris, *Metal Butterflies*, pp. 101–2.

26   Harris, *Federico García Lorca*, p. 31.

27   García-Posada, *Lorca*, p. 92.

28   http://www.walternelson.com/dr/charleston

29   García-Posada, *Lorca*, p. 112.

30   Onis, *El surrealismo*, p. 110.

31 Harris, *Metal Butterflies*, p. 97.

32 Onis, *El surrealismo*, p. 138.

33 Harris, *Metal Butterflies*, p. 97.

34 Ibid.

35 Richard Stammelman, "The Relational Structure of Surrealist Poetry," *Dada/Surrealism*, No. 6 (1973), pp. 76–7.

7

J. V. Foix

Although the Principality of Catalonia was absorbed into Spain in the fifteenth century, the region has always had close ties to France. For one thing, the northern part of Catalonia comprises the modern French département of the Pyrénées-Orientales. For another, the Catalan language shares more similarities with French than with Spanish. Not surprisingly, therefore, news of the latest avant-garde movements in Paris arrived in Barcelona earlier than it did in Madrid. After experimenting with Cubism, Italian Futurism, and Dada, the Catalan avant-garde naturally turned to Surrealism.[1] While Joan Miró and Salvador Dalí were the most important artists, the most talented poet was J. V. Foix. Not only was he "uno de los más rotundos y originales poetas catalanes" ("one of the most original and well-rounded Catalan poets"), as Enrique Badosa declares, but he was also one of the best Surrealist poets anywhere.[2] Refusing to be formally associated with Breton's movement in order to preserve his independence, Foix preferred to be known simply as an "investigador en poesia."[3] He began his career by contributing Surrealist prose poems to L'Amic de les Arts, published at Sitges from April 1926 to March 1929. These texts were later collected in two volumes: Gertrudis (1927) and KRTU (1932), which according to Enric Bou, rank among the best examples of Catalan surrealist prose.[4] In 1956, both volumes were included in a longer book entitled Diari 1918 (Daily Journal 1918). Interestingly, Bou believes the poems were originally inspired by Apollinaire's proto-Surrealist text "Onirocritique" ("Oneirocriticism"), with which they share several traits.[5] Like the latter, he adds, they attempt to reproduce the free flow of dreams.

Discussing the "prodigious lyrical and verbal concentration" that characterizes the early works, Joaquim Molas is struck by the way in which Foix transforms the daily reality of Sarrià or the Port de la Selva into "a universe of fiction, full of strange associations and substitutions and, in the long run, violent transformations."[6] Now a suburb of Barcelona, Sarrià is where the poet lived and worked. Situated on the northeast coast near the French border, Port de la Selva is where he liked to vacation. Like Molas, Pere Gimferrer also notes that his fantastic poems are anchored in physical reality. "El rasgo más caricaturesco del onirismo de la poesia foixiana," he remarks, "es su deliberada cotidianidad" ("The most characteristic feature of Foix's poetry is its deliberate mondanity").[7] Indeed, it is the tension between familiar and unfamiliar, ordinary and extraordinary, and reality and dream that generates much of the interest. Despite the ordinary style and unremarkable premises of many of the texts in *Gertrudis*, for example, Patricia Boehne concludes that it is probably Foix's most avant-garde book.[8]

As Laurent Jenny declares, "le récit surréaliste ne se constitue que par greffes de procédés poétiques sur des matrices narratives" ("Surrealist narrative consists of poetic devices that have been grafted onto narrative matrices").[9] This is especially true of the following texts, which depend heavily on substitution. Time and time again, Foix takes a simple declarative statement and gives it a Surrealist twist by inserting a word that is illogical, irrational, or inappropriate. Whereas the streets in the following untitled text are *straight*, for example, the second clause makes it clear that they were originally *steep*. Substituting one word for the other increased the general sense of *dépaysement* ("bewilderment") that pervades the composition, which is one of the hallmarks of Surrealism:

> Les cases, de roure i de caoba, s'enfilaven turó amunt i formaven una piràmide caprici d'un artífex ebenista. Aquell era el poble on, sota el signe d'Escorpió, sojornava Gertrudis. Eren tan drets els carters, que em creia, abans d'ésser al cim, defallir. De l'interior de les cases sortien

rares músiques com d'un estoig de cigars harmònic. El cel, de pur cristall, es podia tocar amb les mans. Blava, vermella, verda o groga, cada casa tenia hissada la seva bandera. Si no hagués anat carregat d'un feixuc bidó de vernís, inelegant, m'hauria estret més el nus de la corbata. Al capdamunt del carrer més ample, al vèrtex mateix del turó, sota una cortina blau cel, seia, en un tron d'argent, Gertrudis. Totes vestides de blau cel també, les noies lliscaven, alades, amunt i avall dels carrers, i feien com si no em veiessin. Cenyien el cabell amb un llaç escocès i descobrien els portals i les finestres on vidrieres de fosques colors innombrables donàven al carrer el recolliment de l'interior d'una catedral submergida a la claror de les rosasses. El grinyol del calçat em semblava un cor dolcíssim, i la meva ombra esporuguia l'ombra dels ocells presoners de l'ampla claraboia celeste. Quan em creia d'atènyer el cim, dec haver errat la passa: em trobava en el tebi passadís interminable d'un vaixell transatlàntic. M'han mancat forces per cridar i, en clourem la por els ulls, desplegada en ventall, una sèrie completa de cartes de joc em mostrava inimaginables paisatges desolats.[10]

(The oak and mahogany houses clustered together on the hillside to form a pyramid, the whim of a crafty cabinetmaker. This was the town where Gertrude lived, beneath the sign of Scorpio. The streets were so straight I thought I would collapse before reaching the top. Strange melodies emerged from the houses' interiors as if from a harmonious cigar box. I could reach out and touch the crystal sky with my hands. Blue, red, green, or yellow, every house was flying a flag. If I hadn't been carrying a heavy, inelegant pail of varnish, I would have adjusted the knot in my necktie. At the end of the widest street, at the very top of the hill, Gertrudis was sitting on a silver throne beneath a sky-blue curtain. Dressed entirely in blue as well, winged girls were gliding up and down the streets who pretended to ignore me. Their hair secured with a plaid ribbon, they were opening doors and windows whose innumerable panes, tinted in somber colors, gave the street the secluded appearance of a cathedral's interior submerged in the glow of its rose windows. The squeaking of shoes seemed to me like sweet choirs, and my shadow frightened the shadows of the birds imprisoned in the wide celestial clerestory. When I thought I had finally reached the top, I must have taken a wrong turn: I found myself in the warm, endless corridor of an ocean liner. I could not muster the strength to cry out, and, as fear closed my eyes, a deck of playing cards spread out before me in a fan, revealing unimaginable desolate landscapes.)

Although the imaginary town could conceivably be modeled on Sarrià, which is situated near the foot of Mount Tibidabo, the first line is immediately disconcerting. Whereas oak trees are found all over Spain, including Catalonia, mahogany is a tropical hardwood that grows only in the New World. More importantly, the wooden houses are obviously out of place in Spain, where buildings are traditionally made of stone and covered with stucco. As incredible as it sounds, they appear to have been imported from another country—perhaps from the tropical Americas like the mahogany. Or perhaps they were simply assembled on site, as Foix suggests, by an ambitious cabinetmaker. It is hard to tell if his suggestion is meant to be taken literally or metaphorically. As Arthur Terry remarks, "per a Foix els límits entre el real i l'imaginari són molt flexibles" ("for Foix the borders between the real and the imaginary are very flexible").[11] What further complicates the poem, Boehne points out, is that it adopts a dual perspective.[12] Foix is present simultaneously as a witness and as a participant. In addition, of course, he is also the text's creator.

The second line introduces us to a mysterious figure whose name graces the volume and who appears in a number of other poems: Gertrudis. Although the relationship between Foix the participant and Gertrudis is never clarified, it vaguely resembles that between a would-be lover and the object of his passion. Although Foix the author treats Gertrudis like a real person, she is actually a hybrid creation: a symbolic female created from his early experiences with women. Although her present role is relatively benign, her nature changes from one poem to the next. That Gertrudis was born under the sign of the Scorpion speaks for itself—she is an ambiguous femme fatale whom Foix finds irresistible in his role as a naive participant. Surrounded by strange melodies issuing from nearby houses, he dutifully trudges up the mountain until he reaches the top, where he finds Gertrudis seated on a silver throne beneath a blue canopy. That he is able to reach out and touch the sky along the way is puzzling until one realizes that his journey is modeled on a religious pilgrimage. Just as the strange tunes resemble liturgical music, his tactile encounter represents a mystical experience—perhaps even a miracle. This interpretation is confirmed by the presence of winged schoolgirls, who not only seem to represent angels but who are wearing blue, the color of the Virgin Mary. That the visual effects recall the interior of a cathedral and the sound effects resemble a musical choir completes the religious parallel.

As soon as this parallel is established, the focus shifts to the clerestory rising above the nave, choir, and transept where, attracted by the light coming through the windows, a number of birds are trying to get out. Projected onto the cathedral floor below, their fluttering shadows intermingle with Foix's own shadow, which for some reason they find frightening. This latest development is totally unexpected. Comparing his climb up the hill toward Gertrudis to entering a cathedral, Foix pauses to explore the imaginary cathedral he has just conjured up! The suddenly shift in perspective recalls that of an M. C. Escher drawing. The transition from the initial simile to an actual cathedral boggles the mind. It's as if we have entered another spatiotemporal dimension.

Returning—or attempting to return—to the original dimension where he left Gertrudis, Foix unexpectedly finds himself in the corridor of an ocean liner. This sudden change of scenery, which is typical of dreams, occurs frequently in his poetry. "Lo que propiamente defini[e] el carácter visionario de la poesia foixiana," Gimferrer declares, "[son] las transiciones ... son metáforas del carácter cambiante de una realidad que se ve constantemente sobrepasada por sus secretas fuerzas latentes" ("What really defines the visionary character of Foix's poetry [are] the [abrupt] transitions, ... metaphors for the changing nature of a reality that is constantly surpassed by its secret latent forces").[13] Since the ocean liner's corridor is long and warm, a Freudian analyst might conclude that Foix unconsciously wishes to escape from Gertrudis by returning to the womb, which is exactly how it looks to the un-tutored eye. For that matter, the ship floating on the ocean resembles a baby immersed in amniotic fluid. At this point, Foix is overcome by a terrible fear that renders him blind and mute—once again like a baby in the womb. The last thing he glimpses as he continues to reverse the birthing process is a fan-shaped deck of cards—symbolizing fate—that portray hopelessly barren landscapes. As he disappears symbolically into the uncharted nothingness from which he originally came, the reason for his fear becomes clear: the process may be irreversible. He may never be able to return again.

As the previous text demonstrates, dream plays a major role in the elaboration of Foix's prose poems, which unfold according to a paralogical scenario.[14] Sometimes they recount imaginary adventures, other times they incorporate memories or past experiences that the poet manipulates in various ways. "Utilisés comme herméneutique," Montserrat Prudon explains, "le rêve ou le pré-rêve font surgir des images, des visions plus ou moins déformées de la réalité qui les nourrit. Elles sont souvent reflet/rappel du monde de l'enfance ou de l'adolescence" ("Utilized as a hermeneutics, dreaming or half-dreaming conjures up certain images, more or less distorted visions of the reality that nourishes them. They are often reflections/memories of childhood or adolescence").[15] Entitled "La Vila" ("The Town"), the next poem is filled with memories, both real and imaginary, of Foix's teenage years in Sarrià:

> La meva vila és sobre una plataforma circular. Totes les cases donen per llurs portals a la plaça i, perpendiculars, els deu carrers sense sortida. Al mig de la plaça, alta de cent metres, s'alça una torre mil·lenària sense cap obertura. Al cim oncia una bandera negra teixida d'estels retallats de paper d'argent. No sap hom de ningú que hagi anat més enllà de la plaça i tothom ignora què hi ha més enllà dels murs que tanquen els carrers. No cal dir com de segle en segle augmenten les llegendes que fan més paorosa l'existència exterior. El cel del meu poble, com els gonfanons del Via Crucis, té de nit i de dia, immòbils, el sol, la lluna i els estels, pàl·lidament lluminosos. En desvetllen-nos, tots els joves del poble muntern les bicicletes i, a grans tocs de botzina,

desvetllern el veïnat. Les noies treuen les cadires als portals s'hi asseuen. Miren tendrament com, els joves fem les nostres curses al voltant de la plaça, i es cobreixen el pit de medalles perquè guanyi llur amic. Tots portem brodat al jersei amb fil de seda de colors, el nom de l'estimada. Acabades les curses deixem els bicicles recolzats a la torre i anem a seure a costat del nostre amor. Ens donem les mans, i així passern hores i hores. Les mares obren els balcons i hi estenen els domassos.

(My town is on a circular platform. The doors of all the houses open onto the central square, along with ten dead-end streets that are perpendicular to it. In the middle of the square, rising one hundred meters, stands a thousand year old tower without a single opening. A black flag flutters at its top sown with stars cut from tinfoil. No one is known to have ever penetrated beyond the square, and nobody knows what lies on the other side of the walls that enclose the streets. Naturally, various legends have accumulated over the centuries that paint an even more fearful picture of outside existence. Emitting a pale light, the sun, the moon, and the stars are immobilized in my town's sky day and night, and on the banners in the Via Crucis. All the young men ride bicycles and prevent the neighborhood from sleeping by honking their horns. The girls drag chairs to the doorways and sit there. They watch tenderly as we young men run races around the square, and they cover their chests with medals awarded to their boyfriends. We all wear jerseys with our girlfriends' names embroidered in silk thread of different colors. When the races are finished, we leave our bicycles leaning against the tower and go sit with our girlfriends. We spend hours and hours holding hands. The mothers open the balconies and hang out their wash.)

As Dominic Keown remarks, "humor and playfulness are ... at the very center of Foix's expression."[16] Indeed, this is one of the things that make his poems such a delight to read. Like Buster Keaton, who fascinated a whole generation of Surrealists, he specializes in deadpan humor.[17] Regardless of what happens, Foix the participant and Foix the observer display no emotion whatsoever. Although the author clearly derives much amusement from the outrageous scenario, neither of his alter egos bats an eye. "La Vila" itself is divided into three unequal parts, the first of which occupies nearly two-thirds of the poem. After calmly describing the imaginary cityscape, Foix the observer cedes the stage to Foix the participant who, employing the present tense, recalls what it was like to live in a small town at the beginning of the twentieth century (Sarrià had about 13,000 inhabitants). To be sure, the first statement is a complete fabrication. Even if a large enough platform could be constructed to support the fictional town, it is hard to imagine what would support the platform itself. By contrast, the second statement accurately describes the Plaça de Sarrià, which is surrounded by buildings and from which radiate ten streets.

Any resemblance to Foix's hometown ceases at this point as the portrait expands to include a tower as tall as the one constructed by Gustave Eiffel in Paris. As Gimferrer mentions, this image may have been inspired by the smokestacks in many of Giorgio de Chirico's paintings.[18] Since Foix's tower has no door or windows, one wonders who tends the starry black flag at the top and how they are able to reach it. Astonishingly, none of the town's inhabitants have ever attempted to discover what lies beyond their precincts, apparently because they are afraid of what they might find. In this, they resemble many inhabitants of small towns, who are content simply to stay home. Nevertheless, Gimferrer hastens to point out, the themes of enclosure and claustrophobia are also found elsewhere in Foix's poetry.[19] So too the sun, the moon, and the stars are recurring motifs. Permanently suspended overhead in "La Vila," they appear to be some kind of emblems. The remaining lines are devoted to adolescent mating rituals. Like medieval knights jousting in a tournament, the boys wear their girlfriends' colors as they participate in racing and bicycling competitions. Any medals they receive they give to their girlfriends, who wear them proudly on their blouses. The ultimate prize is being able to hold their hands while their mothers hang out the laundry.

> En acostar-se l'hora del repès, en un angle de la plaça s'obre una trapa
> i enmig d'una fumerola d'encens surt el pare Fèlix. Porta tot de llibres

sota un braç i es passa l'altra mà per la barbassa. I diu, un dia: —Déu
es dóna sempre tot. Mai no dóna un braç, o una galta, o una cama.
Ni mai no dóna un braç a un altre braç, o una galta a una altra galta,
ni una cama a una altra cama. I, un altre dia, diu: —La nostra vila és
un acte d'amor de Déu, i totes les coses són filles de l'amor. Aleshores
ens mirem llargament als ulls i estrenyem més les mans amoroses.
Fra Fèlix, entre una nova fumerola d'encens, se'n torna pel cotilló,
carregat amb les bicicletes. El cel, amb el sol, la lluna i els estels, es mou
suaument com una bambolina.

(As the hour to retire approaches, a trapdoor opens in a corner of the
square, and Father Felix emerges in a cloud of incense. He carries a pile
of books under one arm and caresses his thick beard with the other
hand. And one day he said: "God gives himself wholly to us. He never
gives just an arm, a cheek, or a leg. Neither does he give an arm to
another arm, nor a cheek to another cheek, nor a leg to another leg."
And another day he said: "Our town is an act of God's love, and all the
things in it are the offspring of love. Let us therefore gaze at length into
each others' eyes and extend our loving hands more often." Surrounded
by a new cloud of incense, Brother Felix makes his way back through
the cotillion loaded down with the bicycles. Together with the sun, the
moon, and the stars, the sky sways gently like a theater curtain.)

The second section revolves about the figure of Father Felix, who is
attached to a church bordering the square. The latter is probably based
on the Església de Sant Vicenç de Sarrià, which occupies a similar
position in Foix's hometown. All we know about Father Felix is that
he has a thick beard and that he loves to read. While his chief function
in the poem seems to be to provide some comic relief, he also appears
to be something of a controversial figure. Unlike most parish priests,
who enter and leave the church by the front door, he emerges from a
trapdoor set into the corner of the square as if he were an emissary of
the devil. Emerging in a thick cloud of incense, he resembles a genie
right out of the *Arabian Nights*. Indeed, he seems to be surrounded by
incense wherever he goes. Any doubts about Father Felix's identity,
however, are quickly assuaged by the fact that he immediately begins

to preach the word of God. The latter is not some nefarious lord of the underworld, he explains, but rather God the Loving Father, who holds the whole universe in his warm embrace.

The poem concludes on a rather unexpected note. Father Felix has apparently been demoted to janitor and no longer enjoys the perquisites of the priesthood. Surrounded by a cloud of what smells like incense but is probably sulphur, Brother (not Father) Felix carries the bicycles encountered previously through a group of dancing teenage couples and stores them in the church basement, where they came from previously. The last line finally explains why the sun, the moon, and the stars are always present overhead. The fact that they sway like a theater curtain suggests that the entire town, platform and all, is covered by a huge fabric decorated with celestial images on the inside. From the outside, it looks like the big tent at the Barnum and Bailey circus.

In 1932, five years after *Gertrudis* appeared, Foix published another collection of Surrealist prose poems entitled *KRTU*, which like those in the previous volume were taken from *L'Amic de les Arts*. As we will see in a moment, the enigmatic title seems to have appeared to him in a dream. Although a few critics have attempted to find a hidden meaning, the poet himself has stated that there is none.[20] For those readers who are not content simply to enjoy the poems, who want to know what Foix is doing and why, he describes the texts in *KRTU* as "l'objectivació literària dels meus estats psíquics" ("the literary objectification of my psychic states."[21] Presumably this also describes the works in *Gertrudis* and perhaps some other poems as well. The poet in general, Foix adds in his "Letter to Clara Sobirós," is a "mag, especulador del mot, pelegrí de l'invisible, insatifet, aventurer o investigador a la ratlla del son" ("magician, a speculator in words, a pilgrim of the invisible, unsatisfied, an adventurer or investigator on the edge of sleep").[22] At least, that's the kind of poet Foix strives to be and the only kind, in his opinion, that is worthy of the name. The last item in the list confirms his allegiance to Surrealism and the importance of dream. In this role, Terry explains, Foix seeks to "destruir les aparences familiars de la realitat per a donar accés a una vida més autèntica" ("destroy the familiar appearances of reality in order to access a more authentic life").[23] Dressed to the nines, the woman in the following poem has come to join Foix, who is supposed to accompany her to a fancy ball:

S'havia posat, com quan d'infant anava a les processons, un vestit de llustrina rosa amb una escampadissa d'estels retallats de paper d'estany, perruca rossa cenyida amb una corona de roses naturals, xinelles blanques amb els monogrames de Jesús i Maria brodats amb fil d'or, i dues minses ales esgrogueïdes. M'esperava, com sempre, al celobert, entre el safareig, del qual sobreeixia una roja sabonera, i un bell paisatge de bidons de llauna, esbotzats, i negres atuells d'ús indeterminat. —¿Per què—li hauria dit, si m'hagués estat possible de reprendre la paraula —t'has posat un vestit tan llarg? No se't veu el tornassol dels genolls i, a l'envelat, no et podré amanyagar les cames. —¿Per què una sabonera tan espessa cobreix l'aigua del safareig? Els vaixells de paper no hi podran navegar i, ni removent-la amb totes les meves forces amb el picador de rentar la roba, no hi podrem simular un oceà agitat. Em prengué per la mà i, silenciosament, em féu davallar per una escala d'esglaons desiguals. Dues estives de travesses de via fèrria formaven un passadís fresquívol que il·luminaven irregularment diminutes bombetes enteranyinades. Com li agraïa tanta de sol·licitud a mostrar-me els meus paisatges dilectes! Foradades a mig fer, murallats riberencs, galeries subterrànies amb arbredes d'eixades i picots gegantins, reraeixides on pengen mil cordes inútils. Més que els panorames alpestres o els cims pirinencs, més que l'ample buc o la cova i la caverna naturals, em plau el desendreç de tants d'estris inútils on el rovell seductor brilla com una rosada providencial sota la claror moradenca que la meva companya hi aparia. —¿Per què lloen els homes les muntanyes, els boscs, els rius i les fontanes, i menyspreen, hipòcrites!, els laberints que en llurs projeccions metàl·liques realitzen?

(As she used to do for processions when she was a girl, she had put on a pink lamé gown sprinkled with stars cut from tinfoil, a blond wig with a crown of real roses, white slippers bearing the monograms of Jesus and Mary embroidered in gold, and two slender yellowish wings. As usual she was waiting for me in the central patio, between the tub where the clothes were washed, which was overflowing with red foam, and a lovely landscape of mangled tin cans and black containers of indeterminate use. "Why," I would have asked her had I been able to speak, "have you put on such a long dress? The sunflower of your knees is no longer visible, and I won't be able to caress your legs." "Why does such a thick foam cover the wash tub? No one will be able to sail paper boats, and even if I move the washing paddle with all my might, we won't be able to simulate the ocean's waves.")

Like the two previous poems, "S'havia posat" consists of an "inextricable blend of reality ... and fantasy," to quote C. B. Morris, "which [Foix] authenticates ... by his cool, almost detached narration of incident and by his recording of detail."[24] Although the anonymous woman is all dolled up for the occasion, she is dressed rather bizarrely. Her gown is sprinkled with tinfoil stars (like the black flag in the second text), she is wearing a blond wig, and her slippers are decorated with the monograms of Jesus and Mary. While the latter assume a great many different forms, usually involving the letter M, the former commonly feature the letters IHS, originally an abbreviation of the name of Jesus in Greek. Like the winged girls gliding up and down the street in the first text, moreover, she wears a pair of wings herself. Perhaps she has been invited to a masquerade ball. Although she is nameless in the present poem, she is beginning to look more and more like Gertrudis. In both works, wings seem to be a symbol of divinity. While she does not wear wings in "Les cases, de roure i de caoba," she is surrounded by acolytes who do. Equally importantly, she is sitting on a silver throne in the latter poem and wearing a crown in this one. Thus divinity and royalty are combined in her person exactly as in the Virgin Mary.

The second, third, and fourth paragraphs take place around a large tub where the clothes are normally washed, which for some reason is overflowing with a disgusting red foam. This last fact will keep everyone from sailing their toy boats and Foix from making waves to sink them by. Not only is the poet unable to speak, we learn, but he and Gertrudis are on rather intimate terms, at least enough for him to enjoy caressing her bare legs (and for her to let him). However, the most significant discovery is the pile of old tin cans and miscellaneous containers that he finds "bell." The modern age demands a new aesthetics, he seems to imply, one that reflects the new concept of industrial beauty formulated at the beginning of the twentieth century. This then is the "literary objectification of [his] psychic state"—the conviction that the ugly possesses a beauty all of its own. This conclusion is confirmed by the following paragraph.

En ple monòleg interior no m'havia adonat que acabàvem d'arribar a la sortida d'un túnel que duia a una vasta explanada on els homes gosaven exterioritzar llur divina aversió a la natura tot estrafent-ne la desordenada espontaneïtat amb figuracions tubulars de plom i d'argila. Uns altres homes, infatigables, escampaven per terra cabassades de graciosos utensilis de ferreteria i, al fons de tot, quatre homes més es perdien per la línia de l'horitzó, carregats cadascun d'ells amb una feixuga lletra diversa de l'alfabet, la lectura conjunta de les quals donava el nom misteriós: KURT,URKT, TRUK, UKRT, TURK, KRUT ...—del personatge central dels meus somnis.—Farem tard al ball—hauria dit encara, si la paraula m'hagués respostal pensament. La meva companya no era ja a costat meu. Reclosa per sempre dins el vehicle productor del generador trifàsic, vestida amb el seu vestit de ball fet de múltiples gases blau cel, s'allunyava tot acomiadant-se'm amb el somriure de mil blanques margarides i sense plànyer-se de la dissort que la condemnava a un càrcer tan llòbreg. Jo, acotat més que mai en terra, fet un pellingot enquitranat de borra, aplicava unes pinces de soldadura elèctrica a un suport metal-lic i il-luminava la desolada vall d'inefables clarors celestes.

(She took me by the hand and, silently, led me down a staircase with uneven steps. Two railroad ties formed a cool path which was illuminated irregularly by tiny light bulbs covered with spider webs. How pleased she was to exhibit such solicitude by showing me my favorite landscapes! Half-finished tunnels, riverside walls, subterranean galleries with groves of gigantic hoes and pickaxes, rear patios where a thousand useless cords hang. More than Alpine panoramas or the peaks of the Pyrenees, more than broad depressions or natural coves and caverns, I like the disorder of so many useless tools whose seductive rust shines like a providential dew beneath the purplish light prepared by my companion. "Why do men praise mountains, woods, rivers, and springs and, hypocrites, despise the labyrinths they achieve in their metallic projections?" Lost in an internal monologue, I had not noticed that we had arrived at a tunnel's exit leading to a vast esplanade where men dared to exhibit their divine aversion to nature by mocking its disorderly spontaneity with tubular shapes of lead and clay. Some other men were tirelessly scattering basketfuls of graceful metal utensils on the ground, and in the background four more men were disappearing along the edge of the horizon, each weighed down by a separate letter of the alphabet which, taken together, spelled the mysterious name: KURT, URKT, TRUK, UKRT, TURK, KRUT ...—of the central figure in my dreams. "We will be late for the ball," I would have observed if my words had corresponded to my thoughts. My companion was no longer by my side. Enclosed forever within the three-phase generator's mass produced vehicle, dressed in a ball gown made of multiple sky-blue gauzes, she said goodbye with the smile of a thousand white daisies without lamenting the misfortune that condemned her to such a gloomy prison. Bending closer and closer to the ground, transformed into a tarred and lint-covered rag, I applied some arc welding pliers to a metal beam and illuminated the desolate valley with an ineffable celestial brightness.)

Taking his hand, Gertrudis leads him down into an underground cavern containing some of his favorite objects, which are arranged to form informal "still-lifes": thousands of useless cords, heaps of rusty tools, and so on. It is hard to tell which he finds the most seductive—the tools' disorderly piles or the fact that they are useless. Each principle appears to complement the other. Contrary to artists like Charles Sheeler and Charles Demuth, who worshipped the sleek lines and precision of modern machinery, Foix adopts an art for art stance and an anti-utilitarian aesthetic. Why do people admire nature, he wonders, and turn their back on machinery? As the cavern narrows into a tunnel that opens onto a vast square, he witnesses men exhibiting their "divina aversió a la natura" while mocking its disorderly spontaneity by making precisely manufactured tubes. Although they share Foix's dislike of nature, they evidently do not share his love of disorder. At this point,

Foix spies four men in the distance who are each carrying one of the following letters: K, U, R, or T, which spell the name of a mysterious dream figure. The only problem is deciding how they should be combined. Eventually, he settles on KRTU, which becomes the title of the book of poetry he is writing.

As Foix turns around to silently urge Gertrudis to hurry, he discovers that she is no longer there. Having somehow (and somewhere) discarded her earlier gown, she is wearing the same sky blue outfit that she had in the first poem, where she was seated on a silver throne. Her current seat is much less elegant. She has hitched a ride on a truck delivering a large electric generator and is smiling as she departs. The fact that the truck has been mass produced, following Henry Ford's recent invention of the assembly line, emphasizes its modernity as does the fact that the generator has replaced the earlier single-phase model, which was less efficient and required more copper wire. By choosing to associate herself with these two machines, Gertrudis has become a symbol of the modern age herself.

The final stanza is somewhat problematic. Suddenly and with no preparation whatsoever, Foix finds himself magically transformed into "a tarred and lint-covered rag." This is not the first time that one of his poems has concluded with his reduction in size or importance, which has received considerable attention. Thus Boehne calls attention to "the theme of physical smallness and childishness" in his work,[25] Gimferrer notes that the theme is widespread,[26] and Morris concludes it sometimes represents an act of "conscious humility."[27] Although this is not the place to discuss the subject in detail, it is worth noting that Foix goes on to wield a pair of arc welding pliers—which as we saw in Chapter 2 had a special significance for the Surrealists—which he could not do if he were merely a dirty rag. The inescapable conclusion is that the latter represents a metaphor expressing his disappointment at being abandoned by Gertrudis. Basically Foix concludes, he means no more to her than a dirty rag. The question remains, nevertheless, as to why she decided to reject him. In the light of the preceding discussion, it seems reasonable to conclude that he was not modern enough for her, and so, in an effort to change her mind, he decided to learn arc welding—yet another recent mechanical invention. Since the specialized pliers are used mainly for holding something, touching a metal beam should not have had any effect. Whatever the explanation, the latter action produces a spark of such magnitude that it lights up the entire valley and transforms the occasion into a celebration. Hopefully, this will compensate, at least partially, for his earlier disappointment.

The middle years of the twentieth century in Spain were chaotic initially and then oppressive. Following the Civil War, which raged from 1936 to 1939, and the triumph of Generalísimo Francisco Franco, Catalonia was systematically stripped of its Catalan identity as punishment for supporting the other side. Although Foix's third book *Sol, i de dol* (*Alone and in Mourning*) was finished in 1936, it did not appear in print until 1947. While he continued to write after the war began, he did not attempt to publish his writings until 1949, when *Les Irreals Omegues* (*The Unreal Omegas*) finally appeared. Thereafter he resumed publishing on a regular basis until his death thirty-eight years later. In 1972, he published a book of poetry entitled *Tocant a mà* (*Within Reach*), many of whose themes and images are borrowed from *Gertrudis* and *KRTU*. Entitled "Somnis immòbils amb ròssec de cabellera" ("Immobile Dreams with Ponytail"), one of the most interesting poems is dedicated to Pere Gimferrer:

> Que el mar de temps en temps té aparença de sòlid, ho hem vist i ho hem constatat més d'una vegada. Recordo aquell dia que voltats de foc i de fumassa, tot vogant indolents pels escullats de Cala Torta, la barca i els rems van encallar en un sec que desconeixíem, Distrets tot caçant gumies, coltells i d'altres deixalles del temps de la pirateria—al ventre de les ones quan desfalleixen i escumen—no ens havíem adonat que el mar s'enduria. Ni havíem advertit que el Sol, d'un vermell insurgent, modificava el color dels farallons i dels penyals, i que l'ombre dels cosos esbiaixava talment que no era gens fàcil d'encertar l'hora que era. Van sentir-nos aturats en un món encantat. La mar era un vidre de gruix sense esquerdes ni trencs. No sabíem què fer, quan vam descobrir

que tot era areny, de la costa a la ratlla de l'horitzó, i que nosaltres i l'embarcació érem en terra compacta, a immense distància del mar que havíem solcat fressós. Les nostres ombres es projectaven invertides, com si el Sol fos de llevant. Tinc encara presents els tràfecs que vam passar per tornar a casa, a peu, amb la barca i els rems a coll. Però que, avui, un mar lívid i exsangüe—com els llavis de Camilla als confins del plaer—porti a poc a poc a la platja i a les cales estranyes arrels erectes de mal escriure, ocelles dissecades amb els ulls desvetillats, lletres de l'alfabet grosses, impúdicament arrenglerades com en els titulars d'un diari del vespre, robes llibertines barrejades am pallels i moises, singulars estrelles de mar agressives, i somnis immòbilis, empal·liats, amb ròssec de cabellera, m'ullprèn i m'espanta.[28]

(That the sea has a solid appearance from time to time we have seen and witnessed more than once. I remember the day when, surrounded by fire and thick smoke, while rowing lazily along the outcroppings of Cala Torta beach, the boat and the oars ran aground on a high spot we didn't know about. Distracted by hunting for curved daggers, knives, and other items of pirate days—in the bellies of the waves when they foam and ebb—we hadn't noticed that the sea was hardening. Nor had we noticed that the sun, of insurgent crimson, was modifying the color of the pebbles and the peaks, and that all the shadows extended diagonally so that it wasn't easy to be sure what time it was. We felt immersed in an enchanted world. The sea was a deep glass without cracks or breaks. We did not know what to do when we discovered that everything was sand, from the coast to the horizon, and that we and the boat were on solid land, at an immense distance from the sea that we had noisily furrowed. Our shadows were upside-down, as if the Sun were in the East. I can still recall our laborious efforts to return home, on foot, with the boat and the oars on our shoulders. However, I am enchanted and terrified by the ability of a livid and bloodless sea (like Camilla's lips in the throes of passion) to gradually carry strange, erect, and indescribable roots to the beach and the coves, together with desiccated birds with sleepless eyes and fat, shamelessly aligned alphabetical letters—like those in an evening newspaper's headlines— libertine dresses mixed with straw and moss, unusually aggressive starfish, immobile dreams, and wall hangings with ponytails.)

"A brilliant word-painting" in Patricia Boehne's words, "Somnis inmòbils" demonstrates that Foix was still going strong forty-five years after publishing his first book of poetry.[29] This particular composition seems to have been generated by an actual experience—introduced here by a personal observation serving as a preamble. An avid sailor, Foix was familiar with the innumerable appearances the Mediterranean could assume and with its innumerable personalities. On particularly calm days and under the right conditions, he reports, it looks as if someone could walk on it. This thought reminds him of a unique experience when, despite a wildfire burning on some nearby hills, he decided to go boating off the Cala Torta beach, between Port Lligat and Port de la Selva. Not to be confused with a similarly named beach in Majorca, the Catalan version resembles a mini fjord with a small pebble beach at the far end. Although several photographs of Foix show him at the helm of a sailboat, on this particular day he and his friend(s) find themselves in a rowboat. Supposedly hunting for pirate artifacts, they run aground and have to carry the boat back home on their shoulders. As so often in his poetry, Foix reveals himself to be a past master of spatio-temporal metamorphosis. At first, solid water appears to be no more than an amusing concept. Or rather, since it is the product of a visual experience, it is an amusing *percept*. However, since Rudolf Arnheim has shown that visual perception and visual thinking are identical, the percept instantaneously becomes a concept.[30]

Next Foix the author unexpectedly transforms this concept into a reality. Mesmerized by the interplay between the crimson sunlight and the lengthening shadows, Foix the participant fails to notice that the sea is gradually hardening until it becomes solid glass. Presumably "glass" is a metaphor for solid water, but the sea could conceivably have been changed into a vitreous substance. Be that as it may, the reader scarcely has time to absorb this surprising development before a rapid shift in perspective reveals that the sea has suddenly retreated. Foix and his friends are surrounded by dry land as far as the eye can see. While the transitions between the water's various stages are abrupt, they are also surprisingly subtle. Three different operations are necessary to overcome three persistent binary oppositions: that between liquid and solid, that between the sea and the land, and that between wet and dry. Before we have time to think about what has just happened, however, Foix and his companions notice that their shadows are upside-down. Unfortunately it is not entirely clear what that actually means. Since the sun is in the western sky, it may mean that the shadow it would normally cast has been moved wholesale from the eastern side of objects to the western side without changing its original orientation. Or alternatively, it may mean that the shadow is acting as if the sun were on the eastern side, in which case it would naturally fall on the left side of an object. Moving from left to right, the shadow would begin with a person's feet in the first instance or with his head in the second. In either case, it represents yet another miraculous transformation.

At this point, Foix reveals that he has moved on from Gertrudis and has become the ardent lover of someone named Camilla. Progressing from the particular to the general, he focuses on the sea's ability to carry all sorts of strange debris to the shore, which he finds simultaneously enthralling and frightening. Not just any sea, he explains, but one that is livid and bloodless. What frightens him is not the water's pale color, which resembles Camilla's lips pressed tightly together in a moment of passion, but rather the grotesque objects that it deposits on the beach. He is especially fascinated by uprooted stumps that have washed up, whose erect roots seem vaguely obscene. Other objects elicit a similar, fetishistic response including desiccated birds, sexy dresses covered with weeds and moss, and aggressive starfish. Although it is hard to see how "immobile dreams" could be washed up on shore, perhaps that is simply a metaphor for attractive objects. If the wall hangings with ponytails are the most bizarre combinations, finally, the alphabetical letters are the most familiar contributions. Appearing regularly in the poet's works going back to *KRTU*, they testify to his fascination with material language from the very beginning. Patricia Boehne provides an excellent summary of his poetic progress over the years. Foix has evolved from being the victim of unreality in *Gertrudis*, she declares, "to the mastery of its enchantment, with an ability to confront it directly, describe it, comprehend unreality, and use it as his passport ... to another dimension."[31]

Like Hinojosa, whose works we examined in Chapter 5, Foix was a brilliant practitioner of Surrealist narrative. Each in his own unique way managed to appropriate an essentially realistic genre (the prose poem), subvert its initial premises, and convert it into a major vehicle for Surrealist inspiration. Hinojosa's compositions are particularly noteworthy for the density of their imagery. Text after text contains a concatenation of marvelous images that practically overwhelms the reader. By contrast, Foix's poetry is more restrained and is concerned with actions more than with images. Whereas Hinojosa delights in creating fantastic scenes that boggle the imagination, Foix transforms ordinary scenes into surprising encounters with unexpected figures in equally unexpected situations. As Jacqueline Chénieux-Gendron reminds us, "au centre de la pratique surréaliste se trouve l'activité ludique" ("playful activity is at the center of Surrealist practice").[32]

Notes

1   See Serge Salaün and Elisée Trenc, *Les Avant-gardes en Catalogne* (Paris: La Sorbonne Nouvelle, 1995).

2   Enrique Badosa, *Antologia de J. V. Foix*, 2nd ed. (Madrid: Plaza and Janés, 1975), p. 9.

3   Preface to *Les irreals omegues* (1948), repr. in his *Obres completes* (Barcelona: Edicions 62, 1984), Vol. 1, p. 119.

4   Enric Bou, "From Foix to Dalí: Versions of Catalan Surrealism between Barcelona and Paris," *ARTL@S BULLETIN*, Vol. 6, No. 2 (Summer 2017), p. 47.

5   Ibid., pp. 47–8.

6   Joaquim Molas, "J. V. Foix or Total Investigation," *Catalan Review*, Vol. I, No. 1 (1986), p. 119.

7   Pere Gimferrer, "Aspectos de la poesia de J. V. Foix," *Destino* (January 27, 1973), p. 23.

8   Patricia J. Boehne, *J. V. Foix* (Boston: Twayne, 1980), p. 26.

9   Laurent Jenny, "La Surréalité et ses signes narratifs," *Poétique*, No. 15 (1973), p. 501.

10 J. V. Foix, *Diari 1918*, ed. Carmen Arnau (Barcelona: Edicions 62 and La Caixa, 1987), p. 23.

11 Arthur Terry, "La idea de l'ordre en la poesia de J. V. Foix," in *Les avanguardes literàries a Catalunya: bibliografia i antologia crítica*, ed. Joaquim Molas et al. (Madrid and Frankfurt am Main: Vervuert, 2005), p. 196.

12 Boehne, *J. V. Foix*, p. 29.

13 Gimferrer, "Aspectos de la poesia," p. 23.

14 Josep Miquel Sobrer, "Deformation, Mutilation, and Putrefaction: The Early Foix," *Journal of Iberian and Latin American Studies*, Vol. 9, No. 2 (2003), p. 179.

15 Montserrat Prudon, "J. V. Foix, un singulier pluriel," in *Les Avant-gardes en Catalogne (1916–1930)*, ed. Serge Salaün and Elisée Trenc (Paris: Sorbonne Nouvelle, 1995), pp. 65–6.

16 Dominic Keown, "The Ironic Vision of J. V. Foix," in *Readings of J. V. Foix: An Anthology*, ed. Arthur Terry (Barcelona: Anglo-Catalan Society, 1998), p. 131.

17 See for example Willard Bohn, *Marvelous Encounters: Surrealist Responses to Film, Art, Poetry, and Architecture* (Lewisburg: Bucknell, 2005), pp. 126–52.

18 Gimferrer, "Aspectos de la poesia," p. 13.

19 Ibid., p. 16.

20 Boehne, *J. V. Foix*, p. 45.

21 Quoted in C. B. Morris, *Surrealism and Spain 1920–1936* (Cambridge: Cambridge University Press, 1972), p. 257.

22 Ibid., pp. 256–7.

23 Terry, "La idea de l'ordre," p. 194.

24 Morris, *Surrealism and Spain*, p. 94.

25 Boehne, *J. V. Foix*, p. 44.

26 Gimferrer, "Aspectos de la poesia," pp. 26–7.

27 C. Brian Morris, "Gertrudis and the Creative Modesty of J. V. Foix," *Catalan Review*, Vol. 1, No. 1 (Barcelona: Quaderns Crema: June 1986), p. 125.

28   J. V. Foix, *Antologia poètica*, ed. Marià Manent et al. (Barcelona: Proa, 1993), p. 138.

29   Boehne, *J. V. Foix*, p. 101.

30   Rudolf Arnheim, *Visual Thinking* (Berkeley: University of California Press, 1969), p. 14.

31   Boehne, *J. V. Foix*, p. 102.

32   Jacqueline Chénieux-Gendron, "Jeu de l'incipit et travail de la correction dans l'écriture automatique," in *Une Pelle au vent dans les sables du rêve*, ed. Michel Murat and Marie-Paule Berranger (Lyon: Presses Universitaires de Lyon, 1992), p. 126.

8

Portuguese Experiments with Surrealism

That the Surrealist movement is alive and well in Portugal is a well-kept secret—even from many scholars who specialize in Surrealism. As José-Augusto França observes, "le surréalisme portugais ne traverse que difficilement les frontières de son pays" ("Portuguese Surrealism crosses its country's borders only with difficulty").[1] Surrealism made its first appearance in Portugal around 1935, where it attracted the attention of a number of poets and painters. A second phase coalesced around the artist Cândido Costa-Pinto toward the end of the 1940s that witnessed the publication (in 1952) of a manifesto entitled *A afixação proibida* (*Post No Bills*). Because of internal dissension, the group lasted only a few years. Since that time, however, the Surrealist movement has continued to grow in Portugal and to attract a considerable audience. In particular, the Centro Português do Surrealismo has been in existence for at least twenty years. Thanks to its instantaneous visual appeal, Surrealist painting is currently quite popular. As recently as 2013, for example, the Fellini Gallery in Berlin hosted a show entitled "21st Century Portuguese Surrealism" with works by six artists from Portugal. Similarly, the international exhibition "Surrealism Now" opened in the university town of Coimbra on November 17, 2018, and ran until January 10, 2019. Over the years, to be sure, Portuguese Surrealist poetry has also attracted a loyal group of followers. "Nenhum movimento como o surrealismo," Mário Cesariny explains, "propòs tanto, a um só tempo, uma real cidadania para todos e uma real liberdade de cada um consigo" ("No movement like Surrealism proposes so much at the same time: true citizenship for all and true liberty for everyone together").[2] Until 1974, however, Portugal was a right-wing dictatorship that suppressed civil liberties and political freedom.

Fernando Alves dos Santos

Belonging to Surrealism's second Portuguese phase, Alves dos Santos was born and raised in Lisbon, like the other Surrealists examined here. Situated at the mouth of the Tagus river, the capital witnessed extensive modernization and improvements in the quality of life between 1950 and 1970 as much of the rural population gravitated to the city. With around a million and a half people, Lisbon was a sophisticated metropolis that possessed a vibrant cultural life. Although Alves dos Santos was especially attracted to the theater, he was a practicing poet and artist who routinely participated in Surrealist events, such as the *1ª Exposição dos Surrealistas* (1949), *O Cadáver Esquisito Sua Exaltação* at the Galeria Ottolini (1975), and *Três Poetas do Surrealismo* at the Biblioteca Nacional (1981). Besides a number of uncollected texts, his published works include two books of poetry: *Diário Flagrante* (*Flagrant Diary*) (1954) and *Textos Poéticos* (1957). Reviewing the first volume, Antonio Tabucchi praised the poetry's "forza lirica ed evocatrice percorsa da una sottile vena d'ironia" ("lyric and evocative force enlivened by a subtle vein of irony").[3] Entitled "Acordo, adormeço nos braços verticais do vento" ("I Wake up, I Fall Asleep in the Vertical Arms of the Wind"), the following poem is taken from the same volume.[4] Consisting of a series of vignettes loosely cobbled together, it spans the indeterminate space between morning and night:

> Acordo nos braços verticais do vento.
> Numa bandeja dão-me a carícia geométrica da humanidade
> (eu não pedi sequer uma canequinha de café).
> A cidade deixa cair o trajo de teatro
> e mostra-me os seus seios
> Na cálida cólera dos jardins.

No silêncio perplexo do homem e do edifício
o público alivia o peito.
É a hora e a rua feitas para tudo se dar.
Pontualmente comprimido na sua poltrona
o último viajante pensa no momento que perdeu.
Nos braços verticais do vento
os sectários cavalo de tróia
muito castos sobem no elevador
e todas as tardes há concerto.

De cabeça deformada e enorme, enorme
um menino passeia na feira:
—tudo é pequeno e o mundo é sólido.
Os sobreviventes da recente tragédia
beijam-se com ternura
e avisam que não adianta morrer.

Adormeço nos braços verticais do vento.

(I wake up in the vertical arms of the wind.
Give me humanity's geometric caress on a tray
[I didn't even ask for a demitasse of coffee]
The city drops its fancy gown
and shows me its breasts
in the warm anger of the gardens.
In the perplexing silence of man and building
the public sooths its heart.
It is the time and the place where anything could happen.
Punctually compressed in his armchair,
the ultimate traveler ponders the time he has lost.
In the vertical arms of the wind,
religious fanatics Trojan Horse
ascend chastely in the elevator,
and every evening there is a concert.

With an enormous, enormous deformed head
a boy strolls around at the fair:
—everything is small and the world is solid.

The survivors of the recent tragedy
kiss each other tenderly
and warn others that it's no use dying.

I fall asleep in the vertical arms of the wind).

Written in free verse and divided into two unequal stanzas, the
poem is composed almost entirely of isolated references. Except for the
first three lines, which evoke a familiar scene, the rapid succession of
images produces a feeling of *dépaysement*. We have no idea where we
are or what is going on or whom the speaker is addressing. For that
matter, we don't know who the speaker is either. Although the "I" who
wakes up in the first line is presumably Alves dos Santos, there is no
way to be sure. Beginning with an anthropomorphic image of the wind,
the poet rehearses an age-old ritual. Representing the speaker's wife,
the wind wakes him in the morning, fondly caresses his hair, and brings
him his breakfast on a tray. That she has "braços verticais" suggests that
she is bending over him when the poem opens, perhaps to give him a
kiss. Since he knows she will automatically bring him a cup of coffee, he
does not ask for one. Interweaving material and immaterial references,
the initial scene leads to an arresting metaphor in the next two lines.
At the referential level, the image of the city's bare breasts could have
been suggested by the speaker's wife removing her nightgown after
breakfast before changing into her clothes. At the metaphorical level,
the remarkable image reflects the morning's remarkable beauty.

On his way to work, perhaps, the speaker crosses the sunny
municipal gardens and disappears into an urban canyon dominated
by tall buildings. At this point, the unconscious scenario fades away,
and Surrealism begins to assert itself more forcefully. Not only are the
gardens angry for some reason, but the urban center, which would
normally be bustling with activity, is completely silent. Although people
apparently find the eerie silence soothing, the atmosphere is charged
with expectation. Anything could happen at this point, the speaker
confides, where time and space are momentarily frozen. Instead of
waiting for something to occur, however, he decides to enter a nearby

hotel. Besides a professional traveler relaxing in the lobby, he spies a group of religious fanatics entering an elevator "nos braços verticais do vento." This time the wind is represented by an elevator, apparently because its vertical arms resemble the latter's vertical ascent. The author complicates things still further by abruptly inserting a reference to the Trojan Horse between the subject of the main verb and the verb itself. Like the Greek soldiers hidden in the horse's belly, the comparison implies, the fanatics will burst forth when they reach their destination and slaughter their enemies. Unfortunately, we don't know who their enemies are or whether they were ultimately successful.

The action in the second stanza switches to a completely different locale. The author abandons the urban setting in favor of a rural or semi-rural location, where a fair is taking place. The first person we meet is a boy with a huge deformed head, who is strolling around looking at the sights. One wonders if he is simply a visitor or, assuming that the fair exhibits human oddities, if he is part of the freak show. Although the details are lacking, the crowd also includes several survivors of a recent accident, who are extremely happy to be alive and who warn others not to risk their lives. Again, one wonders where the accident happened and whether it involved any of the attractions at the fair. Perhaps the roller coaster flew off the track, or the Ferris wheel tipped over. Whatever the explanation, the poem concludes with the speaker surrendering to the vertical arms of his windy Morpheus. Whether he falls asleep at home or stretched out on a bench at the fair is impossible to say.

So much for my preceding attempt to transform this strange little poem into a coherent narrative. However, the ease with which it was possible to do so inevitably raises a red flag. The value of an automatic text—which is what this composition pretends to be—depends on the extent to which it resists translation. The problem with this example is that it is not bizarre enough, too transparent, even verging on the allegorical. The first line and its variants are the only lines that follow the Surrealist model: "Acordo nos braços verticais do vento" ("I wake up in the vertical arms of the wind"). Unfortunately, even the breasts of the city metaphor seem to be contrived. A practiced Surrealist would simply have written "The city shows me its breasts." Since there is no reliable way of differentiating between an actual automatic text and a skillful imitation, Michael Riffaterre prefers to speak of an "automatism effect."[5] Perhaps this text was simply an early attempt to write automatic poetry.

Mário-Henrique Leiria

Like Fernando Alves dos Santos, Leiria belongs to the second Surrealist phase. A talented artist as well as a writer, he is best known today for a series of popular short stories he published during the 1970s. From 1949 to 1951, he studied at the Escola de Belas Artes in Lisbon, where he was finally expelled for political reasons. He and his fellow Surrealists seem to have been involved in an absurdist plot to overthrow the dictatorship of Antonio Salazar. Following an interview with the secret police, known familiarly as PIDE (Polícia Internacional e de Defesa do Estado), he decided it was time to move to Brazil, where he spent the next nine years. "Cidade adormecida" ("Sleeping City") first appeared in an anthology published in 1954.[6] The previous poem by Fernando Alves dos Santos is Surrealist to the extent that it evokes an imaginary reality. By contrast, Leiria's composition exploits a totally different Surrealist vein: black humor—"black" in the French sense rather than the American. Unlike the latter, which tends toward the morbid, it is fanciful and deliberately absurd. Serving as an escape valve from societal pressures, according to André Breton, *l'humour noir* represents a "révolte supérieure de l'esprit" ("superior revolt of the mind").[7]

> Foi decretada a mobilização geral,
> Bom, isso não teve importância nenhuma
> tanto mais que era simplesmente
> por causa de haver guerra.
> Era uma guerrazinha pequena
> que estava metida numa gaiola.

Davam-lhe alpista,
mas arroz nunca lhe davam-e
por isso,
foi decretada a mobilização geral.
A guerra piava cada vez mais.
Trouxeram-lhe um cunhado
muito lavado,
muito engomado
e zaís, comeu-o.
Então começou a tocar o tambor
e lá fomos todos,
com a espingarda na algibeira
e a mochila cheia de não-fazer-nada.

(A general mobilization was declared,
Good, this is of no importance
all the more so because it was simply
because of the war.
It was a little war
that was put in a cage
and chirped a lot,
continually asking for birdseed and rice from Xiao.

We gave it birdseed,
but never gave it rice,
therefore,
the general mobilization was declared.
The war chirped more and more.
We brought it a brother-in-law,
very clean,
very starched,
and it ate him just like that.
Then it began to play the drum,
and we all went to see,
with a shotgun in our pockets
and a backpack full of doing nothing.)

The first example of *humour noir* is the poem's title. Although readers don't recognize the initial disconnect until much later, they eventually discover that "Ciudade adormecida" does not portray a sleeping city at all. They have been lured into reading the text under false pretenses. The first line sets the stage for the rest of the poem. Troops have been called up to fight in a mysterious war for unknown reasons. Fortunately, the second line assures the reader that there is no cause for concern. Whereas wars are generally hideous experiences, this one is too small to do any damage—which ironically undercuts the idea of waging war in the first place. Indeed, this turns out to be the poet's principal strategy: to attack the idea of war by systematically belittling it. By transforming it into a tiny canary—so small that it can be confined to a cage—the threat of war is reduced to virtually nothing. Although the bird continually asks to be fed birdseed and rice from Xiao, a dedicated pacifist would let it starve to death, thus eliminating the threat of war entirely.

That the canary is able to communicate its nutritional preferences to its handlers is remarkable to say the least. It requests not just any rice, moreover, but rather a Chinese variety from an area west of Shanghai. Since Portugal produces a great deal of rice itself, one wonders how the bird acquired a taste for this specific strain. Insofar as cereals are concerned, at least, it seems to be an avian gourmet. Although Leiria and his colleagues continued to feed the canary birdseed, the second stanza reveals, they reserved the exotic rice for themselves. Contradicting what he said previously, the speaker now claims that the mobilization was the result of their selfishness. Since the canary seemed to need a companion, he continues, they put another bird in the cage, which it attacked and ate almost immediately. Apparently a nation at war makes a dangerous bedfellow (or cage-fellow). Pleased with itself, the canary chooses to celebrate its recent victory by banging on a drum as loudly as it can. Inadvertently contributing to the general humor, Leiria and his friends go to see what is happening but are pathetically ill-equipped to fight a war. Each carries a shotgun (instead of a rifle), which he

supposedly crams into a pocket (which is physically impossible) as if it
were a pistol, and an empty backpack.

Na guerra só o que se fazia era comer,
comiam-se nabos,
comiam-se lições de inglês
e comia-se muito medo
que nos era dado todos os dias
pelos majores que lá não iam
porque ali era longe.
No fim
comeu-se o decreto de mobilização geral
com o arroz do Sião
que não foi posto na gaiola da guerra.
Voltamos todos a tocar corneta
e sem a espingarda na algibeira
pois se tinha gasto toda
com o andar,
porque não lhe tinham dado botas.

(In the war, all one did was eat.
we ate turnips,
we ate English lessons,
and we ate much fear
which was given to us everyday
by the majors who did not go
because it was far away.
In the end
we ate the declaration of mobilization
with the rice from Xiao
which was not put in the war's cage.

We all returned to play the bugle
and without the shotgun in our pocket
because it completely disintegrated
from all the walking
because they did not give you boots.)

Between the second and third stanzas, a lot has happened. Leiria and his colleagues have apparently been involved in the war after all and have already returned home. At this point, the poet abandons his initial efforts to ridicule war in general and paints a somber portrait of the recent battle. The third stanza consists entirely of war stories, which, probably because the men were starving much of the time, are almost exclusively concerned with food. Indeed, that seems to be the sense of the very first line. The soldiers seem to have spent all their time looking for something to eat. Turnips, language lessons, Chinese rice, even the declaration of mobilization—everything served to stem their voracious appetites. Unlike the officers, who distributed their meager rations and then quickly disappeared, they experienced fear (and perhaps death) on a daily basis. Returning home without their weapons and nearly barefoot, they long to hear the sound of a musician playing a cornet (*corneta*) in a band instead of a soldier sounding a bugle (also *corneta*) early in the morning.

The mortal enemy of sentimentality, according to André Breton, black humor assumes a great many guises.[8] Indeed, his *Anthologie de l'humour noir* contains no fewer than forty-five examples taken from several different periods and from several different countries. If the word *humour* is basically untranslatable according to Paul Valéry, everyone knows what it means, and everyone has a favorite example or two. Quoting Sigmund Freud, Breton insists on humor's ability to momentarily liberate the listener from his or her cares, be it with a crude joke or a witty observation. For both Baudelaire and Rimbaud, he continues, black humor is associated with emanation and explosion, neither one of which really describes "Cidade adormecida." Instead of gradually building up steam and ending with a brilliant punch line, the latter emits a constant stream of ridicule and satire.

Henrique Risques Pereira

Not much is known about Risques Pereira, who besides being a poet was also an artist and a civil engineer. Associated with the second wave of Portuguese Surrealism, he signed some of the group's most important manifestos, letters, and other documents. Perfecto E. Cuadrado calls him "[uma] cometa dos maiores do firmamento surrealista português" ("one of the major comets in the Portuguese Surrealist firmament")[9]. Like a celestial visitor he appeared out of nowhere, and like the latter he disappeared just as quickly. A close friend of António Maria Lisboa, the two collaborated to produce various manifestos and poetic texts. Following his friend's death in 1953, Risques Pereira abandoned his art and concentrated entirely on engineering. One of his best known poems is entitled "Um Gato partiu a aventura" ("A Cat Set Off on an Adventure"), which was published in 1949.[10]

As palavras de vidro que tu depões em teus seios, para me ofereceres,
    raspam estridentes na camada imarcescível dos meus olhos;
Caem e eu sonho para espalhar plumas nos espaços;
Trago na mão esquerda, hermética, fechada duramente, as delicadas
    linhas epidérmicas,
Leio nesse rendilhado de sensações o roteiro da minha viagem livre,
    o meu voo solitário, que eu inicio saltando dos telhados para as
    janelas;
É na abstracção hipnótica do rosa íris que eu te vejo acompanhar a
    estranha aventura dum albatroz,
e é ao cair da noite que eu aceno longamente os meus braços;
É na harmoniosa vibração azul que eu transmito o Sol vermelho do
    poente e da tristeza,
e, quando as minhas mãos se transformam em pérolas puras, os teus
    olhos gelam para serem os gigantes e a noite;

(The words of glass you offer me on your breasts scrape shrilly against
    the vivid layer of my eyes;
They fall and I dream of spreading feathers in the spaces;
I bring in my left hand, hermetic, tightly closed, delicate epidermal
    lines,
I read in this tracery of sensations the script of my free trip, my lonely
    flight, that I begin by jumping from the rooftops to the windows;
In the hypnotic abstraction of the pink iris I see you accompanying the
    strange adventure of an albatross,
and I wave my arms for a long time at dusk;

In the harmonious blue vibration I transmit the red Sun in the sunset
　　and the sadness,
and when my hands become pure pearls, your eyes freeze in order to
　　become giants and the night;)

What makes this poem so challenging is that it lacks a coherent narrative. The text consists of approximately a dozen discrete parts that have little or nothing to do with each other. Although the cat appears briefly at the beginning, the middle, and the end, it provides no appreciable continuity. On the contrary, its function appears to be largely thematic. The explanation for the work's fragmentary structure stems from the manner in which it was composed—section by individual section. Discussing André Breton's discovery of psychic automatism, Cesariny cites the latter's identification of *Liberdade* ("Freedom") as Surrealism's driving force and his conviction that "o automatismo preside a toda a grande inspiração poética" ("automatism presides over every great poetic inspiration").[11] Indeed, as the present poem demonstrates, the two concepts are closely interrelated. Risques Pereira first evokes liberty in the fourth line, which refers to his forthcoming "viagem livre"—"free" in the sense that the trip will be unconstrained by reality or logic. Fiercely committed to freedom in any form, he chose the Surrealist style that would grant him the most leeway: automatic writing. In the absence of conscious control, as Derek Harris remarks in another context, "the words themselves appear to produce the text and to be in control of the development of the text."[12] Breton makes essentially the same point himself in *Point du jour*.[13]

In practice, the poet seems to have written a sentence or two, paused for a moment, and then continued. Among other things, this accounts for the poem's continual change of subject and its basically additive style. The text is characterized by what might be called *adflatus interruptus* ("interrupted inspiration"). By the time Risques Pereira resumes writing again, he needs to tap a new unconscious vein. Obeying an initial, erotic impulse, he seizes on the marvelous image of glass words, which he places on his female companion's bare breasts. When they eventually fall off, he replaces them with feathers and lustfully massages them with his fingers (or wishes he could). The scraping of the glass against his eyes may represent an unconscious attempt at self-censorship. The next scene transforms the poet into a fortune teller who, perversely, reads the lines in his own hand instead of his client's. Presumably they advise him to emulate the cat in the title because he immediately begins climbing over the rooftops. The next few lines are dominated by mysterious actions and random colors. Pink gives way to blue and then to red as the earlier woman makes a brief appearance with an albatross. Although the latter is a sign of good luck to sailors, it represents bad luck in Coleridge's "The Rime of the Ancient Mariner." Signaling that he is about ready to lower the celestial boom, the poet balances the sun on the horizon and watches it descend into the ocean. Since sunset is traditionally associated with death, he finds himself overcome with sadness. Unexpectedly, a frenzy of metamorphosis takes place as soon as the sun disappears.

> Livre um gato desliza pela goteira escura da cidade,
> livre uma pequena ilha nasce no ponto ignorado do Oceano,
> livres as ondas escorregam na superfície marinha,
> livres os pássaros e os cavalos na noite da lua encantada,
> livre eu chamo-te dos cumes das serras,
> livres as ondas os cavalos e os pássaros;
>
> (Free a cat slips through the city's dark gutter,
> free a small island is born in an unknown spot in the Ocean,
> free waves slip on the surface of the sea,
> free birds and horses in the night of the enchanted moon,
> free I summon you from the mountain summits,
> free the waves the horses and the birds;)

The central stanza celebrates the overriding principle of freedom, which, as we have seen, is the key to the Surrealist enterprise. Although the litany is not extensive, it touches on some of the more significant kinds of liberty. Despite its association with human beings, the cat is free because it is essentially independent. The island is free, in turn, because it has had the good luck to remain undiscovered. Since no one is aware of its existence, no one can harvest its coconuts or drop a hydrogen bomb on it. The waves are free because it is physically impossible to contain or restrain them. They arise at the whim of the wind and the tides and disappear just as readily. Although Risques Pereira includes birds and horses in the list, he is obviously not thinking of chickens or plow horses but rather of their wild cousins. In their undomesticated state, both animals are free to live their lives as nature intended.

Although they vary widely in every other respect, all the poems cited in this chapter have one thing in common: their subjects are free from human interference. They are free because they are either independent, undiscovered, impossible to control, or wholly natural. To a considerable extent, these four principles describe the unconscious, whose existence was also unsuspected until relatively recently. Because it is impervious to human tampering, the unconscious possesses an oracular purity all of its own.

> Abandono a terra da ilha para viver nos abismos, nas cidades que crescem, nos beijos que enchem o vento,
> e oiço a imensa máquina que esmaga o ferro da estrada construída, a cortina sedosa dos teus cabelos, eu e tu,
> e vejo o cego que avança com os braços levantados para o mundo incompreensível,
> e liberta os corpos visíveis: os teus lábios, os teus seios, o teu sexo;
> e mães batem às janelas e imploram: LAMA!;
>
> A um canto morre em agonia o primeiro grito;
>
> O gato parte à aventura pelos telhados, pelos vales e pelos Sonhos.
>
> (I abandon the island to live in the abysses, in the growing cities, in the kisses that fill the wind,
> and I hear the immense machine that crushes the road's iron, the silken curtain of your hair, you and I,
> and I see the blind man advancing with his arms raised to the incomprehensible world
> and free your visual attributes: your lips, your breasts, your vagina;

and mothers knock on the windows and implore: LAMA!;

At one corner the first cry dies in agony;

The cat sets out on an adventure over rooftops, valleys and Dreams.)

Rather than continue to live an isolated existence, the poet chooses to leave his metaphorical island in order to engage with humanity, symbolized by the expanding cities, and to experience the delights of erotic love, which he unabashedly describes. Although the blind man confronting "o mundo incompreensível" symbolizes the pitiful human condition, the latter is occasionally alleviated by a few momentary joys. While mothers knock on windows and utter agonizing cries, the symbolic cat returns and sets off on a new adventure. Since life is harsh and the future uncertain, the poet insinuates, our most precious possession is freedom.

António Maria Lisboa

Perhaps because some of their poems have been set to music, two Surrealist poets have become surprisingly popular in Portugal. One of these is António Maria Lisboa, who created a small Surrealist group in 1947 that included Pedro Oom, Henrique Risques Pereira, and Fogueiredo Sobral. The other is Mário Cesariny, the fourth member of the group, who was also a talented Surrealist artist. Together with Lisboa, he composed an important manifesto entitled *Afixação Proibida (Post No Bills)*, which initiated the second wave of Surrealism in Portugal. In the opinion of Natalia Correia, a prominent poet and activist, these two men represent "the spirit and soul" of Portuguese Surrealism.[14] Entitled "Comutador" ("Switch"), the following poem by Lisboa was published in 1952.[15]

Ergo-me de ti no zimbório
de folhas na penedia do castelo medieval
de limos na umidade da praia
de cristais entre os rochedos do Cabo Horn.

Caminho de gelo na floresta
de sôfrego na vastidão do deserto
de louco na brancura do hospicio.

Eu abismo, eu cratero
inclinei-me e vi um espectáculo caprichoso: uma unha branca
una unha branca a viver assim despreocupada

(I rise from you in the leafy dome
on the Medieval castle's mossy rock
in the humidity of the crystal beach
between the Cape Horn cliffs.

Path of ice in hunger's forest
in the desert vastness
of madness in the asylum's whiteness.

I abyss, I crater
I bent over and saw a whimsical spectacle:
a white finger nail a white finger nail living
so carefree.)

Like the title of the previous work by Mário-Henrique Leiria, that of the present composition is totally gratuitous. Nothing in the entire poem has anything to do with a *comutador* except the electric fan, which can presumably be turned on and off. However the fan is a silent witness rather than an active participant, which is why it is only mentioned in passing. Although false titles were more typical of Dada than of Surrealism, they clearly appealed to Lisboa and his friends. If elaboration and repetition are the two structures by which a Surrealist poem advances, as Richard Stamelman argues, the first two stanzas illustrate the former principle.[16] In both cases, apparently random nouns are linked together by a seemingly endless series of prepositions. As soon as the poet completes a prepositional phrase, he tacks on another one and then another one again.

At first glance, the initial stanza strikes the reader as highly romantic. It possesses three of the genre's traditional hallmarks: Lisboa and his lady friend live (1) in a leafy bower (2) near a Medieval castle (3) on a craggy peak. In addition, they have a beach made of crystals instead of sand at their disposal. All this would be very attractive were it not for one problem: they live near Cape Horn, at the southern tip of South America, which is famous for its horrendous weather. According to one source, there are 278 days of rainfall in a typical year and seventy days of snow. In contrast to the events in the first stanza, which seem to suggest that the season is summer, the second stanza clearly takes place in winter. Perhaps this finally explains the poem's enigmatic title. The transition between the two seasons is unexpected and abrupt—as if someone had flicked a magic switch. Wearing white robes like mental patients, hunger and madness converge in the vast monotony of the icy landscape. The cold is so pervasive that even their fingernails have turned white.

OGIVA-BORBOLETA
Arco-de-Cor caldo muito triste
Casulo de quem ninguém falou
Teia-de-Aranha exposta à loucura e ao tempo
Andorinha-Azul de chapéu mole e baratas na cama
VENTOINHA

A CONS
TRU
ÇÃO DOS
POEMAS

é como matar muitas pulgas com unhas de oiro azul
é como amar formigas brancas obsessivamente junto ao peito
olhar uma paisagem em frente e ver um abismo
ver o abismo e sentir uma pedrada nas costas
sentir a pedrada e imaginar-se sem pensar de repente.

NUM TÚMULO EXAUSTIVO.

(GOTHICARCH-BUTTERFLY
Arch-of-Color very sad broth
Cocoon about which nobody spoke

Spider-Web exposed to madness and time
soft hat's Blue-Swallow and cockroaches in the bed
ELECTRIC FAN

THE CON-
STRUCT-ION
OF
POEMS

it's like killing lots of fleas with blue and gold finger nails
it's like loving white ants obsessively close to one's chest
looking at a landscape in front and seeing an abyss
seeing the abyss and feeling a rock in your back
feeling the rock and imagining yourself without suddenly thinking

IN THE EXHAUSTING TOMB.)

Suddenly the mysterious hand flicks the climate switch again, and the weather improves dramatically. The allusion to butterflies and swallows suggests that it may even be springtime and thus that the cocoon may be about ready to open. Although much of the fourth stanza is difficult to decipher, the reference to a Gothic arch seems to indicate that the scene is much the same as in the first stanza. Once again, Lisboa finds himself by the same medieval castle on the same craggy peak. Whether the leafy bower and his lady friend are still there is impossible to say. That he compares one of the castle's Gothic arches to a butterfly, however, suggests that the edifice has several stained glass windows. Indeed, this is confirmed by the reference to the "Arco-de-Cor" in the next line. Instead of an architectural element the arch represents a stylistic feature. It is designed to serve as a window frame not as a load-bearing structure.

Although the cocoon is obviously related to the butterfly, the spider web and the cockroaches are associated with the theme of madness, which was introduced previously. Interestingly, the poem's last seven lines are devoted to an entirely different subject—to the creation of poetry. Why Lisboa places this discussion in an exhausting (or exhaustive) tomb is far from clear. Nevertheless, each of the five central lines contains a provocative simile describing the creative process from an unusual point of view. The first one compares the process to trying to kill fleas, which are hard to locate and extremely agile. Like them, the right words are also difficult to find and easily elude capture. For this reason, poets explore a number of different possibilities before settling on a final choice. However, once they manage to find the right words, the next line continues, the latter invade their hearts like white ants (termites) and influence their future actions. By contrast, the third line evokes the poet's ability to perceive the truth of things while ignoring their superficial aspects. Line 4 describes the creative artist's balancing act not as walking a tightrope, but as inching along on a narrow mountain ledge. The fifth line, finally, compares the creative act to a skilled mountain climber. Disregarding the danger all around him, he lets it stimulate his senses and his imagination.

Early in the First Manifesto, Breton proclaims: "Le seul mot de liberté est tout ce qui m'exalte encore" ("The word 'liberty' is the only thing that continues to excite me").[17] Inspired by this pronouncement, like Risques Pereira in the preceding poem, Lisboa values Surrealist freedom above everything else. Not only does he refuse to give his text a unifying theme, but he also makes no attempt to satisfy the reader's thirst for meaning. Although this idiosyncratic approach has its obvious pitfalls, it provides glimpses of a Surreal world in which miscellaneous snapshots are arranged to form a rudimentary mosaic. In the last analysis, "Comutador" is not a bad poem so much as an unsuccessful one. Not every automatic text turns out to be a success.

Mário Cesariny

Natalia Correia speaks for most connoisseurs of Portuguese poetry when she calls Mário Cesariny "the most significant poet of the Surrealist impact."[18] Not only is he one of the most popular Surrealist poets, but he has arguably done more than anyone else to advance the movement's cause in Portugal. Technically, his poetry is characterized by continual experimentation and innovation. As Vicente Araguas observes, "recurre a inventarios caóticos, neologismos, diálogos inconexos y tambien, pero con moderación, a ejercicios automatistas" ("he utilizes chaotic inventories, neologisms, disconnected dialogues, and—with moderation—automatic exercises").[19] Although much of his poetry is perhaps best described simply as "avant-garde," when the Surrealist muse strikes him he responds with great passion and remarkable inventiveness. This describes one of his most famous poems, for example, which is entitled "You Are Welcome to Elsinore."[20]

> Entre nós e as palavras há metal fundente
> entre nós e as palavras ha hélices que andam
> e podem dar-nos morte violar-nos tirar
> do mais fundo de nós o mais útil segredo
> entre nós e as palavras ha perfis ardentes
> espaços cheios de gente de costas
> altas flores venenosas portas por abrir
> e escados e ponteiros e crianças sentadas
> à espera do seu tempo e do seu precipício

> (Between us and words there is molten metal
> between us and words there are revolving propellers
> that can kill us violate us extract
> the most useful secret from our deepest recesses
> between us and words there are burning profiles
> spaces filled with people seen from the back
> tall venomous flowers closed doors
> and stairs and clock hands and seated children
> awaiting their time and their precipice)

If the English title seems familiar to some readers, that's because it comes from *Hamlet* (Act 2, Scene 2), when the Danish prince welcomes his childhood friends Rosencranz and Guildenstern. Hamlet actually says "*Gentlemen*, welcome to Elsinore," but Cesariny expands the greeting to include everyone. As Richard Zenith notes, the poem is a scathing indictment of Portugal under António Salazar, who ruled the country from approximately 1932 to 1970. Infecting daily life, Zenith explains, his fascist dictatorship stood "like an impassable wall 'between us and words,' making communication, poetry, and love's free expression all but impossible."[21] And indeed the first few lines seem to complain about precisely that. Not only was there widespread censorship under Salazar, but free speech was suppressed as well. There were no political parties, and simply toasting freedom was enough to get you thrown in jail.[22] As irksome as this was to the general population, it especially infuriated the Surrealists for whom, as we have seen, freedom was sacred.

Before long, however, one discovers that the stanza is only indirectly concerned with freedom of expression. Cesariny's actual target is the systematic practice of torture by the secret police, who operated openly without fear of the law. Consisting of some three thousand individuals, PIDE was largely responsible for propping up Salazar's corrupt government.[23] Horrific stories abound of people being brutally beaten, burned with electricity, or even thrown out of fourth story windows.[24] The molten metal, revolving propellers, and burning profiles in the poem probably refer to similar experiences, while the last four lines evoke the anonymous beaurocracy that facilitated these abuses. Ultimately, therefore, the wall between "nós et as palavras" is constituted by fear, the fear of being arrested and tortured. In view of this situation, the poem's title turns out to be bitterly ironic. Welcome to our police state, Cesariny seems to say, where you can be thrown in jail without a trial, abused, and tortured.

> Ao longo da muralha que habitamos
> há palavras de vida há palavras de morte
> há palavras imensas, que esperam por nós
> e outras, frageis, que deixaram de esperar
> há palavras acesas como barcos
> e há palavras homens, palavras que guardam
> o seu segredo e a sua posição
>
> (Along the wall where we live
> there are words of life there are words of death
> there are immense words that are waiting for us

and others, fragile, that have given up waiting
there are words lit up like boats
and there are masculine words, words that hide
their secret and their location)

If the first stanza is about the difficulty of communicating during an oppressive regime, the second is about the difficulty of writing poetry under the same circumstances. This time Cesariny is separated from words by an actual wall—presumably belonging to Kronborg Castle overlooking the stretch of water between Denmark and Sweden, where Hamlet lived before him. Indeed, this identification is confirmed in the following stanza. The words in question are as inaccessible as before but this time for a different reason. Cesariny is having trouble finding the right words to use in a poem because they are on the other side of the wall where he can't reach them. One wonders if they are planted in a row like flowers. The wall itself not only represents a physical barrier, in any case, but also serves as a convenient metaphor for a mental block. Although he is not able to see the words, he is able to describe them from previous visits. Indeed, the catalogue takes up most of the stanza. There are marvelous words for every conceivable occasion—from life to death and every stage in between. Some of them are described as if they were human, others as if they were simply alive, and still others as if they were physical objects. Representing the endless possibilities of language, they remind us that poetry is capable of some amazing things.

Entre nós e as palavras, surdamente,
as mãos e as paredes de Elsenor
E há palavras e nocturnas palavras gemidos
palavras que nos sobem ilegíveis à boca
palavras diamantes palavras nunca escritas
palabras impossíveis de escrever
por não termos connosco cordas de violinos
nem todo o sangue do mundo nem todo o amplexo do ar
e os braços dos amantes escrevem muito alto
muito além do azul onde oxidados morrem

palavras maternais só sombra so soluço
só espasmos só amor só solidão desfeita

Entre nós e as palavras, os emparedados
e entre nós e as palavras, o nosso dever falar

(Between us and words, softly,
the hands and the walls of Elsinore
And there are words and nocturnal moaning words
illegible words that rise to one's mouth
diamond words unwritten words
words impossible to write
because we don't have any violin strings
nor all the blood in the world nor all the air's embrace
and lovers' arms write high overhead
very far from the blue where they oxidize and die
maternal words only shadow only sobs
only spasms only love only broken solitude

Between us and words, those who are walled in
between us and words, our duty to speak)

The third stanza continues the list of marvelous words that Cesariny would like to obtain, many of which suffer from their own problems. Although diamond words seem promising, words that are illegible, unwritten, or impossible to write are not worth bothering with. The negative cause and effect relationship between the impossible words and violin strings, blood, and air is puzzling to say the least. The intensifier "todo" only makes things worse. Although the lovers are very far away, their words are just as unsuccessful. Nor do maternal words experience any success. The two-line conclusion repeats the initial opposition between "nós" and "palavras" and, echoing Hamlet's own words, compares the castle to a prison. The latter, in turn, serves as a metaphor for Portuguese society, where common liberties are sharply restricted. While acknowledging the dangers inherent in speaking out, finally, Cesariny insists that it is every citizen's duty to do exactly that.

Notes

1   José-Augusto França, "Le Surréalisme portugais," *Mélusine*, No. 7 (1985), p. 267. For a brief history of the movement, see pp. 267–74.

2   Mário Cesariny, *A intervenção surrealista* (Lisbon: Assírio and Alvim, 1997), p. 9.

3   Antonio Tabucchi, *A parola interdetta. Poeti surrealisti portoghesi* (Turin: Einaudi, 1971), p. 73.

4   Reproduced in Cesariny, *A intervenção surrealista*, p. 205.

5   Michael Riffaterre, *Text Production* (New York: Columbia University Press, 1983), pp. 221–2.

6   Alfredo Margarido and Carlos Eurico da Costa, eds., *Diez Jovens Poetas Portugueses* (Rio de Janeiro: Ministerio da Educação e Cultura do Brasil, 1954). Reproduced in ibid, pp. 206–7.

7   *Les Pensées d' André Breton*, ed. Henri Béhar et al. (Lausanne: L'Age d'Homme, 1988), p. 175.

8   André Breton, "Paratonnerre," in *Anthologie de l'humour noir, Oeuvres complètes*, Vol. 2, ed. Marguerite Bonnet et al. (Paris: Gallimard, 1992), p. 873.

9   Perfecto E. Cuadrado, "Risques Pereira: uma apresentação cordial," *Revista de Cultura*, No. 68 (April 2009), n. p.

10 Cesariny, *A intervenção surrealista*, pp. 117–18.

11 Mário Cesariny, preface to *Antologia do cadáver esquisito* (1961), repr. in *A intervenção surrealista*, p. 276.

12 Derek Harris, *Metal Butterflies and Poisonous Lights: The Language of Surrealism in Lorca, Alberti, Cernuda, and Aleixandre* (Arnecroach: La Sirena, 1998), p. 76.

13 Breton, *Oeuvres complètes*, Vol. 2, p. 298.

14 Natalia Correia, "Surrealism in Portuguese Poetry," ed. George Monteiro, *Portuguese Studies*, Vol. 31, No. 1 (2015), p. 129.

15 António Maria Lisboa, *Poesia de António Maria Lisboa* (Lisbon: Assirio & Alvim, 1980).

16 Richard Stamelman, "The Relational Structure of Surrealist Poetry," *Dada/Surrealism*, No. 6 (1976), p. 73.

17 Breton, *Oeuvres complètes*, Vol. 1, p. 312.

18 Correia, "Surrealism in Portuguese Poetry," p. 130.

19 Vicente Araguas, 'Introducción,' in *Mario Cesariny, Antología poética*, ed. Vicente Araguas (Visor: Madrid, 2004), p. 8.

20 Ibid., pp. 86–9.

21 Richard Zenith, "Mario Cesariny deVasconcelos." https://www. poetryinternationalweb.net/pi/site/poet/item/4653/11/Mario-Cesariny-de-Vasconcelos

22 https://www.amnestyusa.org/faqs/how-did-amnesty-international-start/

23 Richard Eder, "Getting Even with Portugal's Gestapo," *New York Times*, May 5, 1974, p. 5.

24 See, for example, *Prison Conditions in Portugal: Conditions of Detention of Political Prisoners* (London: Amnesty International, 1965), pp. 15–24.

9

Octavio Paz

Born and raised in Mexico City, Octavio Paz was a career diplomat who received the Nobel Prize in Literature in 1990 "for impassioned writing with wide horizons, characterized by sensuous intelligence and humanistic integrity." Encouraged by Pablo Neruda, he published an avant-garde journal called *Barandal (Balustrade)* in 1931 and his first book of poetry, *Luna silvestre (Rustic Moon)* in 1933. Paz first became aware of Surrealism in 1936, when he came across an article by André Breton in the June issue of *Minotaure* that, in his words, "me abrió las puertas de la poesía moderna" ("opened the doors of modern poetry for me").[1] Ten years later, he was able to thank the author in person while serving as cultural attaché to the Mexican embassy in Paris. Assigned to the French capital from 1946 to 1950, Paz renewed his acquaintance with Benjamin Péret, whom he had met in Spain in 1937 at the Second International Congress of Anti-Fascist Writers. Péret introduced him in turn to Breton, who invited him to participate in various Surrealist activities and with whom he developed a close relationship. "Breton fut pour lui une sorte de boussole," Lourdes Andráde explains; "le surréalisme offrit à Paz le contexte nécessaire pour faire surgir une série d'inquietudes personnelles, l'aida à voir plus clair en lui-meme et à se liberer de toute sorte de préjugés" ("Breton was a sort of compass for him ... Surrealism offered Paz the necessary context to tap into a series of personal anxieties, helped him to see more clearly in himself and to free himself from various prejudices").[2]

Donald Sutherland theorizes that Paz was able to embrace Surrealist irrationality easily because of his familiarity with Aztec history and the Catholic Church.[3] Be that as it may, Saul Yurkievich notes that Surrealist influence became more flagrant in his work following his experience in Paris, beginning with *Aguila o sol* (*Eagle or Sun*) composed during 1949–50.[4] Like the Surrealists, he adds, Paz sought to establish the primacy of poetry both as a liberating force and as a means of accessing *le point suprême*, where all antinomies finally fuse together.[5] To this end, he adopted Surrealist practices such as objective chance, psychic automatism, simulated mental illness, *humour noir*, verbal violence, and word games. "Coincide con Breton en considerar al deseo, a la pasión amorosa no sólo como conciliador de los contrarios, sino como principio de interpretación del universo" ("He coincides with Breton in considering desire, amorous passion, not only as a mediator of opposites but also as an interpretive principle of the universe"). As a result, according to both Diego Martínez Torrón and Ricardo Gullón, Paz's Surrealism resembles the French version more closely than that of any other poet writing in Spanish.[6] For that matter, Martínez adds, Paz and Breton are more faithful to Surrealism's basic principles than anyone else.[7] Thanks to the Mexican poet, a surprising number of readers and writers of Spanish possess a good knowledge of what constitutes Surrealism.[8]

Unlike many of the Surrealist poets in Spain (including Catalonia), Paz freely acknowledged his debt to the French movement. Writing in *La Gaceta* in 1959, for example, he declared: "La influencia del surrealismo fue decisivo para mi, pero más bien como actitud ... He encontrado ... la idea de rebelión, la idea del amor y de la libertad en relación con el hombre." ("The influence of Surrealism was decisive for me, but rather as an attitude ... I encountered ... the idea of rebellion, the ideas of love and freedom in relation to man").[9] As Jason Wilson points out, Surrealism—which is to say Surrealist poetry—became Paz's long-awaited alternative to his earlier commitment to political revolution.[10] Although his rebellion assumed a radically different form, it was far more subversive than before. While it sought to infiltrate the enemy's lines and to overthrow the existing order, no violence or unwanted force was required.

Like Breton before him, Paz proposed to completely transform not just modern society but also reality itself. His ultimate goal was to "abolir esta realidad que una civilización vacilante nos ha impuesto como la sola y única verdadera" ("abolish this reality that a hesitant civilization has imposed upon us as the one and only truth").[11] Or rather, he sought to transform the way in which we perceive reality, which is obscured by the veneer of civilization. Instead of the cultural reality that surrounds us from the moment we are born, Paz strove to discover the absolute reality that precedes it—a reality uncontaminated by human presence. "En ese momento paradisiaco," he explains, "un instante y para siempre, somos de verdad" ("In this paradisiac moment, we experience a moment of truth that is eternal").[12] Like Marcel Proust's *moment privilegé* in *A la recherche du temps perdu* (*In Search of Lost Time*), the experience is brief but euphoric. Like Proust's narrator, the Surrealist manages to retrieve a precious moment from the past. Together with the concepts of love and freedom, which are evoked in the same sentence, poetry forms the triple axis of the Surrealist enterprise. Ultimately, each of these three entities is equivalent to the other two. "Hablar de la libertad," Paz declares, "será hablar de la poesía y del amor" ("Speaking of freedom is the same as speaking of poetry or love").[13]

Writing in 1989, Manuel Durán discerned three stages in Paz's poetic evolution: (1) an initial period extending from his earliest poems to "El cantáro rota" ("The Broken Water Jar") (1949), (2) a transitional period from "Himno entre ruinas" ("Hymn Among Ruins") (1948) to "Piedra de sol" ("Sun Stone") (1957), and (3) a final period beginning in 1962 in which his poetry underwent "una transformación completa."[14] Writing thirty years later, by which time Paz had published a half dozen more books of poetry, Alberto Ruy Sánchez divided the same period into four stages and added a subsequent stage: "Emergence of the Poet" (1914–43), "Toward the Unexpected" (1944–58), "The Fleeting Paradise" (1959–70), "The New Violent Season" (1971–90), and "The Search for the Present" (1990–8).[15] Published in *Orígenes* in 1947, "Agua

nocturna" ("Nocturnal Water") belongs to the first group identified by
Durán and the second distinguished by Ruy Sánchez.[16]

La noche de ojos de caballo que tiemblan en la noche,
la noche de ojos de agua en el campo dormido,
está en tus ojos de caballo que tiembla,
está en tus ojos de agua secreta.

Ojos de agua de sombra,
ojos de agua de pozo,
ojos de agua de sueño.

El silencio y la soledad,
como dos pequeños animales a quienes guía la luna,
beben en esos ojos,
beben en esas aguas.

Si abres los ojos,
se abre la noche de puertas de musgo,
se abre el reino secreto del agua
que mana del centro de la noche.

Y si los cierras,
un río te inunda por dentro,
avanza, te haré oscura:
la noche moja riberas en tu alma.

(Night with the eyes of a trembling horse in the night,
night with eyes of water in the sleeping field,
is in your trembling horse eyes,
is in your secret water eyes.

Shadow-water eyes,
well water eyes,
dream water eyes.

Silence and solitude,
like two tiny animals guided by the moon,
drink from your eyes,
drink from your waters.

If you open your eyes,
night opens its mossy doors,
water opens its secret kingdom
flowing from the center of the night.

And if you close them,
a river floods you from within,
advances, darkens you:
night laps against shores of your soul.)

Of all the tropes available for poets to utilize, Ovidio C. Fuente remarks, Paz is particularly drawn to symbolism, which plays a predominate role in his poetry.[17] Ramón Xirau seconds this statement and adds that the remaining tropes—in particular metaphors and paradoxes—serve as "puntos de partida para llegar a un mundo simbólico" ("points of departure in order to arrive at a symbolic world").[18] In his attraction to symbolic constructions, Paz resembles García Lorca—and to a lesser extent Neruda—more than any of the French Surrealists, who generally avoid symbolism. The problem with symbols, however, is that unlike metaphors they are often open-ended. Whereas the first term in a symbolic construction is fixed, the second term is completely flexible (at least in theory). Whereas the first is stated explicitly, the second is merely implicit—whence the difficulty of decoding private symbolism like that in "Agua nocturna." In the absence of a key, the reader is faced with a serious impasse. For a particular symbol to work, it must be appropriated from a common pool of symbols, so that it is immediately recognizable. For this reason, symbols are generally drawn from broad cultural repositories such as religion, mythology, or literature.

Despite its private symbolism, "Agua nocturna" is a surprisingly powerful poem. More than anything, this is due to the important role allotted to repetition and parallelism which, as Richard Stammelman notes, "give structure to [its] dynamic discontinuous movement."[19] Paz never repeats a line precisely but changes a word or two each time, so that the text appears to advance line by line. "Drink from your eyes" is followed by "drink from your water" and so forth. Quickly acquiring the character of an incantation, the poem increases in intensity until it is brought up short by the final four lines, which contain no repetition at all. Consisting of five brief stanzas, "Agua nocturna" prefers to communicate indirectly via implication, insinuation, and inference. The composition is basically structured around three images: "noche," "ojos," and "agua," which Paz moves around like checkers on a checkerboard. As he explores different combinations and permutations, they recur again and again in different contexts. Besides the reader's conscious associations, most of the images are meant to awaken unconscious associations as well. The first line, which is enclosed by a pleonasm, emphasizes the association between the night and an anonymous horse. The fact that the animal is trembling adds to the eerie experience. The second line associates the night with water in a field, which could be either good or bad depending on the circumstances.

Although the subject of "Agua nocturna" appears initially to be the night, which is depicted as the repository of hidden forces, the poem turns out to be a portrait of a mysterious woman. The latter is evoked indirectly via her fascinating eyes which, according to the familiar saying, are a window on her soul. It is not their beauty that fascinates Paz, however, but rather the fact that they mirror the first two lines. Not only are her eyes full of apprehension, but they are also hiding something. One wonders who the woman could possibly be. The fact that the poet simply calls her "tú" is not especially helpful. There seem to be three possibilities: she could be someone Paz knows personally, women in general, or an example of a Surrealist woman. The fact that she is associated with silence and solitude in the third stanza rules out the second option unless she is a deaf mute or a nun. By contrast, the last two stanzas reveal that a mysterious connection exists between her, the night, and the water, all three of which are reunited in the fourth stanza. This fact suggests in turn that she is a Surrealist woman—either an imaginary one or a personal acquaintance.

Although Xavière Gauthier argues that "la femme surréaliste est une forgerie des mâles ("the Surrealist woman is a forgery perpetuated by males"), in actuality there is no single Surrealist woman, only a number of different models for Paz to consider.[20] She herself has identified at least ten versions, including *la femme-fleur, la femme-terre, la femme insaisissable, la voyante,* and *la femme fatale* (the "flower-woman," the "earth-woman," the "inscrutable woman," the "clairvoyant woman," and the "deadly woman"). However, none of them describe the woman in "Agua nocturna," who is closely related to night and to water in particular. Since the night symbolizes both the feminine principle and the unconscious, according to J. E. Cirlot, it is her natural dominion.[21] The same thing is true of water, which is feminine according to Paz himself, and is also a universal symbol of life.[22] The poem concludes with two stanzas that explore the intimate relationship between the woman, the night, and the water. Simply by opening or closing her eyes, she is able to control the sluice gates that govern the flow of both natural phenomena. This gift is shared by Surrealist women in general, Paz observes elsewhere, who are able to "abr[ir] las puertas de la noche y de la verdad" ("to open the gates of the night and of truth").[23] That this is an exclusively feminine talent is underlined by the sexual symbolism in the final two stanzas. Whereas the vaginal imagery in the first emphasizes the woman's connection to fertility and birth, the orgasmic imagery in the second depicts her as someone who fully participates in the sexual universe.

"El prisonero"

The following year, while he was visiting Avignon, Paz composed a poem entitled "El prisonero," which was devoted to the Marquis de Sade.[24] Indeed, he seems to have traveled to the former papal city specifically to visit Sade's residence, the Château de Lacoste, which is not far away. While his choice of subject matter was somewhat surprising, it was not entirely without precedent. In 1909, Apollinaire had brought new attention to bear on the "divine marquis" by editing a collection of his works. Marveling at Sade's perverse inventiveness in the scholarly introduction, he called him "[l]'esprit le plus libre qui ait encore existé" ("the freest spirit who ever existed").[25] Following in his footsteps, Breton and the Surrealists considered Sade to be an important precursor. What they admired about him, Marguerite Bonnet explains, was that "[il] a libéré l'homme des préjugés, des inhibitions nées de l'éducation religieuse, en exaltant la liberté sexuelle" ("[he] liberated mankind from prejudices and inhibitions stemming from a religious education, while exalting sexual freedom").[26] One of the most obvious signs of Breton's admiration is an untitled eulogy he published in 1934. Beginning with the verse "Le Marquis de Sade a regagné l'intérieur du volcan en éruption" ("The Marquis de Sade Returned Inside the Erupting Volcano"), it appears to have impelled Paz to write the present poem thirteen years later.[27]

In Jason Wilson's opinion, which he develops in more detail elsewhere, Paz deviates from Surrealist orthodoxy (de Sade as hero, as mentor of revolt) "in order to correct Breton's mistaken admiration for such an inhuman person."[28] Unfortunately, several things are wrong with this statement. For one thing, Wilson confuses the horrific acts described in Sade's novels with the much tamer actions he performed in real life. Like Breton, moreover, Paz admired Sade as a proponent of absolute freedom, unrestrained by morality, religion, or law. Finally, since Paz practically idolized the Surrealist leader, he would never have presumed to correct any of his statements. Although the Mexican poet's first reaction to Sade's writings was one of "asombro y horror, curiosidad y disgusto" ("astonishment and horror, curiosity and disgust"), it also included an element of "admiración y reconocimiento" ("admiration and recognition").[29] Ultimately, Paz perceived that there was much more to Sade's *oeuvre* than met the pornographic eye. Instead of rejecting the latter's role as a Surrealist hero, he simply concentrated on his equally heroic role as a materialist philosopher. The following poem and two later essays focus on philosophical aspects of Sade's work and their implications for the human condition.[30] Since the Marquis spent a large portion of his life confined to various prisons, an insane asylum, and his chateau in Provence, he chose to entitle the poem "El prisonero."

> à fin que ... les traces de ma tombe disparaissent de
> dessus la surface de la terre comme je me flatte que
> ma mémoires'éffacera de l'esprit des hommes ...
> Testamento de Sade.

No te has desvanecido
Las letras de tu nombre son todavía una cicatriz que no se cierra
un tatuaje de infamia sobre ciertas frentes.

Cometa de pesada y rutilante cola dialéctica,
atraviesas el siglo diecinueve con una granada de verdad en la mano
y estallas al llegar a nuestra época.

Máscara que sonrie bajo un antifaz rosa
hecho de párpados de ajusticiado,
verdad partida en mil pedazos de fuego,
¿ que quieren decir todos esos fragmentos gigantescos,
esa manada de icebergs que zarpan de tu pluma y en alta mar enfilan
    hacia costa sin nombre,
esos delicados instrumentos de cirugía para extirpar el chancro de
    Dios,
esos aullidos que interrumpen tus majestuosos razonamientos de
    elefante,
esas repeticiones atroces de relojeria descompuesta,
toda esa oxidada herramienta de tortura?

El erudito y el poeta
el sabio, el literato, el enamorado,
el maníaco y el que sueña en la abolición de nuestra siniestra realidad,
disputan como perros sobre los restos de tu obra.
Tú, que estabas contra todos,
eres ahora un nombre, un jefe, una bandera.

> ("so that … all traces of my grave vanish from the
> face of the earth as I flatter myself that my memory
> will be obliterated in men's minds …"
>   —Sade's last will and testament.

You have not vanished.
The letters of your name form a scar that refuses to heal,
a tattoo of infamy on certain foreheads.

Weighty comet with your bright dialectical tail,
You zoom through the nineteenth century holding a grenade,
finally exploding when you reach our era.

Mask that smiles beneath a pink surface,
composed of executed prisoners' eyelids,
truth divided into a thousand flames,
what do all those giant fragments mean?
that pack of icebergs emerging from your pen and heading for nameless
    coasts across the high seas?
those delicate surgical instruments for excising the cancer of God?
those howls interrupting your majestic elephantine thoughts?
those atrocious sounds of broken clockwork?
all those rusty tools of torture?

The intellectual and the poet,
the scholar, the man of letters, the lover,
the maniac and the man dreaming of our sinister reality's destruction,
fight like dogs over your work's last few scraps.
You who despised them all,
are today a name, a leader, and a banner.)

The first four stanzas of "El prisonero" were written in response to the epigraph cited above. Not only have all traces of Sade *not* disappeared from the face of the earth, along with his memory, but the term *sadisme* was attested in French as early as 1834 (in the *Dictionnaire universel*) and was adopted by Richard von Krafft-Ebing, the first sexologist, fifty-eight years later. After that, it was quickly incorporated into the popular lexicon. As Paz declares, the marquis has become "un nombre, un jefe, una bandera." He is famous (or infamous) primarily for deriving sexual pleasure from the infliction of pain—on himself as well as on others. This proclivity is evoked primarily in the first stanza, although there are scattered references to blood elsewhere. The scar that refuses to heal probably refers to Sade's fondness for flagellation, which seems to have been his favorite means of inflicting and receiving pain. It is important, in any case, to differentiate between the historical figure and the author of the horrifying stories that have come down to us. Ironically, apart from his love of whipping, it is tempting to conclude that Sade was basically a nonviolent sadist. For one thing he was imprisoned during most of his adult years and thus rendered powerless. For another, he obtained most of his sexual gratification by frequenting prostitutes, arranging orgies, violating various sexual taboos, and imagining obscene stories to include in his novels. Other favorite activities included masturbation, sodomy, and blasphemy. While his actions in real life were certainly reprehensible, they were not nearly as heinous as those he invented for his books—which is what most people remember. Despite the howls of some flagellants in the third stanza of the poem, Sade never killed anyone or tortured them with surgical instruments. The latter reference is to a scene in *120 Days of Sodom*, where several individuals perform "surgery" on a young woman named Augustine. (The mask made from cadavers' eyelids presumably comes from there as well.) In any case, the fact that Paz's instruments are used to "extirpar el chancro de Dios" means they are basically metaphors. A lifelong atheist and fanatical enemy of Christianity, Sade employed *dialectical* instruments to disprove the existence of God.

Since Sade's works were banned for more than a century by governments all over the world, Paz depicts him as a comet zooming harmlessly over the nineteenth century. Not until the following century, when his writings became more available, did the grenade of truth it was carrying finally detonate. Indeed, his masterpiece *120 Days of Sodom* was published for the very first time in 1904. Among the explosive truths that Sade's comet revealed were the darker side of human nature and the fictitious nature of God. However, as Wilson notes, the true subject of "El prisonero" is not Sade's salacious works but rather his philosophical writings, which continue to attract considerable attention today.[31] Among the intellectuals and scholars evoked by Paz, for example, Colette V. Michael calls Sade "one of the most important figures of the 18th Century." And Alice Laborde believes that he is "as important as Diderot, Rousseau, Voltaire and Montesquieu."[32] The reference to the comet's dialectical tail is puzzling until one realizes that Paz is alluding to a celebrated work entitled *Dialogue entre un prêtre et un moribond* (*Dialogue between a Priest and a Dying Man*) (1782). Instead of repenting his sins, as the priest requests, the man regrets not having satisfied his natural passions more often. Lawrence W. Lynch calls it "a powerful exposition of the moribund's atheism, followed by the destruction of the validity of theology and the degradation of the interviewer."[33] Very much a product of the Enlightenment, Sade was a materialist philosopher who believed in nature, reason, and finite explanations. Paz calls his philosophical writings "icebergs" because they are lucid, precise, and dispassionate.

Inclinado sobre la vida como Saturno sobre sus hijos,
recorres con fija mirada amorosa
los surcos calcinados que dejan el semen, la sangre y la lava.
Los cuerpos, frente a frente como astros feroces,
están hechos de la misma substancia de los soles.
¿Lo que llamamos amor o muerte, libertad o destino,
no se llama catástrofe, no se llama hecatombe?
¿Donde están las fronteras entre espasmo y terremoto,
entre erupción y cohabitación?

Prisionero en tu castillo de cristal de roca
cruzas galerías, cámaras, mazmorras,
vastos patios donde la vid se enrosca a columnas solares,
graciosos cementerios donde danzan los chopos inmóviles.
Muros, objetos, cuerpos te repiten
Todo es espejo!
tu imagen te persigue.

(Bent over life like Saturn over his sons,
you focus your constant loving gaze
on the scorched furrows left by semen, blood, and lava.
Face to face like ferocious stars, our bodies
are made of the same substance as the suns.
What we call love or death, liberty or destiny,
isn't it also called catastrophe or massacre?
Where is the dividing line between spasm and earthquake,
between eruption and orgasm?

Prisoner in your castle of rock crystal
you encounter galleries, rooms, dungeons,
vast patios where grapevines coil around sunny columns,

gracious cemeteries where motionless poplars dance.
Walls, objects, bodies repeat you.
Everything is a mirror!
your image pursues you.)

The next two stanzas evoke Sade's daily life inside and outside the Château de Lacoste, where he appears to be confined. The reference to the mythical Saturnus, who was the Roman version of the Greek Cronos, is curious to say the least. Since it was foretold that he would be overthrown by one of his children, he chose to eat each one as it was born. Like him, Paz declares, Sade has a voracious appetite for life. Nevertheless, the image of the latter gazing at the grounds surrounding his chateau clashes horribly with that of Saturnus devouring one of his children (immortalized in a famous painting by Goya). Whereas Sade's gaze is "loving" (*amorosa*), Saturn's action is plainly horrifying. Neither is it clear how semen, blood, and lava can gouge out furrows in the ground nor how they happen to be scorched. Seeking to establish a parallel relationship between man and nature, the next six lines are uttered by Paz, who appears to agree with Sade's view. Just as there is no difference between love and death or between liberty and destiny, viewed from the *point suprême* envisioned by Breton, other oppositions are united by commonalities too. No difference exists between our bodies and the sun because both are made of atoms, between love and catastrophe because both are cataclysmic experiences, and between death and massacres because both involve extinctions. Viewed from this angle, earthquakes and muscle spasms, like volcanic eruptions and orgasms, appear to be parallel phenomena if not identical. The dividing line separating the two phenomena all but disappears.

That Paz chose to transform the Chateau de Lacoste into a castle made of rock crystal was not entirely without precedent. Gemstones appear with some regularity in Surrealist texts, and the Crystal Palace in London had been in existence since 1851. Nonetheless, Paz's decision provided Sade with a worthy home and a brilliant symbol. Like his philosophical writings, the castle is characterized by clarity, precision, and transparency. It is not only a valuable jewel but also a work of art and an impressive monument. As Sade wanders through the palace, inspecting various rooms and observing its impressive architectural features, the structure gradually becomes a house of mirrors. Seen from certain angles and under certain lighting conditions, glass—and presumably crystal—can actually reflect light. An equation even exists that can predict the amount of reflectivity. As Sade strolls around the palace, therefore, his image is reflected everywhere he looks. Like him, Paz seems to say, his historical counterpart left an indelible imprint on everything around him.

El hombre está habitado por silencio y vacío
¿Cómo saciar esta hambre,
cómo acallar este silencio y poblar su vacío?
¿Como escapar a mi imagen?
Sólo en mi semejante me trasciendo,
sólo su sangre da fe de otra existencía.
Justina solo vive por Julieta,
las víctimas engendran los verdugos.
El cuerpo que hoy sacrificamos
¿no es el Dios que mañana sacrifica?

La imaginación es la espuela del deseo,
su reino es inagotable e infinito como el fastidio,
su reverso y gemelo.
Muerte o placer, inundación o vómito,
otoño parecido al caer de los días,
volcán o sexo,
soplo, verano que incendia las cosechas,
astros o colmillos,
petrificada cabellera del espanto,
espuma roja del deseo, matanza en lta mar,
rocas azules del delirio,
formas, imágenes, burbujas, hambre de ser,
eternidades momantáneas,
desmesuras: tu medida de hombre.
Atrévete:
la libertad es la elección de la necesidad.

Sé el arco y la flecha, la cuerda y el ay.
El sueño es explosivo. Estalla. Vuelve a ser sol.

En tu castillo de diamente tu imagen se destroza y se rehace, infatigable.

(Man is inhabited by silence and emptiness
How can this hunger be assuaged,
how can this silence be quieted and its emptiness populated?
How can I escape my image?
Only in others like me can I transcend myself,
only their blood gives proof of another existence.
Justine only lives through Juliette,
victims engender their executioners.
The body that we sacrifice today
isn't it the god who will sacrifice tomorrow?

Imagination is the spur of desire,
its kingdom is inexhaustible, as infinite as boredom,
its opposite and twin.

Death or pleasure, flooding or vomit,
autumn like the succession of the days,
volcano or sex,
a puff of air, summer that fires the harvests,
stars or canines,
petrified hair of fear,
red foam of desire, slaughter on the high seas,
blue rocks of delirium,
forms, images, gurgles, lust for life,
momentary eternities,
excesses: your measure as a man.
Go ahead and dare:
freedom is choosing necessity.
Be the bow and the arrow, the cord and the cry.
Dream is explosive. It bursts. It becomes a sun again.

In your diamond castle your image destroys and remakes itself,
    tirelessly.)

Inspired by the image of Sade presiding over his palace of mirrors, Paz devotes the last three stanzas to a meditation on life in general and his own role in particular. The central problem from an existential perspective is man's essential solitude, which seems to be especially acute for artists and writers. At least, Paz claims elsewhere that solitude is what defines the modern poet.[34] The subject is introduced in the very first line: "el hombre está habitado por silencio y vacío." And since everything is a mirror, as he exclaims in the preceding stanza, the situation quickly becomes more complicated. "La consciencia del vacío de no ser y la imagen de un hombre escindido," Hugo J. Verani observes, "reflejan una soledad multiplicada por espejos" ("The consciousness of the emptiness of not existing and the image of a divided man reflect a solitude multiplied by mirrors").[35] This is precisely Paz's problem; everywhere he turns he is constantly reminded of his predicament. However, the greatness of his poetry, as Rachel Phillips observes, "lie[s] in its direct confrontation of the human condition, and in his expression of the evolving consciousness of the poet as he searches for his own answers and his own break-throughs."[36] In more than one respect, his continual search for meaning resembles that of Albert Camus, in whose books he took a keen interest.

Perceiving several similarities between Sade's situation and his own, Paz identifies four problems before presenting his own solution. Part of the difficulty facing him is that man is an inquisitive animal. He possesses enough intelligence to wonder about his situation vis-à-vis the rest of the world. In order to find peace, he needs to eliminate either his existential hunger, the silence that oppresses him, his persistent feeling of emptiness, or the omnipresent image of himself. The question that remains, of course, is how to accomplish that. Paz's answer, based on his own experience, was to let another person—in this case his wife—into his daily life. Only through a close relationship with somebody else—preferably of the opposite sex—does existence begin to make sense. In the absence of absolute meaning, we have to create our own meaning via other people. The only way to get outside ourselves, Paz declares, is by forming meaningful reciprocal connections. So far, so good. At this point, however, he attempts to translate this important lesson into a universal principle governing situations that are clearly not interpersonal. The three examples that he gives involve reciprocal relationships between Sade's novels *Justine* and *Juliette*, between an executioner and his victim, and between a sacrificial victim and the god whom he eventually becomes. For example, *Justine* will always be known as a book that influenced *Juliette* and *Juliette* as a book that was influenced by *Justine* and so forth. By definition, each could not exist without the other. Unlike personal interrelationships, however, these are necessarily imposed *a posteriori* by outside observers. Essentially the product of semantic games, they have no intrinsic worth.

The penultimate stanza continues Paz's musings on the interrelatedness of things, although the reason certain things are paired with others is not always clear. The first three lines apply to Sade and to Paz alike. Imagination is indeed the spur of desire as the author of *120 Days of Sodom* knew very well. It is not the opposite of boredom so much as located at the other end of the continuum linking them together. Here again, at least theoretically, each could not exist without the other. For similar reasons, death is juxtaposed in Paz's mind with pleasure, volcanoes with sex, stars with canine teeth, and desire with slaughter. Since much of the list is incoherent, it may have been generated automatically.

Paradoxically, Paz concludes, freedom and necessity are not incompatible, since after a certain point freedom becomes an absolute necessity. In urging readers to adopt a holistic point of view, like Breton before him, he sought to create a new relationship between the individual and the world. Like the Surrealist leader, he recommended that they strive to embrace the total picture—not just the bow or the arrow but both objects working together. "Rappelons que l'idée de surréalisme tend simplement à la récupération totale de notre force psychique," Breton remarked in The Second Manifesto, "par un moyen qui n'est autre que la descente vertigineuse en nous" ("Remember that the idea of Surrealism simply seeks to accomplish the total recuperation of our psychic force by means of a dizzying descent into ourselves").[37]

The last time we glimpse Sade in the poem, his crystal palace has suddenly been transformed into a diamond palace. As he walks through various rooms, his image appears and disappears every time he passes a mirror. The continual alternation between presence and *vacío* anticipates the Hindu cycle of death and rebirth that he would encounter a few years later in India, which would play an important role in his poetry.

"Noche en claro"

Among the various figures who populated French Surrealism, Paz felt the closest to Breton and Benjamin Péret, whose moral authority he respected as much as their poetry. "Many times when I write," he confided in an obituary written for the first poet, "it is as if I held a silent dialogue with Breton."[38] Finding himself in Paris again in 1959, Paz spent an enjoyable evening chatting with both men at the Café d'Angleterre. This experience was memorialized in a poem written soon after entitled "Noche en claro" ("Clear Night"), which he dedicated to Breton and Péret.[39]

> A las diez de la noche en el café de Inglaterra
> salvo nosotros tres
> > no había nadie
> Se oía afuera el paso húmedo del otoño
> pasos de ciego gigante
> pasos de bosque llegando a la ciudad
> Con mil brazos con mil pies de niebla
> cara de humo hombre sin cara
> el otoño marchaba hacia el centro de Paris
> con seguros pasos de ciego
> Las gentes caminaban por la gran avenida
> algunos con gesto furtivo se arrancaban el rostro
> Una prostituta bella como una papisa
> cruzó la calle y desapareció en un muro verduzco
> la pared volvió a cerrarse

Todo es puerta
basta la leve presión de un pensamiento
Algo se prepara
              dijo uno entre nosotros

(At ten o'clock at night in the Café d'Angleterre
except for us three
              there was no one
outside one could hear autumn's damp footsteps
the footsteps of a blind giant
the footsteps of a forest reaching to the city
with a thousand arms with a thousand misty feet
a face of smoke a faceless man
autumn walked toward the center of Paris
with the steady steps of a blind man
People were strolling along the wide avenue
some plucking at their faces with furtive gestures
A prostitute as lovely as a female pope
crossed the street and disappeared behind a greenish wall
that closed behind her
Everything is a door
the slight pressure of a thought suffices
Something is about to happen
              one of us said)

The title of the poem refers to Paz's obituary for Péret, which concludes: "Depuis lors la nuit universelle et ma nuit personnelle sont devenues plus claires" ("Since then the universal night and my personal night have become clearer").[40] Although "Noche en claro" is usually translated as "Sleepless Night," a better translation would be "Clear Night" or "Bright Night." Whatever it was that was troubling Paz in the past seems to have disappeared. At least he feels better about the world and about his personal situation. Although the composition is fairly long, it is divided into three sections of different lengths. Much of the first seventeen lines is essentially anecdotal. The poem begins with the three poets sitting around a table in the empty Café d'Angleterre, while outside the autumn mist envelopes Paris in a damp cloak. No longer in existence, the café may have been the establishment of the same name that was situated at 37, rue des Capucines on the Right Bank. Autumn itself is portrayed as a blind giant with countless arms and legs. As such he personifies the Bois de Boulogne, which stretches eastward from the Seine near Suresnes to the western edge of the city. The fact that the poet calls him an "hombre sin cara" explains why he is blind—he has no face. Like the protagonist of Apollinaire's "Le Musicien de Saint-Merry," which Paz was fond of, he is a man with no eyes, no nose, and no ears. Interestingly, Paz published a translation and an analysis of the Apollinaire poem in 1965, which was included in *Puertas al campo* the next year.[41] While the faceless man, the prostitute, and her final disappearance are borrowed from the French poem, the people plucking at their faces are entirely Paz's invention.

The final three lines conclude the first half of the initial section, introduce the second half, and create an expectant note. Prompted by the prostitute's disappearance into what looks like a solid wall, Paz turns philosophical. Through the power of thought, he declares with a metaphorical flourish, anything can be a door that opens onto another domain. That the refrain is uttered by "uno entre nosotros," finally, suggests that he and the other two poets have left the café and are continuing their conversation outside. The refrain "Algo se prepara" marks the transition from one part to the next.

> se abrió el minuto en dos
> leí signos en la frente de ese instante
> Los vivos están vivos
> andan vuelan maduran estallan
> los muertos están vivos
> oh huesos todavía con fiebre
> el viento los agita los dispersa
> racimos que caen entre las piernas de la noche
> La ciudad se abre como un corazón
> como un higo la flor que es fruto

más deseo que encarnación
encarnación del deseo
Algo se prepara
     dijo el poeta

(The minute split into two halves
I read the signs on the face of that moment
The living are alive
they walk fly ripen burst
The dead are alive
oh still feverish bones
the wind shakes and scatters them
clusters falling between the night's legs
The city opens like a heart
like a fig the flower that is a fruit
more desire than incarnation
the incarnation of desire
Something is about to happen
     the poet said)

At this point, Rachel Phillips explains, "an expansion of consciousness seems to take place, and the poet sees with clairvoyant eyes."[42] More precisely, Paz experiences one of his famous epiphanies like that in "Agua nocturno." Alberto Ruy Sánchez describes the experience as "the sudden apparition of a clarity that vanishes one instant later."[43] The poet himself describes it as a minute split into two halves, one of which perceives everyday reality, the other a preexisting reality stripped of its civilized veneer. What he glimpses during the thirty seconds allotted to this second view is that life and death occupy different points on a sliding scale. "Tout porte à croire qu'il existe un certain point de l'esprit," Breton declared in the Second Surrealist Manifesto, "d'où la vie et la mort … cessent d'être perçus contradictoirement" ("Everything tends to indicate that a certain point in the mind exists where life and death … cease to be perceived contradictorily").[44] The last five lines introduce the theme of the city, which will be taken up in more detail in the next section.

While the first simile anticipates open heart surgery, the second echoes the conclusion of Apollinaire's poem "Les Fenêtres": "La Fenêtre s'ouvre comme une orange / Le beau fruit de la lumière" ("The window opens like an orange / The lovely fruit of light"). Since the fig is a well-known female sex symbol, it represents the object of male desire. The section concludes with the familiar refrain: "Algo se prepara." This time the speaker is identified as Paz himself.

Este mismo otoño vacilante
este mismo año enfermo
fruta fantasmo que resbala entre las manos del siglo
año de miedo tiempo de susurro y mutilación
Nadie tenía cara aquella tarde
en el underground de Londres
En lugar de ojos
          abominación de espejos cegados
En lugar de labios
          raya de borrosas costuras
Nadie tenía sangre nadie tenía nombre
no teníamos cuerpo ni espíritu
no teníamos cara
El tiempo daba vueltas y vueltas y no pasaba
no pasaba nada sino el tiempo que pasa y regresa y no pasa
Apareció entonces la pareja adolescente
él era rubio "venablo de Cupido"
gorra gris gorrión callejero y valiente
ella era pequeña pecosa pelirroja
manzana sobre una mesa de pobres
pálida rama en un patio de invierno
Niños feroces gatos salvajes
dos plantas ariscas enlazadas
dos plantas con espinas y flores súbitas
Sobre el abrigo de ella color fresa
resplandeció la mano del muchacho
las quatro letras de la palabra Amor
en cada dedo ardiendo como astros

(This same hesitating autumn
this same sick year
phantom fruit that slips between the century's hands
year of fear time of whispering and mutilation
No one had a face that afternoon
in the London Underground
Instead of eyes
      an abomination of blind mirrors
Instead of lips
      a line of blurred stitches
No one had blood no one had a name
we had neither body nor spirit
we had no faces
Time spun around and around without passing
nothing passed except time which passes and returns and doesn't pass
Then a teenage couple appeared
he was a blond "Cupid's arrow"
a scrappy street-smart sparrow
she was a little freckled redhead
an apple on a poor man's table
a pale branch in a winter patio
Ferocious children stray cats
two wild plants entwined together
two thorny plants with sudden flowers
The boy's hand was emblazoned
on her strawberry jacket
with the four letters of the word Love
burning like stars on each finger)
[the drawing of a hand with the word "Love]

At the beginning of section 2, Paz's vision morphs into a memory of a time when he was experiencing a crisis, sometime before the *noche* became *claro*. Everything he looked at was contaminated by his depression. Not only did the season itself look unhealthy, he confesses, but the whole year was characterized by fear and confusion. Even the people in the London Underground seemed repulsive. Immersed in a sea of anonymous individuals with mutilated faces, he seemed to be caught in a time warp where nothing ever changed. Interestingly, Paz includes himself among the zombies with mirrors instead of eyes and scars instead of lips. As he is staring absently into space, however, he glimpses a pair of teenagers with their arms around each other who reaffirm the value of love despite the poverty and ugliness all around them. Indeed, the boy has the letters L.O.V.E. tattooed on the fingers of the right hand, which are visible from the back when he wraps his arms around her. In this way, as Wilson notes, Surrealist values are opposed to the night that threatens to consume humanity.[45] "Al mundo de 'robots' de la sociedad contemporanea," the poet declares elsewhere, "el surrealismo opone los fantasmas del deseo, dispuestos siempre a encarnar en un rostro de mujer" ("To the 'robot' world of contemporary society, Surrealism juxtaposes the phantasms of desire, incarnated always in a woman's face").[46] Paz includes a drawing of the boy's hand with the letters across the back of his fingers and adds a brief Surrealist meditation:

> Tatuaje escolar tinta china y pasión
> anilllos palpitantes
> oh mano collar al cuello ávido de la vida
> pájaro de presa y caballo sediento
> mano llena de ojos en la noche del cuerpo
> pequeña sol y río de frescura
> mano que das el sueño y das la resurrección

> (Student tattoo Chinese ink and passion
> palpitating rings
> oh hand collar around life's eager neck
> bird of prey and thirsty horse
> hand full of eyes in the body's night
> tiny sun and cool river
> hand that conveys dreams and renewal)

Following the conclusion of the London sequence, which contains some powerful memories, Paz returns to the present. While he has been reliving his experience underground, the three men have been strolling in the direction of the Seine, which leads to the next segment. The first sentence reprises a previous statement and adds an equally optimistic observation. Doors exist to be opened, Paz insists, and bridges exist to be crossed. As if to prove the truth of this statement, he and his two friends cross over the river in order to reach the Left Bank.

> Todo es puerta
> todo es puente
> ahora marchamos en la otra orilla
> mira abajo correr el río de los siglos
> el río de los signos
> Mira correr el río de los astros
> se abrazan y separen vuelven a juntarse
> hablan entre ellos un lenguaje de incendios
> sus luchas sus amores
> son la creación y la destrucción de los mundos
> La noche se abre
> mano inmensa
> constelación de signos
> escritura silencio que canta
> siglos generaciones eras
> sílabas que alguien dice
> palabras que alguien oye
> pórticos de pilares transparentes
> ecos llamadas señas laberintos
> Parpadea el instante y dice algo
> escucha abre los ojos ciérralos
> la marea se levanta
> Algo se prepara
>
> Nos dispersamos en la noche
> mis amigos se alejan
> llevo sus palabras como un tesoro ardiendo
> Pelean el río y el viento del otoño
> pelea el otoño contra las casas negras
> Año de hueso
> pila de años muertos y escupidos

estaciones violadas
siglo tallado en un aullido
pirámide de sangre
horas royendo el día en año el siglo el hueso
Hemos perdido todas las batallas
todos los días ganamos una

(Everything is a door
    everything is a bridge
now we are walking to the other bank
look down there where the river of the centuries runs
the river of signs
Look where the river of stars runs
they embrace they separate and they rejoin again
they speak a language of fire among themselves
their struggles their loves
are the creation and destruction of whole worlds
The night opens
    an immense hand
constellation of signs
writing silence that sings
centuries generations eras
syllables that someone says
words that someone hears
porticoes with transparent pillars
echoes calls signs labyrinths
The moment blinks and says something
listen open your eyes close them
the tide is rising
    Something is about to happen

We scattered in the night
my friends disappeared
I carried their words like a burning treasure
the river and the autumn wind fought
A year of bones
a pile of dead years spat out

violated seasons
century carved into a scream
pyramid of blood
hours gnawing at the day the year the century the bone
We have lost every battle
each day we win one)

As they are crossing one of the bridges that span the Seine, Paz tells his companions to look at the river below, which in his mind actually constitutes three rivers. Bearing the weight of the centuries, a multitude of signs, and countless stars respectively, they mingle and converse in a secret language. Nicely defined as silence that sings, writing joins the other means of communication in an elaborate semiotic dance. Created by a mysterious being, the very stars spell out a silent message. Everything signifies, the poet seems to say, if we were only able to decipher it. Since all good things must come to an end, however, the three men go their separate ways, leaving a grateful Paz with warm memories and a certain optimism. Wilson hypothesizes that his "tesoro ardiendo" was Surrealism, which sustained him during the Cold War period despite the threat of nuclear war and the memory of previous wars.[47] Indeed, this is why Paz calls the twentieth century a "siglo tallado en un aullido." We may have lost every humanitarian battle, he remarks, but every day that we resist the forces of evil we win one.

Poesia
La ciudad se despliega
su rostro es el rostro de mi amor
sus piernas son piernas de mujer
Torres plazas columnas puentes calles
río cinturón de paisajes ahogados
Ciudad o Mujer Presencia
abanico que muestras y ocultas la vida
bella como el motín de los pobres
tu frente delira pero en tus ojos bebo cordura
tus axilas son noche pero tus pechos día
tus palabras son de piedra pero tu lengua es lluvia

tu espalda es el mediodía en el mar
tu risa el sol entrando en los suburbios
tu pelo al desatarse la tempestad en las terrazas del alba
tu vientra la respiración del mar la pulsación del día
tú te llamas torrente y te llamas pradera
tú te llamas pleamar
tienes todos los nombres del agua
Pero tu sexo es innombrable
la otra cara del ser
la otra cara del tiempo
el revés de la vida
aquí cesa todo discurso
aquí la belleza no es legible
aquí la presencia se vuelve terrible
replegada en sí misma la Presencia es vacío
lo visible es invisible
Aquí se hace visible lo invisible
aquí la estrella es negra
la luz es sombra luz la sombra
Aquí el tiempo se para
los quatro puntos cardinales se tocan
es el lugar solitario el lugar de la cita

Ciudad Mujer Presencia
aquí se acaba el tiempo
aquí comienza

     (Poetry
The city unfolds
its face is the face of my love
its legs are the legs of a woman
Towers plazas columns bridges streets
river belt of drowned landscapes
City or Woman Presence
fan that reveals or conceals life
as beautiful as the revolt of the poor
your brow is delirious but I drink sanity in your eyes

your armpits are night but your breasts are day
your words are stone but your tongue is rain
your back is midday on the sea
your laughter is the sun entering the suburbs
your loose hair is a storm on the dawn's terraces
your stomach is the breath of the sea the pulse of the day
your name is torrent and your name is meadow
your name is high tide
you have all the names of water
But your vagina is unnamable
the other face of being
the other face of time
the reverse of life
here all discourse ceases
here beauty is illegible
here presence becomes terrible
folded into itself Presence is empty
the visible is invisible
Here the invisible becomes visible
here the star is black
light is shadow and shadow light
Here time stops
the four cardinal points touch each other
it is an isolated place and a meeting place

City Woman Presence
here time ends
here it begins)

The final section of "Noche en claro" consists of a poem in which Paz
eulogizes the City, Woman, and Presence, which are roughly equivalent
to each other. Together they represent a folding fan of life that is
alternatively open or closed. Like the Comte de Lautréamont, whose
poetry the Surrealists adored, Paz creates an outrageous simile. Like the
former, who wrote "beau comme ... la rencontre fortuite sur une table
de dissection d'une machine à coudre et d'un parapluie" ("beautiful
as ... the chance encounter of a sewing machine and an umbrella on a

dissecting table"), he contributes the phrase "bella como un motín de los pobres."[48] In a similar fashion, the next eleven lines are modeled on a poem by Breton entitled "L'Union libre" (1931).[49] Like the latter poet, Paz has drawn up a list of imaginary attributes belonging to his ideal woman. Like those on Breton's list, they represent a series of metaphors that compare her to natural phenomena—in this case night, day, rain, the sea, the sun, a storm, water in general, and a meadow. In both instances, the female subject corresponds to the first type of Surrealist woman that Gauthier identifies: *la femme-nature*.[50] Every positive characteristic associated with nature can be applied to her, depending on the phenomena chosen to represent her.

Interestingly, Paz draws the line at attempting to find a metaphor for his ideal women's vagina. Instead, he decides to evoke the experience of making love and experiencing an orgasm. According to him, the experience is so awesome that it is impossible to describe. Nevertheless, he ventures that it is unearthly, timeless, and a bit like dying. Speech is rendered impossible, he continues, beauty no longer matters, and everything is eclipsed by the intensity of the moment. So miraculous is this experience that it constitutes a spatiotemporal *point suprême*. So powerful is it that traditional oppositions completely disappear, including those between visible and invisible and between light and dark. Not only does time come to a standstill, but space essentially collapses as north, south, east, and west lose all meaning. It is hard to imagine a more moving tribute to the physical and emotional power of sex. Throughout Paz's work, the role of erotic love is consistently as important as that played by Woman, poetry, and imagination.

Notes

1   Octavio Paz, "André Breton o la búsqueda del comienzo," in *Octavio Paz: la búsqueda del comienzo*, ed. Diego Martínez Torrón, 2nd ed. (Mexico City: Fundamentos, 1980), p. 62. Entitled "Le Chateau étoilée," the article would become chapter 5 of *L'Amour fou* the next year. In April 1936, a Spanish translation appeared in *Sur*, published in Buenos Aires.

2 Lourdes Andráde, "Regards convergents' Paz, Breton, et Péret," tr. Henri Béhar, *Mélusine*, Vol. 19 (1999), p. 153.

3 Donald Sutherland, "Excursiones, incursiones, y retornos de un craneo de azucar," in *Octavio Paz*, ed. Pere Gimferrer (Madrid: Taurus, 1982), p. 207.

4 Saul Yurkievich, "Octavio Paz: Indagador de la palabra," in *Octavio Paz*, ed. Pere Gimferrer (Madrid: Taurus, 1989), p. 106.

5 Ibid., pp. 97–8.

6 Martínez Torrón, "El surrealismo de Octavio Paz," *Octavio Paz: la búsqueda del comienzo*, p. 7 and Ricardo Gullón, "El universalismo de Octavio Paz," in *Octavio Paz*, ed. Pere Gimferrer (Madrid: Taurus, 1982), p. 230.

7 Martínez Torrón, Diego, "El Surrealismo de Octavio Paz," p. 19.

8 Ibid., p. 7.

9 *La Gaceta*, No. 55 (1959). Repr. in ibid., p. 17.

10 Jason Wilson, Octavio Paz (Boston: Twayne, 1986), p. 38.

11 Octavio Paz, "El surrealismo," *Octavio Paz: la búsqueda del comienzo*, p. 34.

12 Ibid.

13 Ibid., p. 31.

14 Manuel Durán, "Hacia la otra orilla: La ultima etapa en la poesía de Octavio Paz," in *Octavio Paz*, ed. Pere Gimferrer (Madrid: Taurus, 1989), p. 120.

15 Alberto Ruy Sánchez, *An Introduction to Octavio Paz*, tr. Jeannine Marie Pitas (Oakville, ON: Mosaic, 2018). pp. 5–6.

16 Octavio Paz, *Obra poética* (1935–1988) (Barcelona: Seix Barral, 1990), pp. 127–8.

17 Ovidio C. Fuente, "Teoria poetica de Octavio Paz," *Cuadernos Americanos*, Vol. 31 (1972), p. 234.

18 Ramón Xirau, *La poesía de Octavio Paz, Aproximaciones a Octavio Paz*, ed. Angel Flores (Mexico City: Mortiz, 1974), p. 28.

19 Richard Stammelman, "The Relational Structure of Surrealist Poetry," *Dada/Surrealism*, No. 6 (1976), p. 73.

20 Xavière Gauthier, *Surréalisme et sexualité* (Paris: Gallimard, 1971), p. 190.

21 J. E. Cirlot, *A Dictionary of Symbols*, tr. Jack Sage, 2nd ed. (London: Routledge and Kegan Paul, 1985), p. 228.

22   Paz, "André Breton o la búsqueda del comienzo," p. 62.

23   Paz, "El verbo desencarnado," *La búsqueda del comienzo*, p. 81.

24   Paz, *Obra poética*, pp. 120–2.

25   Guillaume Apollinaire, ["Le Divin Marquis"], in *Oeuvres en prose completes*, Vol. 3, ed. Pierre Caizergues and Michel Décaudin (Paris: Gallimard, 1993), pp. 799–800. See Michel Delon, "Apollinaire, Sade," in *La Place d'Apollinaire*, ed. Anja Ernst and Paul Geyer (Paris: Garnier, 2014), pp. 81–95.

26   Marguerite Bonnet note to André Breton, *Oeuvres complètes*, Vol. 2, ed. Marguerite Bonnet et al. (Paris: Gallimard, 1992), p. 1556.

27   Ibid., p. 399.

28   Wilson, *Octavio Paz*, p. 40.

29   Octavio Paz, Un más allá erótico: Sade (Mexico: Vuelta, 1993), p. 7.

30   Ibid.

31   Wilson, *Octavio Paz*, p. 40.

32   Both figures are quoted in https://www.latimes.com/archives/la-xpm-1991-07-15-mn-1641-story.html

33   Lawrence W. Lynch, *The Marquis de Sade* (Boston: Twayne, 1984), p. 22.

34   Paz, *La busqueda del comienzo*, p. 79.

35   Hugo J. Verani, *Octavio Paz: el poema como caminata* (Mexico: Fondo de Cultura Económico 2013): p. 115.

36   Rachel Phillips, *The Poetic Modes of Octavio Paz* (Oxford: Oxford University Press, 1972), p. 7.

37   André Breton, *Second manifeste du surréalisme*, *Oeuvres complètes*. Vol. 1, p. 791.

38   Cited in Wilson, *Octavio Paz*, p. 38.

39   Paz, *Obra poetica*, pp 349–53.

40   Octavio Paz, "Benjamin Péret," *Les Lettres Nouvelles*, new series, Vol. 1, No. 24 (October 7, 1959), pp. 26–7.

41   Octavio Paz, "El músico de Saint-Merry," *Inicio*, No. 2 (October 1965), pp. 21–4. See the English translation of both by Margaret Peden in *L'Esprit créateur*, Vol. 10, No. 4 (Winter 1970), pp. 269–84. For analysis of Apollinaire's poem, see Willard Bohn, *Reading Apollinaire's "Calligrammes"* (New York: Bloomsbury, 2018), pp. 61–79.

42   Phillips, *The Poetic Modes*, p. 90.

43   Alberto Ruy Sánchez, *An Introduction to Octavio Paz*, tr. Jeannine Marie Pitas (Oakville, ON: Mosaic, 2018). p. 9.

44 André Breton, *Second Manifeste du surréalisme, Oeuvres complètes,* Vol. 1, ed. Marguerite Bonnet et al. (Paris: Gallimard, 1988), p. 781.

45 Wilson believes the letters are on the girl's hand rather than the boy's. See. *Octavio Paz,* p. 37.

46 Paz, "El Surrealismo," p. 29.

47 Wilson, *Octavio Paz,* p. 37.

48 Isidore Ducasse, *Les Chants de Maldoror, Oeuvres complètes,* ed. Maurice Saillet (Paris: Livre de Poche, 1963), p. 322.

49 André Breton, *Oeuvres complètes,* Vol. 2, ed. Marguerite Bonnet et al. (Paris: Gallimard, 1992), pp. 85–7.

50 Gauthier, *Surréalisme et sexualité,* pp. 98–99. See also Ann Marie Remley Rambo, "The Presence of Woman in the Poetry of Octavio Paz," *Hispania,* Vol. 51, No. 2 (May 1968), pp. 259–64.

10

South American Surrealism

Following the publication of André Breton's *Manifeste du surréalisme*, which received surprisingly widespread notice, the movement quickly acquired an international dimension. "Pour surprenant que cela puisse être," Robert Ponge declares, "les informations sur le surréalisme arrivent en Amérique latine avec une extrême rapidité et les débats ne tardent pas à éclater" ("As surprising as it may seem, information about Surrealism arrived in Latin America extremely rapidly and immediately elicited heated discussions").[1] Latin Americans who were well off spent their summers in Paris as well, where a few of them encountered Surrealism for the first time. Of all the places that provided fertile ground for Surrealism to blossom, Hispanic America was perhaps the most fruitful and at the same time the most frustrating. Fruitful because Surrealism found a receptive audience; frustrating because this audience was so small. To be sure, the sheer size of the area virtually guaranteed that it would eventually produce a number of homegrown Surrealists. Today the region comprises some sixteen countries divided between South America, Central America, and North America—to which should be added three Spanish-speaking countries in the Caribbean: Cuba, Puerto Rico, and the Dominican Republic. When Stefan Baciu published his invaluable anthology in 1974, he included Surrealist poetry from the four nations that were the earliest to embrace Surrealism: Argentina, Chile, Mexico, and Peru.[2] Since then the list has grown to include Venezuela, Cuba, the Dominican Republic, and other countries as well.[3]

Something about these countries caused a few perceptive and adventurous young men to be receptive to the young movement—perhaps because the countries were still young themselves. Even sixty years later, Anna Balakian was struck by the youthful quality of Surrealist poetry in Latin America: "Je n'en connais pas," she declared, "de plus lumineuse, vibrante, dynamique, realisant certaines des promesses du surrealisme des annees 20" ("I don't know any poetry that is more luminous, vibrant, dynamic, that realizes certain promises of Surrealism in the 1920s").[4] Even so, Latin American Surrealists—including Octavio Paz—had a hard time interesting their fellow citizens originally and remained voices crying in the wilderness. Thus Surrealism never gained ground as a widespread cultural or artistic movement in Hispanic America. Interestingly, given their geographical proximity, the different Surrealist centers developed independently from each other.[5] Since their host countries were so culturally isolated, poets and painters derived their knowledge of Surrealism directly from France—either through journals such as *La Révolution Surréaliste* or by visiting the country itself. Despite Hispanic America's long association with Spain, the avant-garde capital of the world was situated not in Madrid or Barcelona but in Paris. It was from there that not only Surrealism but also numerous other movements emanated.

Aldo Pellegrini

Not surprisingly, since Buenos Aires was a thriving cosmopolitan city, the first Surrealist group in Latin America was founded there in 1926. Known as the "Paris of South America" because of its broad avenues and spacious plazas, the Argentine capital has always had a very European feeling. In addition, one-half of its two million inhabitants at the time actually came from Europe, mostly arrivals from Spain and Italy. Headed by Aldo Pellegrini, who came from an immigrant family himself, the group was composed entirely of medical students, who were intrigued by the Surrealist documents he had obtained from the French publisher Gallimard. According to Melanie Nicholson, these included the *Manifeste du surréalisme* and the journal *La Révolution Surréaliste*.[6]

Not surprisingly, everyone was immediately tempted to try his hand at automatic writing. Two years later the group published a journal entitled QUE (WHAT) containing the fruit of their investigations, and a second issue appeared in 1930. For reasons that seem to be mostly political, Surrealism lay dormant after that until the end of the Second World War, when a larger group relaunched the original program and created several new journals. The major event during those years was the emergence of the gifted poet Enrique Molina, who, together with Pellegrini, dominated Argentine Surrealism until his death in 1997. Composed by Pellegrini, "La mujer transparente" ("The Transparent Woman") is taken from *El muro secreto* (*The Secret Wall*), published in 1949.[7]

Tu voz era una bebida que yo sorba silencioso
ante las miradas asombradas
un pájaro de luz
salió de tu cuerpo transparente
pájaro de luz
       instante que revolotea
a una velocidad vertiginosa
atravesando calles y calles
persiguen tu cuerpo que huye
¿cuándo podrás alejar a la jauría enloquecida?
desamparada
te has destrozado al caer
los restos de tu cuerpo se arrastran por todos los rincones del mundo
ah un día renacerás tú
       la transparente
única, inconfundible
levemente inclinada, nunca caída
rodeada de impenetrable silencio
avanzando tu pie frágil entre la vacilante monotonía
ah un día renacerá tu risa
tu risa de pájaro transparente
tu risa herida.

(Your voice was a drink that I sipped silently
before amazed glances
a bird of light
flew out of your transparent body
a bird of light
        a fluttering instant
at a dizzying speed
crossing more and more streets
they chase your fleeing body
when can you drive the rabid pack away?
helpless
you broke into pieces when you fell
your remains are scattered all over the world
one day you will be reborn,
        transparent
unique, unmistakeable
slightly bent over, having never fallen
surrounded by impenetrable silence
advancing your fragile foot among the flickering monotony
one day your laughter will be reborn
your transparent bird laughter
your wounded laughter.)

One would love to know more about the genesis of this remarkable poem, especially how Pellegrini arrived at the concept of a woman made entirely of glass. Although glass breasts appear in various Surrealist texts, for example, glass women are conspicuous by their absence.[8] Perhaps the woman was modeled on a glass figurine or, since the poet compares her voice to a drink of some kind, on a Coca Cola bottle. Unfortunately, Mrs. Butterworth syrup—Señora Jarabe de Mantequilla—is not a candidate for this honor, since this product dates from many years later. Since he was a doctor (or soon would be), Pellegrini may also have been familiar with an extraordinary psychiatric phenomenon called "the glass delusion." The most famous example is King Charles VI of France, who wore padded clothing because he feared he would shatter if anybody touched him. Interestingly, Cervantes invokes this bizarre disorder on at least two occasions. The first is in a short story entitled *El licenciado Vidriera* (*The Glass Lawyer*), in which the hero suffers from a glass delusion after consuming a quince. The second, which is very possibly the source of Pellegrini's woman, occurs in *Don Quixote* (part 1 chapter 33), where a short poem begins as follows:

> Es de vidrio la mujer;
> Pero no se ha de probar
> Si se puede o no quebrar,
> Porque todo podría ser.
> Y es más fácil el quebrarse … .
>
> (Woman is made of fragile glass; / but do not put
> her to the test/ to see if she will break, / for that
> might come to pass. // She is too apt to shatter …)

As a group of bystanders look on with amazement, a marvelous bird emerges from the woman's transparent body and immediately disappears. Since the bird is composed entirely of photons, it flies at the speed of light, disappearing before the human eye can even register it. After comparing the woman's voice to a refreshing drink in the first line, Pellegrini implicitly compares it to birdsong in the third. That the bird itself is made of light indicates that it is a positive symbol. Perhaps it represents the woman's soul; then again, perhaps she is a source of life, goodness, truth, or joy. The *Illustrated Encyclopedia of Traditional Symbols* lists many more attractive possibilities.[9] One thing is certain: subsequent events suggest that she is an important source of vitality, someone who enjoys life to the fullest.

At this point, however, the story gets a little confusing. Several people, presumably the former bystanders, pursue the woman with the transparent body, who for some reason is desperate to get away from them. We never learn why they are chasing her or why she is afraid of them. Calling back over her shoulder, she asks Pellegrini—since he is the author of the poem and thus omnipotent—to save her from her determined pursuers. Unfortunately, because she is distracted, she trips and falls and shatters into a million pieces. The impact is so severe that fragments are scattered all over the surface of the globe. Like Osiris but unlike Orpheus, Pellegrini assures us, she will be reborn someday slightly the worse for wear but otherwise as good as new. Somehow all the fragments will be located, collected, and reunited. In the meantime, since her unfortunate accident, Buenos Aires has become a very dull place in which to live. Not only is the pervasive silence unbearable, but without the transparent woman around to liven things up, life is unbelievably boring. Everyone is waiting for the day when she will finally return, bringing with her the bird of light, her infectious laughter, and her *joie de vivre*. Although her marvelous voice will apparently be a little sadder than before, it will still resemble birdsong as well as a refreshing drink.

Entitled "Mármoles" ("Marbles"), the next poem by Pellegrini is centered around several women as opposed to a single individual.[10] In contrast to the previous woman who is made of glass, her sisters have been carefully carved from marble.

> Nadie podrá olvidar
> la voz velada del arqueólogo en cuclillas
> buscando entre antiguas ruinas
> las huellas de la angustia de los siglos
> hundidas en la arena
> sólo prosperan las prostitutas petrificadas
> que conservan a través de los siglos
> un inagotable deseo de amor
> la voz velada y lejana busca lo viviente en lo
> muerto
> a la sombra de la voz
> la más deliciosa de las doncellas se desnuda de sus
> heridas
>
> piadosamente
> cae una noche rota
> piadosamente
> sopla sobre los antiguos mármoles
> el gran viento de los acoplamientos

en cada instante nacen y mueren de un modo
infinito
seres invisibles que fecundan al tiempo
la voz lejana llama
al misterio derramado entre los monumentos
arqueológicos
una tempestad de mordiscos
hace sangrar los mármoles
sangre coagulada del tiempo inalcanzable
sangre inalcanzable del vacío.

(Nobody will forget the veiled voice of the squatting archaeologist
    searching among the ancient ruins for traces of the centuries'
    anguish
buried in the sand
only the petrified prostitutes thrive
who have embodied inexhaustible desire
across the centuries
the veiled and distant voice searches for the living in the dead
in the voice's shadow
the most delicious of the maidens undresses her
wounds
a broken night falls
piously
the connections' powerful wind
blows piously on the ancient marbles
at every moment they are born and die
infinitely
invisible beings who fertilize time
the distant voice calls
to the mystery spilled among the archaeological
monuments
a biting storm
makes the marbles bleed
coagulated blood of unattainable time
unattainable blood of the void)

The poem opens to reveal an archaeologist sifting through the scattered remains of an ancient civilization. His voice is muted ("velada"), we eventually learn, because the site he is excavating is some distance away. As the reference to "la angustia de los siglos" implies, many of the things that archaeologists uncover bear traces of ancient misfortunes—civic as well as personal. There may be indications that a city has been sacked or that it has experienced a flood. There may be a broken dish or a coin someone lost on the way to the market. Since the ruins here are buried in sand, one surmises that the scene takes place in Egypt or somewhere in the Middle East. Among other things, it includes the remains of a temple whose marble pillars have been carved to resemble standing women. Like the caryatids decorating the Erectheum on the Greek Parthenon, they presumably help to support the building's roof. That the poet calls the columns "prostitutas petrificadas" introduces an unexpected note. These are not just statues of any women but rather statues of temple prostitutes, whose sacred duty required them to have sex with anyone who had a coin to offer the god.[11] An extremely old institution in the Middle East, it dates from well before *Gilgamesh* (*c.* 2000 BC), in which a sacred prostitute named Shamhat plays an important role. Thanks to these ancient erotic pillars, Pellegrini interjects, the inexhaustible power of desire has been publically acknowledged for thousands of years. As he well knew, sexuality was also one of the cornerstones of Surrealism, especially insofar as it exerted pressure on the Freudian unconscious. In addition, as Mary Ann Caws reminds us, *l'amour fou* ("delirious love") was "the founding tenet" of Surrealist poetry.[12]

While the archaeologist interprets the various artifacts that he encounters—essentially bringing them back to life—one of the female pillars also comes to life, exemplifying the Surrealist principle of *le merveilleux*. While she takes off several bandages acquired previously, night falls bit by bit, bathing the marble columns in a strong wind. The fact that both natural phenomena occur "piadosamente" creates a religious aura that transforms the pillars into religious artifacts. Continually fluctuating in time and space, they connect the present to the past in an infinite loop. This is the mystery that the archaeologist finally acknowledges at the edge of his excavation. Heralded by the wind, a desert sandstorm suddenly moves in whose stinging particles provide a glimpse of the statues' "blood." The latter are powered by time, it turns out, which Pellegrini defines as the blood of the cosmos. Since we have already seen that the reverse is true, that the columns "fertilize" time, a second infinite loop connects these two entities as well. Time and pillars are locked in a reciprocal embrace for all of eternity.

César Moro

César Moro was the first Peruvian to join the Surrealist movement and the only Latin American author to publish a poem in *Le Surréalisme au Service de la Révolution*.[13] As Gaëlle Hourdin notes, he was "la parfaite incarnation de l'entre-deux" ("the perfect incarnation of an intermediary") between Europe and the Americas.[14] After studying at the Colegio de la Inmaculada in Lima, Moro traveled to Paris in 1925, where he continued to pursue his twin interests: painting and poetry. A few years later, he met Breton and his colleagues, enthusiastically adopted their cause, and participated in many of their activities.[15] Indeed, Baciu even calls him the "Benjamin Péret of hispanoamerican Surrealism."[16] When Moro finally returned to Lima, after an absence of eight years, he brought his enthusiasm for Surrealism with him and founded a local branch, composed largely of himself and his fellow Peruvian Emilio Adolfo Westphalen. In 1935 he and Westphalen organized the First Latin American Surrealist Exhibition at the Academia Alcedo de Lima, which attracted art from all over Latin America.

Known as the "City of the Kings," because it was founded during the Three Kings holiday (Epiphany) in 1535, Lima was where the Peruvian ruling class lived, which was largely of European descent. Home to perhaps 500,000 people, it possessed a flourishing economy but was racked by bloody political violence during the 1930s. As far as cultural activities were concerned, the city was hopelessly provincial—not just unresponsive but hostile to any kind of avant-garde activity. For that reason, Moro calls it "Lima la horrible" in a poem of the same name written in 1949.[17] (Ironically, the phrase has become a common refrain today in the Peruvian capital.) One understands why he spent so much time in Paris, which by comparison must have seemed like heaven to him. Although Moro was forced to leave Peru in 1938, for complicated political reasons, he found an excellent refuge in Mexico, where he spent the next ten years of his life. Welcomed by his Mexican counterparts, he was able to continue his Surrealist activities unabated.[18] Entitled "Libertad-Igualdad" ("Liberty-Equality"), the following poem is dated April 26, 1940:[19]

> El invierno recrudece la melancolía de la tortuga ecuestre
> El invierno la viste de armiño sangriento
> El invierno tiene pies de madera y ojos de zapato
> La esmeralda puede resistir la presencia insólita del tigre
> Acoplado a la divina tortuga ecuestre
> Con el bramido de la selva llorando por el ojo fatal de la amatista
> La generación sublime por venir
> Desata las uñas de las orquídeas que se clavan en la cabeza de los
>   angélicos ofidios
>
> La divina tortuga asciende al cielo de la selva
> Seguida por el tigre alado que duerme reclinada la cabeza
> Sobre una almohada viviente de tenuirrostros
>
> (Winter worsens the equestrian tortoise's melancholy
> Winter dresses her in bloodstained ermine
> Winter has wooden feet and shoe eyes
> The emerald can resist the tiger's unexpected presence
> Coordinated with the divine equestrian tortoise
> With the jungle loudly lamenting the amethyst's fatal eye
> The sublime future generation loosens the orchids' claws embedded in
>   the angelic serpents' heads
>
> The divine tortoise ascends to the jungle's sky
> Followed by the winged tiger asleep with its head on a living pillow
>   of birds)

While a poem's title ordinarily prepares the reader for what is to come, this is no ordinary poem. Sooner or later, one perceives that it has nothing to do with liberty and even less with equality. Instead of a guide, the title is little more than a temporary distraction. Like most if not all of Moro's poetry, it is an example of automatic writing. The first of four unequal stanzas introduces us to the two main characters: the tortoise and the tiger. That the former is able to ride horseback is not only completely unexpected but nearly impossible to imagine. Moro liked the image so much, however, that he used it as the title of a collection of poetry published posthumously in Lima in 1957. By contrast, nothing about the tiger particularly signals it out for attention. We know even less about the striped quadruped than we do about the tortoise—except that its presence is unexpected. One wonders whether the two of them can coexist peacefully. Although the tortoise seems to always have a melancholy personality, her depression deepens every winter—perhaps because she suffers from seasonal affective disorder. Mimicking the weasel's yearly transformation, she wears a white coat in winter to keep herself warm. The fact that it is stained with blood suggests either that she has been attacked by a predator or that she has become a predator herself, which seems unlikely. Moro's attempt to portray winter as a wooden puppet is remarkably daring but not entirely successful. The gap between the abstract tenor and the concrete vehicle is too difficult to bridge.

For some reason, lines 4 and 6 introduce two gemstones whose symbolism is far from traditional. While the emerald is usually associated with immortality or hope, Moro's example defends its possessor from attacks by tigers.[20] This suggests in turn that it is intended to protect the tortoise from her unexpected visitor, who may or may not be dangerous. Although the amethyst normally symbolizes humility, here it appears to represent the evil eye, which will hopefully be directed at the tortoise's enemies. The last two lines contain several additional revelations. The discovery that the tortoise is a divine being comes as a complete surprise—as does the fact that it and the tiger possess wings. Presumably this means that the latter also enjoys divine status. For better or worse, their ascension into heaven recalls that of

Jesus and several other biblical personages. Cushioning the tiger's head, the pillow of living birds is a nice touch. Although Moro makes no mention of it, they are almost certainly doves. The next stanza returns to the subject of winter:

El invierno famélico se vuelve un castillo
El invierno tiene orejas de escalera un peinado cañón
Tiene dientes en forma de sillas de agua
Para que los soldados ecuestres de la tortuga
Beban las sillas y suban las orejas
Desbordantes de mensajes escritos en la nieve
Como aquel que dice: "a su muy digno cargo elevado
Como el viento participe en un % mínimo, me es grato
Dirigir un alerta de silencio"

En vano los ojos se cansan de mirar
La divina pareja embarcada en la cópula
Boga interminable entre las ramas de la noche
De tiempo en tiempo un volcán estalla
Con cada gemido de la diosa
Bajo el tigre real

(The famished winter turns into a castle
Winter has staircase ears, a canyon hairstyle
It has teeth in the shape of water chairs
So the tortoise's equestrian soldiers
Can drink the chairs and raise their ears
Overflowing with messages written in the snow
For example "in its very worthy charge the wind participates in a
    minimum %, I am pleased
To direct a silent alert"

In vain eyes grow tired of looking
The divine couple engaged in copulation
Sail interminably among the night's branches
From time to time a volcano erupts
With each of the goddess's moans
Beneath the royal tiger)

Up to this point, the poem has been reasonably coherent—unusual, to be sure, but still reasonably coherent. Although the third stanza continues to observe the grammatical niceties, however, it makes very little sense. It is hard to decide whether Moro is experimenting with automatic writing or experiencing a Dada relapse. There are examples of gratuitous metamorphosis, bizarre combinations, physical impossibilities, and strange hybrids. One wonders how winter can suddenly turn into a castle, for example, and how chairs can be made of water. This explains why Mirko Lauer and Abelardo Oquendo classify Moro among the "rabid" practitioners of Surrealism.[21] That the tortoise possesses a troop of equestrian soldiers suggests she enjoys earthly power as well as that which accompanies her divine status. Indeed, the final stanza confirms that she and the tiger preside over a royal kingdom. Not only are they intimately related to nature, moreover, but they also represent natural forces themselves. As they fly through the night air, they copulate like eagles and trigger a series of volcanic eruptions. More than anything, they seem to be autochthonous beings who have been elevated to a god-like level.

Although the previous poem was in Spanish, Moro wrote largely in French while he was living in Mexico. This fact alone sets him apart from all the other poets in Hispanic America. Since it necessarily restricted his readership among the Spanish-speaking public, it has taken a while for critics to gauge his true worth. According to Gabriel Ramos, however, Moro is "el mejor representante del surrealismo en el continente [sud] americano" ("the best representative of Surrealism on the [South] American continent").[22] In Westphalen's judgment, moreover, he is also the most orthodox of the hispanophile Surrealist poets.[23] He learned his lesson very well during the years that he resided in Paris. "Le culte du caractère analogique du langage poétique est évident partout dans [sa] poésie" ("The cult of the analogical nature of poetic language is evident everywhere in [his] poetry") Anna Balakian declares.[24] With its systematic pairing of body parts and natural phenomena, Breton's poem "L'Union libre" ("Free Union") served as a model for many of his works. This is especially true of a poem entitled "Lettre d'amour"

("Love Letter"), which Moro wrote in French and Westphalen later translated into Spanish.[25] Composed in Mexico in 1942, it was addressed to Antonio Acosta, a young Mexican official who had been his lover.[26] Although their relationship was brief—from November 1938 to the beginning of 1939—the memory of their *amour fou* ("delirious love") haunted him for many years thereafter.[27] Interestingly, Moro later confided, the tortoise and tiger in "Libertad-Igualdad" represent the two of them enjoying a celestial idyl.[28] Something very similar occurs at the beginning of "Lettre d'amour":

Je pense aux holoturies angoissantes qui souvent nous entouraient à
    l'approche de l'aube
quand tes pieds plus chauds que des nids
flambaient dans la nuit
d'une lumière bleue pailletée
Je pense à ton corps faisant du lit le ciel et les montagnes suprêmes
de la seule réalité
avec ses vallons et ses ombres
avec l'humidité et les marbres de l'eau noire reflétant toutes les étoiles
dans chaque oeil

Ton sourire n'était-il pas le bois retentissant de mon enfance
n'étais-tu pas la source
la pierre pour des siècles choisie pour appuyer ma tête?
Je pense à ton visage
immobile braise d'où partent la voie lactée
et ce chagrin immense qui me rend plus fou qu'un lustre de toute
    beauté balancée dans la mer

Intraitable à ton souvenir la voix humaine m'est odieuse
toujours la rumeur végétale de tes mots m'isole dans la nuit totale
où tu brilles d'une noirceur plus noire que la nuit
Toute idée de noir est faible pour exprimer le long ululement du noir
    sur noir éclatant ardemment

(I think of the alarming sea cucumbers that often surrounded us at the
    approach of dawn
when your feet flamed in the night

hotter than nests
with a spangled blue light
I think of your body transforming the bed into the sky
and the supreme mountains
of the only reality
with its vallies and its shadows
with the humidity and marbles of the black water reflecting all the stars
in each eye

Wasn't your smile the resounding wood of my youth
weren't you the source
the centuries' stone chosen to support my head?
I think of your face
immobile ember from which springs the Milky Way
and this immense grief that makes me crazier than a gorgeous
    chandelier balanced in the sea

Intractable at your memory the human voice is hateful to me
the vegetal sound of your words still isolates me in the total night
where you shine with a blackness blacker than night
Every idea of black is insufficient to express the long ululation of black
    on black ardently bursting)

The poem opens with an intimate portrait of the lovers in bed together as the sun begins to rise. Because their love was taboo and probably even punishable by law, Moro never mentions Antonio by name. Instead, utilizing a series of anonymous pronouns, he lets the reader assume that the latter is a beautiful woman. Insofar as the first stanza is concerned, Jason Wilson notes, "the lover's body is the sole reality."[29] All that matters is his magnificent frame which, at least for Moro, magically transforms their bed into a celestial landscape with its own unique mountains, valleys, and lakes. If the fact that they both have stars in their eyes testifies to their mutual passion, the fact that they have *all the stars in the universe* in each eye testifies to the intensity of that passion. Completing this unearthly landscape in the second stanza, Moro compares his lover's face to a glowing ember, which in turn becomes the source of the Milky Way. The poem shifts from the idyllic past at this point to the flawed present, from memory to reality. Counterbalancing the luminous joy that pervades the first two stanzas, an immense grief overcomes the poet at the thought of what he has lost forever. The original experience may be over, but it is far from forgotten. Instead of deriving joy from the thought of his lover's voice, Moro finds that thought hateful because it emphasizes how alone he finds himself. Instead of the luminosity associated with his earlier happiness, he is surrounded by an impenetrable darkness—the symbol of absence, depression, and mourning.

Uttered in a moment of deep frustration, the final ululation expresses his torment but also his underlying passion.

Je n'oublierai pas
Mais qui parle d'oubli
dans la prison où ton absence me laisse
dans la solitude où ce poème m'abandonne
dans l'exil où chaque heure me trouve
je ne me réveillerai plus
je ne résisterai plus à l'assaut des grandes vagues
venant du paysage heureux que tu habites
Resté dehors sous le froid nocturne je me promène
sur cette planche haut placée d'où l'on tombe net

Raidi sous l'effroi de rêves successifs et agité dans le vent
d'années de songe
averti de ce qui finit par se trouver mort
au seuil des châteaux désertés
au lieu et à l'heure dits mais introuvables
aux plaines fertiles du paroxysme
et de l'unique but

de nom naguère adoré
je mets toute mon adresse à l'épeler
suivant ses transformations hallucinatoires
Tantôt une épée traverse de part en part un fauve
ou bien une colombe ensanglantée tombe à mes pieds

devenus rochers de corail support d'épaves
d'oiseaux carnivores

(I will not forget
but who is talking about forgetfulness
in the prison where your absence leaves me
in the solitude where this poem abandons me
in the exile where each hour finds me
I will no longer awaken
I will no longer resist the assault of the great waves
coming from the happy countryside that you inhabit
remaining outside beneath the nocturnal cold I stand
on this dangerous high diving board

Rigid from the fright of successive dreams and shaken in the wind of
years of dream
warned about what ends in death
on the threshold of deserted chateaus
at the arranged place and time but impossible to find
on the fertile plains of the paroxysm and of the single goal

It takes all my skill to spell
a formerly adored name
following its hallucinatory transformations
Now a sword pierces a wild animal through and through
or else a bloody dove falls at my feet
become cliffs of coral the support of wrecked boats
of carnivorous birds)

Left with nothing but memories, Moro feels cut off not only from his lover but also from society and from his country of origin. His precarious psychological state threatens his identity as a human being. Not surprisingly, given his present circumstances, thoughts of suicide and death frequently cross his mind. He dreams of finding permanent relief, for example, by falling into a permanent sleep. He also thinks of drowning himself in the ocean or a swimming pool. However, thoughts of actually committing suicide literally scare him stiff. Moro is so upset in any case that his attempts to spell Antonio's name lead to bloody hallucinations involving wild animals. Returning to the theme (and the temptation) of death, he fantasizes that his feet have been transformed into coral reefs and thus that he is powerless to act.

Un cri répété dans chaque théâtre vide à l'heure du spectacle
    inénarrable
Un fil d'eau dansant devant le rideau de velours rouge
aux flammes de la rampe
Disparus les bancs du parterre
j'amasse des trésors de bois mort et de feuilles vivaces en argent corrosif
On ne contente plus d'applaudir on hurle
mille familles momifiées rendant ignoble le passage d'un écureil
Cher décor où je voyais s'équilibrer une pluie fine se dirigeant rapide
    sur l'hermine
d'une pelisse abandonnée dans la chaleur d'un feu d'aube
voulant adresser ses doléances au roi
ainsi moi j'ouvre toute grande la fenêtre sur les nuages vides
réclamant aux ténèbres d'inonder ma face
d'en effacer l'encre indélébile
l'horreur du songe
à travers les cours abandonnées aux pâles végétations maniaques

Vainement je demande au feu la soif
vainement je blesse les murailles
au loin tombent les rideaux précaires de l'oubli
à bout de forces
devant le paysage tordu dans la tempête

(A cry repeated in each empty theater at the time of its hilarious
    performance
A stream of water dancing to the flaming footlights
before the red velvet curtain
No benches in the orchestra
I gather treasures of dead wood and lively corrosive silver leaves
No longer content to applaud they yell
a thousand mummified families render despicable the passage of a
    squirrel

Beloved scenery where I witnessed a fine rain falling rapidly on the
    ermine
a fur abandoned in the heat of a dawn fire
wishing to address its complaints to the king
thus I open the window wide onto the empty clouds
demanding that the shadows inundate my face
in order to remove the indelible ink
the horror of the dream
across the courtyards abandoned to pale maniacal vegetation

Vainly I ask the fire for thirst
vainly I wound the walls
in the distance the precarious curtains of forgetfulness descend
exhausted
before the twisted landscape in the storm)

Distancing themselves from Moro's former love affair, the final
three stanzas are constructed around theatrical conceits. Although
the antepenultimate stanza evokes multiple theaters and multiple
performances, the theaters in question are empty. In each instance,
the entertainment appears to consist of a vertical stream of water
dancing "hilariously" before the theater curtain illuminated by flaming
footlights. As Moro sets about collecting wood and silver leaves, an
audience materializes out of nowhere and, tired of clapping, begins
to yell "encore!" For better or worse, contradictions and nonsensical
events abound in automatic writing. Thus a squirrel passing through
the branches is denounced by a group of mummies. As a fine rain
drenches an irate abandoned fur, the poet opens the window and asks
the shadows to wash the indelible ink off his face, which by definition
is impossible. Or perhaps this is simply a dream like the overgrown
courtyards filled with unruly vegetation. According to Wilson, the
poem ends with a plea for more storms and more fire, which he takes to
be metaphors for more passion.[30] However, it is difficult to square this
interpretation with the words on the page. The only request that Moro
actually makes is, strangely enough, for more thirst. As he pounds on
the walls around him, a theatrical curtain of forgetful rain falls on the

storm-wracked landscape in the distance. In the absence of a formal conclusion, the poem finally stops at this point. Like the rain, it has simply become exhausted.

Braulio Arenas

Like Cesar Moro, Braulio Arenas was both a poet and an artist. His family moved from the north of Chile to Santiago in 1929 when he was sixteen. At the time, the capital was a busy metropolis with a population of one million people, many of whom were Spanish and Italian immigrants. Although the whole country was deeply affected by the Great Depression, there were more opportunities there than in the hinterland. During the 1930s, while the government implemented policies based on the United States' New Deal, Arenas studied at the Liceo Abate Molina and prepared to enroll in law school. In this he resembled a great many avant-garde artists and writers, especially those writing in Spanish, who earned a law degree as a form of unemployment insurance. After a brief stint in law school, however, Arenas dropped out in order to devote himself to writing. In 1938, inspired by what was happening in Europe, he founded a Surrealist group in Santiago called Mandrágora ("Mandrake") along with Teófilo Cid and Enrique Gómez Correa.[31] From 1938 to 1941, they published a magazine of the same name that helped to advance the cause of Surrealism in Latin America. Some measure of their commitment to experimental poetry can be gauged from an event that occurred at the Universidad de Chile in 1940. Angered by Pablo Neruda, whom he accused of catering to bourgeois tastes, Arenas ripped his speech from his hands and tore it into a thousand pieces.

Around 1942, Arenas was excited to discover the existence of *VVV*, a Surrealist magazine edited in New York by David Hare, André Breton, and several other colleagues. With Breton's permission, he reprinted a document from the first issue (June 1942) entitled *Prolégomènes à un troisième manifeste du surréalisme ou non* (*Introduction to a Third Manifesto of Surrealism or Not*) in a magazine entitled *Leitmotiv*, which had replaced *Mandrágora* by that time. Fired with enthusiasm, he contributed two items of his own to the next issue of *VVV* (March 1943): a collage poem and a "Letter from Chile" in which he proclaimed his allegiance to Surrealism, which he defined as "a moral passion." Neutral up until that point, Chile entered the Second World War the same year on the side of the Allies.

Attempting to come to grips with the Mandrágora poets, the intrepid chronicler of Spanish American literature Enrique Anderson-Imbert chose the adjective "hallucinatory," which was not necessarily the best term to describe them.[32] However, his second attempt was much closer to the mark. In his opinion, Arenas and his colleagues sought to create "a weird marriage between an unreal world and an irrational poetry." Employing techniques allied to dreaming and psychic automatism, Arenas invents fanciful beings, transposes points of reference, and constantly contradicts himself. For this reason, Fernando Alegria calls him "un poeta lírico de humor confusionista" ("a liric poet of confusionist humor").[33] In poems such as "Día a Día" ("Day by Day"), for example, readers find themselves continually *dépaysé* (disoriented).[34] Time and space are elastic concepts that vary from one moment to the next:

El vidrio de la ventana se ha quebrado anticipadamente.
Unos decían: "Han sido los colores del prisma al atravesar
la noche para fijarse en el techo." Otros culpaban al pez
lápiz; otros, al pez carta; otros, al pez buzón.
Sólo que a la mañana siguiente el vidrio de la ventana
se veía intacto. Nada, ni la menor trizadura, ni el menor
color, ni el menor sello de correo.
Las olas del mar, como de constumbre.

(The window pane has shattered in anticipation. Some said:
"It was the prism's colors that traversed the night and
settled on the roof." Others blamed the pencil fish; others,
the letter fish; others, the mailbox fish.
Except the next morning the window pane was discovered
to be intact. Nothing, neither the tiniest piece nor the
tiniest color nor the tiniest postage stamp.
The sea's waves as usual.)

As advertised, nothing in the poem makes the slightest sense. Everything varies widely from the first day to the second. Although the sentences are grammatically correct, many of them are patently absurd. Even those that are perfectly straightforward refuse to add up. In the first place, the poem's basic premise is fatally flawed. Windows don't just break by themselves, especially in anticipation of another event. They are not sentient beings and certainly not psychic. Neither is there any way that the colors emanating from a prism could have been responsible for the breakage, especially during the night, when prisms cannot function. And while the postal fish are arranged in a logical progression, from the writing implement to the finished document to the eventual depository, they are not responsible either. No one in their right mind would ever blame any of these things, and yet, according to Arenas, several people have done exactly that. Or have they? The next morning the window has been miraculously restored. Or has it? The fact that no trace remains of the broken glass or the object that broke it is suspicious to say the least. Are we to believe that the window fixed itself? Or that someone came and repaired it during the night? The easiest explanation, according to Ockham's razor, is not only the most likely but also the most convincing. Taking the laws of physics as well as probability into account, it appears that the window was never broken in the first place. This in turn means that Arenas was lying, that he is basically an untrustworthy narrator. Here, as elsewhere in his poetry, he has been amusing himself at our expense by constructing a puzzle that has no solution.

"Poema de memoria" ("Poem from Memory") employs an analogous device:

> Para embellecer al cerezo
> Con un papiro nigromántico
> Esta mañana se ha vestido
> Una silente alondra roja
>
> Yo llevé esta alondra un día
> Entre mis manos enguantadas
> Hasta un Café en el que solía
> Reunirme con mis amigos

Lejano tiempo ya el cereza
Se tumbó al ímpetu del hacha
La alondra roja es un recuerdo
En mi vida de un solo día

Esta mañana se ha vestido
Con un papiro nigromántico
Un silente alondra roja
Para embellecer al cerezo

(To adorn the cherry tree
With a necromantic papyrus
The morning has dressed itself in
A silent, red lark

One day I carried the lark
In my gloved hands
To a Café where I used
To meet my friends

Many years ago the cherry tree
Was felled by the axe's momentum
The red lark is a memory
Of a single day in my life

The morning has dressed itself
In a necromantic papyrus
A silent, red lark
To adorn the cherry tree)

For better or worse, this poem poses many more questions than it answers. Like the previous poem, it utilizes contradictions and semantic incompatibilities to achieve total confusion. The key to grasping the first stanza is to recognize that morning is portrayed as a woman. Since she is carrying a document associated with witchcraft, she is probably not Aurora but apparently some sort of priestess. Judging from the fact that she has put on a special garment, the adornment of the cherry tree (which reminds one of Christmas) must mark an important occasion. A visit to the nearest bird book informs us, moreover, that larks only sing when they are flying, which explains the lark's silence. Up to this point the scraps of information fit together reasonably well. However, the same book contains another piece of information that sabotages this realistic interpretation: larks are brown birds not red ones. More importantly, they are far too small to use as an article of clothing. Indeed, the speaker in the second stanza is able to carry the lark in his hands. Arenas introduces an additional complication in the third stanza, which retroactively situates the episode in the first stanza—narrated in the present tense—in the distant past. Suddenly all these events turn out to have taken place a long time ago. The final stanza completes the systematic mystification by deliberately contradicting the first. Instead of the red lark, morning is wearing the necromantic papyrus! By this time, the hapless reader has no idea what to believe. It is tempting to conclude that Arenas has been playing a Surrealist game called *l'un dans l'autre* ("one in the other"). In order to generate images that possessed the maximum power, Breton and his colleagues would choose two random objects and imagine that one of them was contained in the other. A similar strategy governed their experiments with *contrepets* ("spoonerisms") and with *le cadavre exquis* ("the exquisite cadaver"). As we saw in Chapter 2, anything and everything was valid in their search for the ultimate image.

Fortunately, Arenas' poems are not all exercises in frustration. When the impulse strikes him, as "El corazón" ("The Heart") demonstrates, he can be quite romantic:

Tú hablaste del corazón hasta por los ojos
Tú hablaste del fuego hasta por la nieve
Por ti yo un día me decidí al azar
          Para encontrarte

Yo he desatado el nudo del azar
Una mañana me decidí del súbito
Y sólo quien haya logrado desatarlo
          Podrar entenderme

Yo he desatado el nudo del azar
Un nudo astuto viejo y persistente
Y esta tarea era semejante
    A la belleza

Yo he desatado el nudo del azar
Y tú mujer apareciste entonces
Mujer azar y azar mujer eran en todo
    Tan semejantes

(You spoke of the heart even through your eyes
You spoke of fire even through the snow
For you I decided by chance one day
    To meet you

I have untied the knot of chance
One morning I suddenly decided
And only someone who has managed to untie it
    Will understand me

I have untied the knot of chance
A clever old and persistent knot
And this task was similar
    To beauty

I have untied the knot of chance
And then you appeared woman
Woman chance and chance woman were basically
    So alike)

This apparently simple little poem is actually more complex than it seems at first glance. To be sure, the basic plot is all too familiar. The narrator—who is presumably Arenas—meets a woman, the two of them fall in love, and they presumably live happily ever after. What interests the poet, however, is not *what* happened but rather *how* it happened, what led to these two people meeting and ultimately falling in love. Unfortunately, we learn virtually nothing about the woman except that she has expressive eyes. By contrast, since it is Arenas who is speaking, we learn his side of the story in more detail. At times, his account even has something of a confessional tone about it. Although the first two lines are parallel constructions, they communicate in very different ways. Since the heart is the traditional seat of love, for example, the first verse exploits metonymy. And since fire is traditionally equated with passion, the second verse utilizes metaphor. In both cases, the verb "to speak" is also employed metaphorically, meaning something like "to suggest the possibility of." Similarly, the preposition "through" signifies agency in the first instance and "defiance" in the second. By means of her eyes the woman evokes the possibility of love and, despite all the snow around her, the possibility of passion. The third line introduces the theme of objective chance—an important Surrealist principle—which plays a huge role in the poem. Although deciding something by chance appears to be an oxymoron, the statement contains a deeper truth. Having detected a sign of interest in the woman's eyes, Arenas was determined to meet her, which turned out to be a fortuitous decision.

The next three stanzas revisit his original decision and introduce a curious metaphor. All three begin with the same sentence: "Yo he desatado el nudo del azar," which emphasizes how important his choice was. So far as I know, the decision to portray chance in this manner rather than, say, as a pair of dice or the Sword of Damocles is entirely without precedent. Neither is it particularly easy to visualize. The central idea seems to be that chance is contained in a big bag with a rope around it. As long as the rope is tied in a knot, nothing can escape. However, once the bag is untied, chance becomes readily available. The problem is that the knot is extremely difficult to untie. It takes a huge effort to succeed. In the present instance, the analogy is with a man trying to screw up his courage to approach a woman. Although there is no guarantee, he has to take a chance in order to succeed. This seems to be precisely what Arenas is describing, which he compares to creating beauty. In both the personal and the artistic arena, nothing ventured usually results in nothing gained. In love and art, fortune rewards those who forge ahead. Proof that Arenas' gambit was successful is reserved for the conclusion, where the beautiful woman in the first stanza magically materializes before him. As the poem demonstrates, women and chance are very closely intertwined a least as far as love is concerned.

Notes

1   Robert Ponge, "Notes pour une histoire du surréalisme en Amérique Hispanique des années 20 aux années 50," *Mélusine*, Vol. 24 (2004), p. 316.

2   Stefan Baciu, *Antología de la poesía surrealista latinoamericana* (Mexico City: Mortiz, 1974).

3   See, for example, Ponge, "Notes pour une histoire," pp. 327–8.

4   Anna Balakian, "Réception du surréalisme dans la poésie latino-americaine," *Mélusine*, Vol. 4 (1982), p. 52.

5   Pierre Rivas, "Le Surréalisme au Pérou," *Mélusine*, Vol. 3 (1982), p. 109.

6   Melanie Nicholson, *Surrealism in Latin American Literature: Searching for Breton's Ghost* (New York: Palgrave Macmillan, 2013), p. 48.

7   Baciu, *Antología de la poesía*, p. 169.

8   See, for example, Willard Bohn, *The Rise of Surrealism: Cubism, Dada, and the Pursuit of the Marvelous* (Albany: State University of New York Press, 2002), p. 162.

9   J. C. Cooper, *An Illustrated Encyclopedia of Traditional Symbols* (London: Thames and Hudson, 1978), pp. 96–7.

10 Baciu, *Antología de la poesía*, p. 174.

11 See, for example, B. Z. Goldberg, *The Story of Sex in Religion* (New York: Grove, 1930), pp. 72–3.

12 Mary Ann Caws, ed. *Surrealist Love Poems* (Chicago: University of Chicago Press, 2005), p. 14.

13 Cesar Moro "Renomée de l'amour," *Le Surréalisme au Service de la Révolution*, No.5 (May 15, 1933), p. 38.

14 Gaëlle Hourdin, "Cesar Moro et le surréalisme entre l'ancien et le nouveau monde," *Mélusine*, Vol. 31 (2011), p. 253.

15 For a description of Moro's activities in Paris, see Dawn Ades, "'We Who Have Neither Church Nor Country': César Moro and Surrealism," in

Surrealism in Latin America: Vivísimo Muerto, ed. Dawn Ades et al. (Los Angeles: Getty, 2012), pp. 15–21.

16   Baciu, *Antología de la poesía*, p. 115.

17   Cesar Moro, *La Tortuga ecuestre y otros poemas en español*, ed. Américo Ferrari (Lima: Bibiloteca Nueva, n.d.).

18   See, for example, Juan Pascual Gay, "César Moro y los circulos surrealistas de Mexico (1938–1948)," in *La Nueva Literatura Hispánica*, Vol. 10 (Universitas Castellae, 2006).

19   Baciu, *Antología de la poesía*, pp. 230–1.

20   Cooper, *An Illustrated Encyclopedia*, p. 90.

21   Mirko Lauer and Abelardo Oquendo, eds. *Surrealistas & otros peruanos insulares* (Barcelona: Ocnos, 1973), p. 17.

22   Gabriel Ramos, "La articulación del lengaje surrealista de César Moro," *Lexis*, Vol. 39, No. 1 (2015), p. 102.

23   Emilio Adolfo Westphalen, "Pinturas y dibujos de César Moro," *Amaru*, No. 9 (March 1969), pp. 53–9.

24   Balakian, "Réception du surréalisme," p. 50.

25   César Moro, *Lettre d'amour* (Mexico City: Editions Dyn, 1944).

26   Melanie Nicholson "César Moro: Exile and the Poetic Imagination," *Revista Hispánica Moderna*, Vol. 68, No. 1 (June 2015), p. 47.

27   Perla Masi, "El cuerpo musical de la palabra: erotismo en la poesía de César Moro," *Inti*, No. 54 (Autumn 2001), p. 28.

28   Ramos, "La articulación del lengaje surrealista," pp. 117–18.

29   Jason Wilson, "Spanish American Surrealist Poetry," in *A Companion to Spanish Surrealism*, ed. Robert Havard (London: Tamesis, 2004), p. 265.

30   Ibid.

31   B. Marta Contreras, "Surrealismo en Chile," Atenea: Revista de Ciencia, Arte y Literaturea de la Universidad de Concepción, Chile, No. 452 (1985), pp. 29–55.

32   Enrique Anderson-Imbert, *Spanish-American Literature: A History*, 2nd ed., Vol. 2 (Detroit: Wayne State University Press, 1969), p.705.

33   Fernando Alegria, "Braulio Arenas," *Anales de la Universidad de Chile*, No. 125 (January–April 1962), p. 91.

34   Baciu, *Antología de la poesia*, p. 179. The remaining poems by Arenas may also be found in this volume.

Coda

Seeing as how André Breton once referred to the Surrealist movement as "the prehensile tail of Romanticism," the title of this final section seems particularly apropos.[1] Since 1924, Surrealism has spread to many more countries than those examined in this book. Besides France, Spain, Catalonia, Portugal, Mexico, Argentina, Chile, and Peru, a quick survey of *Mélusine* (published by the Cahiers du Centre de Recherche sur le Surrréalisme) reveals that Surrealism was and/or is also active in Japan, Quebec, Martinique, Egypt, England, Sweden, sub-Saharan Africa, North Africa, Romania, Germany, Austria, Czechoslovakia, Yugoslavia, Hungary, Belgium, Serbia, and the United States.[2] Other countries could easily be added to this impressive list, such as Syria, which apparently harbors an active Surrealist contingent as well (see Chapter 3). Thus no further proof is needed of the movement's worldwide appeal. Indeed, as Octavio Paz declares, "el surrealismo ha contribuido de manera poderosa a formar la sensibilidad de nuestra época" ("Surrealism has contributed powerfully toward forming the sensibility of our era").[3] Traces of Surrealism are to be found everywhere these days—not just in paintings or poems but also in films, advertisements, fashion, furniture, architecture, songs, and miscellaneous accessories. I myself possess a working facsimile of one of the melting watches in Dalí's *The Persistence of Memory*, given to me by my daughter Heather.

For better or worse, not every Surrealist convert embraced the official model wholesale. In contrast to Octavio Paz and César Moro, who regarded Breton's pronouncements as gospel, others simply borrowed the tenets that happened to appeal to them. Indeed, I would argue that Surrealism's adaptability is one of the things that has made it so influential. Like the Catholic Church, the movement has been quick to assimilate some of the characteristics of its adopted countries. One of the best examples is Mexican Surrealism, which borrowed a number of themes from Mexican folklore. While some Surrealist poets chose to ignore certain concepts, such as *le point suprême* or *le hasard objectif*, all of them attempted to reproduce the logic of dreams and/or to replicate *le merveilleux*. Although the Parisian movement was officially dissolved by Jean Schuster in 1966, following Breton's death, another Parisian group sprang up in its place that is still active today. In other countries, Surrealism has continued to prosper with little interruption. In the United States, for example, an interesting offshoot called Afro-Surrealism surfaced as recently as 2009.[4] As of this writing, I am glad to report, the movement's influence shows no sign of abating. Surrealism is as powerful and as influential today as it has ever been.

Although some readers and viewers may not know much about Surrealist theory, they are usually familiar with the Surrealist style(s). Besides various traveling exhibitions and the permanent collections of different museums, a number of web sites have kept the movement continually before the public eye, such as www.surrealismtoday.com and www.surrealism.co.uk. Articles that appeal to special Surrealist constituencies exist as well, such as "Contemporary Women Artists Against Alternative Facts"[5] and "Modern Surrealism and How It Is Used in Design Today."[6] There are even half a dozen web sites that will teach you how to write Surrealist poetry. As Gaëlle Hourdin remarks, "Par son projet de dévoiler les profondeurs de l'esprit humain et de 'transformer le monde' le surréalisme a, dès son apparition, affiché son vocation universelle." ("By striving to unveil the depths of the human mind and to 'transform the world,' Surrealism has displayed its universal appeal ever since its inception").[7] As a result, the past one hundred years have been tremendously exciting—not just for the Surrealists but also for modern poetry fans all over the world. One wonders what exciting developments the next hundred years will bring. New artists and writers will undoubtedly dazzle us with their technical skills and valuable insights. One or two poets may even receive a Nobel Prize. How supremely fitting it would be if one of those individuals just happened to come from France, where it all began a long time ago.

Notes

1 André Breton, *Second Manifeste du Surréalisme, Oeuvres complètes*, Vol. 1, ed. Marguerite Bonnet et al (Paris: Gallimard, 1988), p. 803.

2 For an exhaustive list, see "Surréalistes de tous les pays," http://melusine-surrealisme.fr/site/Surr-ts-pays/somsurr-ts-pays.htm

3 Octavio Paz, "El surrealismo," in *La búsqueda del comienzo (escritos sobre el surrealismo)*, ed. Diego Martínez Torrón, 2nd ed. (Mexico City: Fundamentos, 1983), p.44.

4 See D. Scott Miller, "AfroSurreal Manifesto," *San Francisco Bay Guardian*, May 20, 2009. And see Rochelle Spencer, *AfroSurrealism: The African Diaspora's Surrealist Fiction* (New York: Routledge, 2019).

5 www.artspace.com (February 23, 2019).

6 https://lstwebdesigner.com<modern-surrealism

7 Gaëlle Hourdin "Cesar Moro et le surréalisme entre l'ancien et le nouveau monde," *Mélusine*, Vol 31 (2011), p. 253.

Acknowledgments

Portions of Chapters 2 and 7 appeared previously in the following journals and are reprinted with their kind permission: "Revisiting the Surrealist Image," *Romance Quarterly*, Vol. 66, No. 2 (Fall 2019), pp. 91–106; "André Breton and Three Surrealist Poets," *Philosophy and Literature*, Vol. 44, No. 2 (October 2020), pp. 310–22; and "Investigating Poetry With J. V. Foix," *Forum for Modern Language Studies*, Vol. 58 No. 1 (January 2022), pp. 14–27. For better or worse, all translations are my own.

Bibliography

Ades, Dawn. *Dalí*. London: Thames and Hudson, 1990.

Ades, Dawn. "'We Who Have Neither Church Nor Country': César Moro and Surrealism." *Surrealism in Latin America: Vivísimo Muerto*. Ed. Dawn Ades et al. Los Angeles: Getty, 2012, pp. 15–21.

Alegria, Fernando. "Braulio Arenas." *Anales de la Universidad de Chile*, No. 125 (January–April 1962), pp. 91–3.

Aleixandre, Vicente. *Poesía completa*. Ed. Alejandro Sanz. Barcelona: Lumen, 2017.

Alexandrian, Sarane. *André Breton par lui-même*. Paris: Seuil, n.d.

Alonso, Amado. *Poesía y estilo de Pablo Neruda; Interpretación de una poesía hermética*. Buenos Aires: Losada, 1940.

Alquié, Ferdinand. *Philosophie du surréalisme*. Paris: Flammarion, 1955.

Anderson, Andrew A. "García Lorca's Poemas en prosa and Poeta en Nueva York: Dalí, Gasch, Surrealism, and the Avant-Garde." *A Companion to Spanish Surrealism*. Ed. Robert Havard. Woodbridge: Tamesis, 2004, pp. 163–82.

Anderson-Imbert, Enrique. *Spanish-American Literature: A History*. Tr. John V. Falconieri. 2nd ed. Vol. 2. Detroit: Wayne State University Press, 1969.

Andráde, Lourdes. "Regards convergents." *Paz, Breton, et Péret*. Tr. Henri Béhar. Mélusine, Vol. 19 (1999), pp. 153–62.

Apollinaire, Guillaume. *Oeuvres en prose complète*. Vol. 2. Ed. Pierre Caizergues and Michel Décaudin. Paris: Gallimard, 1991.

Apollinaire, Guillaume. *Oeuvres en prose completes*. Vol. 3. Ed. Pierre Caizergues and Michel Décaudin. Paris: Gallimard, 1993.

Aragon, Louis. "L'Homme coupé en deux." *Les Lettres Françaises*, May 9–15, 1968, p. 7.

Araguas, Vicente. "Introducción." Mario Cesariny. *Antología poética*. Ed. Vicente Araguas. Visor: Madrid, 2004, p. 8.

Arnheim, Rudolf. *Visual Thinking*. Berkeley: University of California Press, 1969.

Audoin, Philippe. *Breton*. Paris: Gallimard, 1970.

Baciu, Stefan. *Antología de la poesía surrealista latinoamericana*. Mexico City: Mortiz, 1974.

Badosa, Enrique. *Antologia de J. V. Foix*. 2nd ed. Madrid: Plaza and Janés, 1975.

Balakian, Anna. *André Breton*. New York: Oxford University Press, 1971.

Balakian, Anna. "Réception du surréalisme dans la poésie latino-americaine." *Mélusine*, Vol. 4 (1982), pp. 43–53.

Balakian, Anna. *Surrealism: The Road to the Absolute*. Chicago: University of Chicago Press, 1986.

Bédouin, Jean-Louis. *La Poésie surréaliste: anthologie*. Rev. ed. Paris: Seghers, 1977.

Béhar et al., Henri. Ed. *Les Pensées d' André Breton*. Lausanne: L'Age d'Homme, 1988.

Benayoun, Robert. "A plus d'un titre … ." Benjamin Péret. *Le Grand Jeu*. Paris: Gallimard, 1969, pp. 7–17.

Billault, Alain. "La Folie poétique: remarques sur les conceptions grecques de l'inspiration." *Bulletin de l'Association Guillaume Budé: Lettres d'Humanité*, No. 61 (December 2002), pp. 18–35.

Boehne, Patricia J. *J. V. Foix*. Boston: Twayne, 1980.

Bohn, Willard. *Marvelous Encounters: Surrealist Responses to Film, Art, Poetry and Architecture*. Lewisburg: Bucknell, 2005.

Bohn, Willard. *Reading Apollinaire's "Calligrammes."* New York: Bloomsbury, 2018.

Bohn, Willard. "Revisiting the Surrealist Image." *Romance Quarterly*, Vol. 66, No. 2 (Fall 2019), pp. 91–106.

Bohn, Willard. *The Rise of Surrealism: Cubism, Dada, and the Pursuit of the Marvelous*. Albany: StateUniversity of New York Press, 2002.

Bohn, Willard. Ed. "Special issue on Surrealism." *Forum for Modern Language Studies*, Vol. 58, No. 1 (January 2022).

Bonnet, Marguerite. *André Breton: Naissance de l'aventure surréalist*. Paris: Corti, 1975.

Bou, Enric. "From Foix to Dalí: Versions of Catalan Surrealism between Barcelona and Paris." *ARTL@S BULLETIN*, Vol. 6, No. 2 (Summer 2017), n. p.

Breton, André. *Entretiens (1913–1952)*. Ed. André Parinaud. Rev. ed. Paris: Gallimard, 1969.

Breton, André. *Oeuvres complètes*. Vols. 1–3. Ed. Marguerite Bonnet et al. Paris: Gallimard, 1988–1999.

Breton, André. *"Signe ascendant" suivi de … "Constellations."* Paris: Gallimard, 1968.

Breton, André and Philippe Soupault. *Les Champs magnétiques: Le Manuscrit original fac- similé et transcription*. Ed. Serge Faucherau and Lydia Lachenal. Paris: Lachenal and Ritter, 1988.

Breunig, L. C. *The Cubist Poets in Paris: An Anthology*. Lincoln: University of Nebraska Press, 1995.

Breunig, L. C. "Le Sur-réalisme." *Revue des Lettres Modernes*, Nos. 123–126 (1965), pp. 25–7.

Cantarelli, Gino. "Lumières de mercure." *SIC*, Nos. 21–22 (September–October 1917), p. 159.

Caws, Mary Ann. *André Breton*. New York: Twayne, 1971.

Caws, Mary Ann. *The Poetry of Dada and Surrealism: Aragon, Breton, Tzara, Eluard, and Desnos*. Princeton: Princeton University Press, 1970.

Caws, Mary Ann. "Prose Poem." *The Princeton Encyclopedia of Poetry and Poetics*. 4th ed. Ed. Roland Greene et al. Princeton: Princeton University Press, 2012, pp. 1112–13.

Caws, Mary Ann. Ed. *Surrealist Love Poems*. Chicago: University of Chicago Press, 2005.

Cayuela González, Carolina. "Metapoesía y pragmática en 'El Poeta' de Vicente Aleixandre." *Espéculo: Revista de estudios literarios*, No. 34 (November 2006–February 2007).

Cesariny, Mário. *A intervenção surrealista*. Lisbon: Assírio and Alvim, 1997.

Champigny, Robert. "The S Device." *Dada/Surrealism*, No. 1 (1971), pp. 3–7.

Chénieux-Gendron, Jacqueline. "Jeu de l'incipit et travail de la correction dans l'écriture automatique." *Une Pelle au vent dans les sables du rêve*. Ed. Michel Murat and Marie-Paule Berranger. Lyon: Presses Universitaires de Lyon, 1992, pp. 125–44.

Chénieux-Gendron, Jacqueline. *Surrealism*. Tr. Vivian Folkenflik. New York: Columbia University Press, 1990.

Cirlot, J. E. *A Dictionary of Symbols*. Tr. Jack Sage. 2nd ed. London: Routledge and Kegan Paul, 1985.

Cohn, Robert Greer. *Toward the Poems of Mallarmé*. Rev. ed. Berkeley: University of California Press, 1980.

Marta, Contreras B. "Surrealismo en Chile." *Atenea: Revista de Ciencia, Arte y literatura de la Universidad de Concepción, Chile*, No. 452, pp. 29–55.

Cooper, J. C. *An Illustrated Encyclopedia of Traditional Symbols*. London: Thames and Hudson, 1978.

Correia, Natalia. "Surrealism in Portuguese Poetry." Ed. George Monteiro. *Portuguese Studies*, Vol. 31, No. 1 (2015), pp. 124–31.

Courshon, W. L. "Salvador Dalí's Expulsion from the Surrealist Group." *Dada/Surrealism*, No. 5 (1975), pp. 80–9.

Cuadrado, Perfecto E. "Risques Pereira: uma apresentação cordial." *Revista de Cultura*, No. 68 (April 2009), n. p.

Debicki, Andrew P. *Spanish Poetry of the Twentieth Century: Modernity and Beyond*. Lexington: University Press of Kentucky, 1994.

Décaudin, Michel. "Autour du premier manifeste." *Quaderni del Novecento Francese*, No. 2 (1974), pp. 27–47.

Delon, Michel. *"Apollinaire, Sade." La Place d'Apollinaire*. Paris: Garnier, 2014, pp. 81–95.

Desnos, Robert. *Oeuvres*. Ed. Marie-Claire Dumas. Paris: Gallimard, 1999.

Ducasse, Isidore. *Les Chants de Maldoror. Oeuvres complètes*. Ed. Maurice Saillet. Paris: Livre de Poche, 1963.

Duhamel, Georges. "Alcools de Guillaume Apollinaire." *Mercure de France* (June 16, 1913), p. 801.

Durán, Manuel. "Hacia la otra orilla: La ultima etapa en la poesía de Octavio Paz." *OctavioPaz*. Ed. Pere Gimferrer. Madrid: Taurus, 1989, pp. 118–28.

Durán Gili, Manuel. *El superrealismo en la poesía española contemporanea*. Mexico City: Universidad Autónoma de México, 1950.

Durozoi, Gérard. *History of the Surrealist Movement*. Tr. Alison Anderson. Chicago: University of Chicago Press, 2002.

Eder, Richard. "Getting Even with Portugal's Gestapo." *New York Times*, May 5, 1974, p. 5.

"Eight Myths about Snakes." https://museumsvictoria.com.au/article/8-myths-about-snakes/

Eluard, Paul. *Oeuvres complètes*. Vol. 1. Ed. Marcelle Dumas and Lucien Scheler. Paris: Gallimard, 1968.

Finkelstein, Haim. *Salvador Dalí's Art and Writing 1927–1942: The Metamorphosis of Narcissus*. Cambridge: Cambridge University Press, 1996.

Foix, J. V. *Antologia poètica*. Ed. Marià Manent et al. Barcelona: Proa, 1993.

Foix, J. V. *Diari* 1918. Ed. Carmen Arnau. Barcelona: Edicions 62 and La Caixa, 1987.

Foix, J. V. *Obres completes*. Vol. 1. Barcelona: Edicions 62, 1984.

França, José-Augusto. "Le Surréalisme portugais." *Mélusine*, No. 7 (1985), pp. 267–74.

Fuente, Ovidio C. "Teoria poetica de Octavio Paz." *Cuadernos Americanos*, Vol. 31 (1972), pp. 226–42.

García Lorca, Federico. *Romancero gitano, Poeta en Nueva York, El Publico.* Ed. Derek Harris. Madrid: Taurus, 1993.

García-Posada, Miguel. *Lorca: Interpretación de "Poeta en Nueva York."* Madrid: Akal, 1981.

Gauthier, Xavière. *Surréalisme et sexualité.* Paris: Gallimard, 1971.

Gay, Juan Pascual. "César Moro y los circulos surrealistas de Mexico (1938-1948)." *La Nueva Literatura Hispánica.* Vol. 10. Universitas Castellae, 2006.

Geist, Anthony L. "'Esas fronteras deshechas': Sexuality, Textuality, and Ideology inVicente Aleixandre's Espadas como labios." *The Surrealist Adventure in Spain.* Ed. C. Brian Morris. Ottawa: Dovehouse, 1991, pp. 181–90.

Gershman, Herbert S. *The Surrealist Revolution in France.* Ann Arbor: University of Michigan Press, 1974.

Gimferrer, Pere. "Aspectos de la poesia de J. V. Foix." *Destino* (January 27, 1973), p. 23.

Goldberg, B. Z. *The Story of Sex in Religion.* New York: Grove, 1930.

Gómez Yebra, Antonio A. "Mujer y erotismo en La Flor de California." *Monographic Review / Revista Monográfica*, Vol. 7, pp. 115–23.

Gratton, Johnnie. "Poetics of the Surrealist Image." *Romanic Review*, Vol. 69, Nos. 1–2 (January–March 1978), pp. 205–21.

Greene, Robert W. *The Poetic Theory of Pierre Reverdy.* Berkeley: University of California Press, 1967.

Greene et al., Roland. Eds. *The Princeton Encyclopedia of Poetry and Poetics.* 4th ed. Princeton: Princeton University Press, 2012.

Gullón, Ricardo. "El universalismo de Octavio Paz." *Octavio Paz.* Ed. Pere Gimferrer. Madrid: Taurus, 1982, pp. 223–35.

Harris, Derek. *Federico García Lorca: Poeta en Nueva York.* London: Grant and Cutler, 1978.

Harris, Derek. *Metal Butterflies and Poisonous Lights: The Language of Surrealism in Lorca, Alberti,Cernuda, and Aleixandre.* Arnecroach, Scotland: La Sirena, 1998.

Higginbotham, Virginia. "La iniciación de Lorca en el surrealismo." *El Surrealismo.* Ed. Victor García de la Concha. Madrid: Taurus, 1982, pp. 240–54.

Hinojosa, José María. *La flor dernía.* Ed. José Antonio Mesa Toré. Madrid: Huerga y Fierro, 2004.

Hinojosa, José María. "Su corazón no era más que una espiga." Published with another poem under the title "Estos dos corazones." *Litoral*, No. 9 (June 1929), pp. 10–13.

Hourdin, Gaëlle. "Cesar Moro et le surréalisme entre l'ancien et le nouveau monde." *Mélusine*, Vol. 31 (2011), pp. 253–64.

"How Did Amnesty International Start?" https://www.amnestyusa.org/faqs/how-did-amnesty-international-start/

"How the Fire Escape Became an Ornament." https://www.theatlantic.com/technology/archive/2018/02/how-the-fire-escape-became-anornament/554174/

Ilie, Paul. "The Term 'Surrealism' and Its Philological Imperative." *Romanic Review*, Vol. 69, Nos. 1–2 (January–March 1978), pp. 90–102.

Jakobson, Roman and Morris Halle. *Fundamentals of Language*. 2nd ed. The Hague: Mouton, 1971.

Jenny, Laurent. "La Surréalité et ses Signes Narratifs." *Poétique*, No. 16 (1973), pp. 499–520.

Keown, Dominic. "The Ironic Vision of J. V. Foix." *Readings of J. V. Foix: An Anthology*. Ed. Arthur Terry. Barcelona: Anglo-Catalan Society, 1998, pp. 119–32.

Kuenzli, Rudolf E. "Surrealism and Misogyny." *Surrealism and Women*. Ed. Mary Ann Caws et al. Cambridge: MIT Press, 1991, pp. 17–26.

Lagmanovich, David. "Las 'Artes poéticas' de Pablo Neruda." *Espéculo: Revista de estudios literarios*, No. 28 (November 2004), n. p.

Lander, Jess. "Say Cheers. Five Unique Toasting Traditions from around the World." https://www.winecountry.com/blog/say-cheers-5-unique-toasting-traditions-from-around-the-world/

Lauer, Mirko and Abelardo Oquendo. Eds. *Surrealistas & otros peruanos insulares*. Barcelona: Ocnos, 1973.

Lecomte, Marcel. "Tension de l'image chez Reverdy." *Le Journal des poètes* (August–September 1960), p. 6.

Lindgren, Kristina. "Professor Offers a Dissenting View of Marquis de Sade." *Los Angeles Times*, July 15, 1991.

Lisboa, António Maria. *Poesia de António Maria Lisboa*. Lisbon: Assirio & Alvim, 1980.

Lista, Giovanni. Ed. *Le Futurisme: Textes et manifestes 1909–1944*. Ceyzérieux: Champ Vallon, 2015.

Lynch, Lawrence W. *The Marquis de Sade*. Boston: Twayne, 1984.

Mallarmé, Stéphane. *Oeuvres complètes*. Ed. Henri Mondor and G. Jean-Aubry. Paris: Gallimard, 1965.

Mandiargues, Pieyre de. *"Préface" to Paul Eluard. Capitale de la douleur suivie de L'Amour la poésie*. Paris: Gallimard, 1966, pp. 5–9.

Margarido, Alfredo and Carlos Eurico da Costa. Eds. *Dez Jovens Poetas Portugueses*. Rio de Janeiro: Ministerio da Educação e Cultura do Brasil, 1954.

Martin, Claude. Ed. *Correspondance Jules Romains Guillaume Apollinaire*. Paris: Jean-Michel Place, 1994.

Martínez Torrón, Diego. "El surrealismo de Octavio Paz." *Octavio Paz: la búsqueda del comienzo*. 3rd ed. Madrid: Fundamentos, 1983, pp. 7–25.

Masi, Perla. "El cuerpo musical de la palabra: erotismo en la poesía de César Moro." *Inti*, No. 54 (Autumn 2001), pp. 27–50.

Matthews, J. H. "Benjamin Péret: Marvelous Conjunction." *About French Poetry from Dada to "Tel Quel": Text and Theory*. Ed. Mary Ann Caws. Detroit: Wayne State University Press, 1974, pp. 126–38.

Matthews, J. H. *Languages of Surrealism*. Columbia: University of Missouri Press, 1986.

Matthews, J. H. *Surrealism, Insanity, and Poetry*. Syracuse: Syracuse University Press, 1982.

Matthews, J. H. *Surrealist Poetry in France*. Syracuse: Syracuse University Press, 1969.

Mead, Gerald. *The Surrealist Image: A Stylistic Study*. Berne: Peter Lang, 1978.

Menarini, Pietro. "Emblemas ideológicos de Poeta en Nueva York." *El surrealismo*. Ed. Victor García de la Concha. Madrid: Taurus, 1982, pp. 255–70.

"Mid-1920s-The Charleston Era." http://www.walternelson.com/dr/charleston

Miller, D. Scott. "AfroSurreal Manifesto." *San Francisco Bay Guardian*, May 20, 2009.

"Modern Surrealism and How It Is Used in Design Today." https:// lstwebdesigner.com<modern-surrealism

"Mohammad Zaza—The Earth Is Blue Like an Orange." *Catalogue to His Exhibition at the Depo Gallery in Istanbul, April 21 to May 18, 2016*. See http://www.depoistanbul.net/en/event/exhibition-mohammad-zaza-the-earth-is-blue-like-an-orange/

Molas, Joaquim. *"J. V. Foix or Total Investigation."* Tr. Louis J. Rodrigues. *Catalan Review*, Vol. I, No. 1 (1986), pp. 107–22.

Moran, Dominic. "Neruda's 'Arte poética': Some Further Thoughts." *Bulletin of Spanish Studies*, Vol. 88, Nos. 249–71 (2011), pp. 249–71.

Morand, Paul. *Lampes à arc*. Paris: Au Sans Pareil, 1920.

Moro, César. *Lettre d'amour*. Mexico City: Editions Dyn, 1944.

Morris, C. B. *Surrealism and Spain 1920–1936*. Cambridge: Cambridge University Press, 1972.

Morris, C. Brian. "Gertrudis and the Creative Modesty of J. V. Foix." *Catalan Review*, Vol. 1, No. 1 (June 1986), pp. 123–39.

Murat, Michel. *Le Surréalisme*. Paris: Librairie Générale Française, 2013.

Neira, Julio. "José María Hinojosa y el primer poema surrealista español." *Insula*, Nos. 452–453 (July–August 1984), p. 17.

Neira, Julio. "Surrealism and Spain: The Case of Hinojosa." Tr. C. Brian Morris. *The Surrealist Adventure in Spain*. Ed. C. Brian Morris. Ottawa: Dovehouse, 1991, pp. 101–18.

Neira, Julio. *Viajero de soledades: estudios sobre José María Hinojosa*. Seville: Fundación Genesian, 1999.

Neira, Julio. "*El surrealismo en José María Hinojosa (Esbozo)*." El surrealismo. Ed. Victor García de la Concha. Madrid: Taurus, 1982, pp. 271–85.

Neruda, Pablo. *Obras completas*. Vol. 1. Ed. Hernán Loyola and Saúl Yurkievich. Barcelona: Galaxia Gutenberg, 1999.

Nevers, Janine. "Salvador Dalí peinture et poésie: de l'automatisme à la paranoia-critique." *Mélusine*, No. 7 (1985), pp. 205–17.

Nicholson, Melanie. "César Moro: Exile and the Poetic Imagination." *Revista Hispánica Moderna*, Vol. 68, No. 1 (June 2015), pp. 39–57.

Nicholson, Melanie. *Surrealism in Latin American Literature: Searching for Breton's Ghost*. New York: Palgrave Macmillan, 2013.

Onis, Carlos Marcial de. *El surrealismo y cuatro poetas de la generación del 27*. Madrid: Porrúa Turanzas, 1974.

Paz, Octavio. "Benjamin Péret." *Les Lettres Nouvelles, New Series*, Vol. 1, No. 24 (October 7, 1959), pp. 26–7.

Paz, Octavio. *Obra poética (1935–1988)*. Barcelona: Seix Barral, 1990.

Paz, Octavio. *Octavio Paz: la búsqueda del comienzo*. Ed. Diego Martínez Torrón. 2nd ed. Mexico City: Fundamentos, 1980.

Paz, Octavio. *Un más allá erótico: Sade*. Mexico City: Vuelta, 1993.

Paz, Octavio. "El músico de Saint-Merry." *Inicio*, No. 2 (October 1965), pp. 21–4.

Peden, Margaret. "The Musician of Saint-Merry" by Apollinaire: A Translation and a Study." *L'Esprit créateur*, Vol. 10, No. 4 (Winter 1970), pp. 269–84.

Peeters, Léopold. "Critique de l'image surréaliste." *French Studies in Southern Africa*, No. 29 (2000), pp. 66–81.

Péret, Benjamin. "La Poésie est UNE et indivisible." *VVV*, No. 4 (February 1944), p. 10.

Personneaux-Conesa, Lucie. "Histoire et historiographie du surréalisme espagnol." *Mélusine*, No. 11 (1990), pp. 133–41.

Phillips, Rachel. *The Poetic Modes of Octavio Paz*. Oxford: Oxford University Press, 1972.

Pierre, José. "Salvador Dalí poète surréaliste." *Mélusine*, No. 12 (1991), pp. 179–98.

Ponge, Robert. "Notes pour une histoire du surréalisme en Amérique Hispanique des années 20 aux années 50." *Mélusine*, Vol. 24 (2004), pp. 315–32.

Predmore, Richard L. *Los poemas neoyorquinas de Federico García Lorca*. Madrid: Taurus, 1985.

Prison Conditions in Portugal: Conditions of Detention of Political Prisoners. London: Amnesty International, 1965, pp. 15–24.

Prudon, Montserrat. "J. V. Foix, un singulier pluriel." *Les Avant-gardes en Catalogne (1916–1930)*. Ed. Serge Salaün and Elisée Trenc. Paris: Sorbonne Nouvelle, 1995, pp. 51–81.

Raaberg, Gwen. "The Problematics of Women and Surrealism." *Surrealism and Women*. Ed. Mary Ann Caws et al. Cambridge: MIT Press, 1991, pp. 1–10.

Rambo, Ann Marie Remley. "The Presence of Woman in the Poetry of Octavio Paz."*Hispania*, Vol. 51, No. 2 (May 1968), pp. 259–64.

Ramos, Gabriel. "La articulación del lengaje surrealista de César Moro." *Lexis*, Vol. 39, No. 1 (2015), pp. 101–32.

Rattray, Jacqueline. "Celebrating Transgression: Blasphemy and Lust in the Work of the Spanish Surrealist José María Hinojosa." *Romance Studies*, Vol. 16, No. 2 (1998), pp. 45–55.

Reverdy, Pierre. "L'Image." *Nord-Sud*, No. 13 (March 1918), p. 1.

Reverdy, Pierre. *Plupart du temps, poèmes 1915–1922*. Paris: Flammarion, 1967.

Riffaterre, Michael. *Semiotics of Poetry*. Bloomington: Indiana University Press, 1978.

Riffaterre, Michael. *Text Production*. Tr. Terese Lyons. New York: Columbia University Press, 1983.

Rivas, Pierre. "Le Surréalisme au Pérou." *Mélusine*, Vol. 3 (1982), pp. 109–14.

Roberts, Stephen. "The Self-adjusting Sonnet: Pablo Neruda's 'Arte poética.'" *The Kate Elder Lecture*. London: Department of Hispanic Studies, Queen Mary University, 2002.

Romains, Jules "La Poésie immédiate." *Vers et Prose*, (October–November–December 1909).

Rodríguez Monegal, Emir. *El viajero inmóvil. Introducción a Pablo Neruda.* Buenos Aires: Losada, 1966.

Rothman, Roger. *Tiny Surrealism: Salvador Dalí and the Aesthetics of the Small.* Lincoln: University of Nebraska Press, 2012.

Ruy Sánchez, Alberto. *An Introduction to Octavio Paz.* Tr. Jeannine Marie Pitas. Oakville, ON: Mosaic, 2018.

Ryan-Kobler, Maryalice. "Pablo Neruda's 'Arte Poética': At the Prophetic Crossroads." *Revista Hispánica Moderna*, Vol. 53, No. 2 (December 2000), pp. 439–48.

Saint-Pol-Roux. *De la Colombe au Corbeau par le Paon. Les Reposoirs.* Paris: Société du Mercure de France, 1904.

Salaün, Serge and Elisée Trenc. *Les Avant-gardes en Catalogne.* Paris: La Sorbonne Nouvelle, 1995.

Salvat-Papasseit, Joan. *Arc-Voltaic*, No. 1 (February 1918).

Sobrer, Josep Miquel. "Deformation, Mutilation, and Putrefaction: The Early Foix." *Journal of Iberian and Latin American Studies*, Vol. 9, No. 2 (2003), pp. 179–89.

Spencer, Rochelle. *AfroSurrealism: The African Diaspora's Surrealist Fiction.* New York: Routledge, 2019.

Stamelman, Richard. "The Relational Structure of Surrealist Poetry." *Dada/Surrealism*, No. 6 (1976), pp. 59–78.

Steiner, Wendy. *The Colors of Rhetoric: Problems in the Relation between Modern Literature and Painting.* Chicago: University of Chicago Press, 1982.

Stewart, Chris. "Watch out for Snakes. They Steal Mothers' Milk You Know." https://www.telegraph.co.uk/expat/expatlife/9535237/Watch-out-for-snakes.-They-steal-mothers-milk-you-know … .html

"Surrealism Today: Contemporary Women Artists Against Alternative Facts." www.artspace.com (February 23, 2019)

"Surréalistes de tous les pays." http://melusine-surrealisme.fr/site/Surr-ts-pays/somsurr-ts-pays.htm

Sutherland, Donald. "Excursiones, incursiones, y retornos de un craneo de azucar." *Octavio Paz.* Ed. Pere Gimferrer. Madrid: Taurus, 1982, pp. 201–14.

Tabucchi, Antonio. *A parola interdetta. Poeti surrealisti portoghesi.* Turin: Einaudi, 1971.

Terry, Arthur. "La idea de l'ordre en la poesia de J. V. Foix." *Les avanguardes literàries a Catalunya: bibliografia i antologia crítica.* Ed. Joaquim Molas et al. Madrid and Frankfurt am Main: Vervuert, 2005, pp. 193–8.

Torre, Guillermo de. "Arco voltaico." *Grecia*, No. 34 (November 30, 1919), p. 3.

Tzara, Tristan. "Bilan." *SIC*, Nos. 49–50 (October 15–30, 1919), p. 385.

Tzara, Tristan. *Oeuvres complètes*. Vol. 1. Ed. Henri Béhar. Paris: Flammarion, 1975.

Wilson, Jason. *Octavio Paz*. Boston: Twayne, 1986.

Verani, Hugo J. *Octavio Paz: el poema como caminata*. Mexico City: Fondo de Cultura Económico, 2013.

Westphalen, Emilio Adolfo. "Pinturas y dibujos de César Moro." *Amaru*, No. 9 (March 1969), pp. 53–9.

Wilson, Jason. *Octavio Paz*. Boston: Twayne, 1986.

Wilson, Jason. "Spanish American Surrealist Poetry." *A Companion to Spanish Surrealism*. Ed. Robert Havard. London: Tamesis, 2004, pp. 253–76.

Xirau, Ramón. "La poesía de Octavio Paz."*Aproximaciones a Octavio Paz*. Ed. Angel Flores. Mexico City: Mortiz, 1974.

Yurkievich, Saul. "Octavio Paz: Indagador de la palabra." *Octavio Paz*. Ed. Pere Gimferrer Madrid: Taurus, 1989, pp. 96–117.

Zenith, Richard. "Mario Cesariny de Vasconcelos." https://www.poetryinternationalweb.net/pi/site/poet/item/4653/11/Mario-Cesariny-de-Vasconcelos

Index